HIL-Stacks
F

Reading and Understanding

D0911094

Reading and Understanding

An Introduction to the Psychology of Reading

Geoffrey Underwood

and

Vivienne Batt

UNIVERSITY
OF NEW BRUNSWICK

MAR 14 1997

LIBRARIES

Copyright © Geoffrey Underwood and Vivienne Batt, 1996

The right of Geoffrey Underwood and Vivienne Batt to be identified as authors of this work has been asserted in accordance with the Copyright, Designs and Patents Act 1988.

First published 1996

2 4 6 8 10 9 7 5 3 1

Blackwell Publishers Ltd
108 Cowley Road
Oxford OX4 1JF
UK

Blackwell Publishers Inc
238 Main Street
Cambridge, Massachusetts 02142,
USA

All rights reserved. Except for the quotation of short passages for the purposes of criticism and review, no part of this publication may be reproduced, stored in a retrieval system, or transmitted, in any form or by any means, electronic, mechanical, photocopying, recording or otherwise, without the prior permission of the publisher.

Except in the United States of America, this book is sold subject to the condition that it shall not, by way of trade or otherwise, be lent, resold, hired out, or otherwise circulated without the publisher's prior consent in any form of binding or cover other than that in which it is published and without a similar condition including this condition being imposed on the subsequent purchaser.

British Library Cataloguing in Publication Data

A CIP catalogue record for this book is available from the British Library.

Library of Congress Cataloging-in-Publication Data

Underwood, Geoffrey (Geoffrey D. M.)
    Reading and understanding: an introduction to the psychology of
reading/Geoffrey Underwood and Vivienne Batt.
        p. cm.
    Includes bibliographical references and indexes.
    ISBN 0–631-17949-6 (alk. paper). – ISBN 0–631-17951-8 (pbk.: alk. paper)
    1. Reading, Psychology of. I. Batt, Vivienne. II. title
BF 456.R2U96 1996
418'.4'019 – dc20

Typeset in 10/12 Sabon
by CentraCet, Cambridge
Printed in Great Britain by Hartnolls Ltd, Bodmin, Cornwall

This book is printed on acid-free paper

Contents

Preface

Reading is a skill essential for formal education and for an individual's success in society. The importance of this ability is reflected in the amount of research that psychologists have dedicated to its understanding. The discussions in this book present the major strands of psychological research on reading, and point to our developing understanding of the processes that make reading possible.

The popular approach taken by psychologists is to view reading as being supported by cognitive systems that act upon printed information and convert it into a form that makes contact with our memories, and that can then be used by our thought processes. This is the approach to be presented here. Reading is the process by which we identify individual words from their printed and written forms, and by which we combine these words into simple ideas or propositions, in order to be able to form a mental model of the text based upon inferences that take us beyond the information given.

Largely implicit in these discussions is the matter of methodology: how can we gain access to the cognitive processes necessary for the development of mental models from printed words? The processes are usually hidden since we usually read silently and the responses to what we have read are not necessarily immediate. Psychologists have devised a number of ways of observing the hidden processes, with methods that identify the components of reading and plot their characteristics. So, the early process of identifying or recognizing individual words is one such component, and the characteristics of words are systematically varied in laboratory experiments in which immediate responses to them are recorded. In these experiments we are able to determine the characteristics of words that result in processing delays and this tells us about the characteristics that are being used by the recognition process. This commonly used methodology is currently being supplemented by the increasingly popular technique of monitoring people's eye movements as they read, and one of our purposes in this book is to demonstrate the power of these investigations. Although psychologists have observed eye movements during reading for a century, only recently has commercially available equipment made these investigations generally accessible. As we read a sentence our eyes move from word to word, pausing for a short time and then moving at great speed to the next word. The length of these pauses, or fixations, varies according to the difficulty with which the inspected word is recognized and according to the difficulty with which the word is integrated with the other words of a sentence. By measuring fixation durations we can therefore gain direct access to the processes of reading as they occur. This methodology is providing an exciting alternative to presenting readers with individual words to which response keys are pressed and reaction times measured. To reflect the importance of eye movement recordings in the investigation of reading, we have dedicated a whole chapter to the methodology and to current research strands.

The chapter on eye movements, by virtue of being based more on the methodology in use than on the nature of the research questions addressed by the techniques, stands apart from the other chapters. This is a difficulty that we recognize, but we consider the opportunities that are afforded by these direct measures of reading processes to be sufficiently important to highlight them. The remaining chapters are organized in a more conventional fashion. Chapter 1 provides an overview and some definitions. Reading is presented as *skilled information processing*, and so each of these terms is defined. This requires a discussion of the information that is available in print, and of orthography, a comment on the notion of skill as it applies to reading, and a summary of the processes that take the skilled reader from the acquisition of information from print to the understanding of sentence meanings. A principal role is reserved here for the possible uses of speech recoding. Chapter 2 concerns the recognition of individual words. As we vary certain characteristics of words it becomes more difficult for the reader to identify them, and these are the characteristics that are being processed. If such a characteristic has no effect upon recognition – the colour in which the word is printed, perhaps – then the cognitive system responsible for recognition is insensitive to this characteristic, and our model of recognition need not take it into account. The final model of word recogniton will be an account of the effects of all of the characteristics of words that are associated with variations in processing difficulty. Chapter 3 continues the discussion of word recognition, and of the controversy over the alleged importance of speech recoding in descriptions of the acquisition of reading skills by children. If speech recoding is an essential part of skilled reading, then there are implications for the ways in which children are taught to read, as proponents of phonics methods and of phonological awareness training point out. Chapter 4 reviews the evidence available from individuals whose reading is in some way defective. This chapter has an emphasis on the acquired dyslexics, individuals who are assumed to have been able to read perfectly well prior to a physical injury such as a stroke but who afterwards show some disruption to their reading ability. The usefulness of the evidence from these patients is not universally accepted, and doubts must be expressed over the significance of defects that vary from patient to patient, and that can change from time to time for an individual patient. This chapter also considers claims for comparability between acquired dyslexics, who could read normally at one time, and developmental dyslexics, who have difficulty in learning to read. Chapter 5 then takes a sideways step to make the case for the use of eye movement methodology in our investigations of reading. As well as describing the basis of the technique and theoretical models of eye guidance during reading, this chapter describes current investigations of the use of sentence contexts in recognizing words and the processes involved in parsing the syntax of sentences. We also describe how eye movements have been used to plot the developmental course of reading acquisition, and their association with explanations of the developmental dyslexia. Chapter 6 concerns text understanding. This account of reading assumes that we can consider separating the stages of reading into descriptions of word recognition, descriptions of the integration of words into basic ideas or propositions, and descriptions of the reader's formation of a mental model of the meaning of the text using his or her own knowledge and making inferences. These processes of reasoning with language are not specific to reading, of course, but they are part of a complete description of the cognitive processes that occur when we extract meaning from print.

These descriptions have been taking shape for some time now, and saw their first expression in lectures presented as part of our undergraduate course. They have benefited from the feedback given to us by several generations of Nottingham students, and more recently their form has developed in response to equally exacting and helpful comments from four anonymous reviewers and from our colleagues at Nottingham. These generations of students and these reviewers deserve our profound gratitude for helping to shape the descriptions here, and for helping us to correct our own misunderstandings and misrepresentations. The remaining problems, of course, are our own responsibility. Thanks are also due in no small measure to the many researchers whose work is described in this book. Without their efforts towards understanding what it means to extract meaning from print we would have had little or nothing to write about. We hope that we have represented some of the excitement that we feel in approaching an understanding of this most important human ability.

Geoffrey Underwood
Vivienne Batt

Nottingham, September 1995

1

Reading as Skilled Information Processing

When we read we do so perhaps to enjoy a novel, or to understand the argument presented by the writer of a scientific article. We also need to read to extract a few ideas from a dictionary or from an encyclopaedia, and to identify the place names on a road map. Reading has many levels, and it usually performed in the service of some other activity. Although we talk of reading as a pastime in its own right, when we read novels, for instance, our enjoyment is one of the end-products of a series of psychological processes that enable us to acquire purely visual information from the page and convert it into meanings. This book is concerned with the psychological processes necessary for reading. Our reasons for reading, the circumstances of reading, and our affective responses to what we have read all lead to valuable research questions, but these questions are beyond the scope of this book. Our aim here is to describe the mental activities that enable us to read – the activities that enable us to see word meanings in printed and written symbols, and to integrate these meanings into the ideas presented in sentences.

Given that the word 'reading' has a number of interpretations, we should start with an outline of the meaning to be used in our discussions. This is the purpose of the first section of this chapter, in which we present reading as an information-processing skill comprising a number of cognitive subskills, and in which we present the laboratory approach to reading research.

Reading is a complex skill that most of us can perform without thought of how it is accomplished. Skilled drivers change gear without thinking about their grip on the gear lever or the position of the heel of their left foot, and reading can also be described as being skilled because the component activities require no thought. In reading the last couple of sentences, you have inspected words and phrases of varying difficulty and you have integrated the words into a mental construction of meaning. Your mind is unlikely to have been occupied with thoughts about the meaning of each word – whether, for example, the word *grip* in the sentence about skilled driving was intended to mean a travelling bag or holdall, or whether it meant the act of grasping. When we read we can be said to transform written language into meanings, but it is only occasionally that we need to worry about the meaning of an individual word. This is not to say that reading is always an continuously smooth activity, because when we do come across unfamiliar words we are disturbed by them and the calm flow of ideas is halted. On these occasions we often resort to inferring their meanings from the context in which they appear, and this interrupts our personal reconstruction of the writer's story in our minds. We can solve the problem of what the word probably means, and we can think about how the word fits in the sentence, about the meaning of the whole sentence, and about the ideas in the paragraph. There is no single activity here that can be identified as reading and this is why we shall regard reading as comprising a set of component subskills. The closest that we can come to defining reading is by use of a generality, by suggesting that it is a form of problem solving that is directed at the integration of words in an attempt to recover the writer's ideas. By describing reading as 'problem solving' we have, of course, used one mysterious activity to describe another, and we present ourselves the difficulty of saying what it means to solve a problem. Reading, like all forms of problem solving, can be described as an information-processing task. In the case of reading we can also observe the acquisition of skill, as most of us become highly skilled information processors. This view, of course, invites a preliminary discussion of the words 'skilled information processing', and this is one purpose of this introductory chapter. Our other main purpose is to introduce the laboratory approach to reading research that will support the discussion throughout the book.

What are the component processes that are necessary for understanding? The sequence of events from letter perception, through word recognition, word integration, and construction of a mental model together describe a very simple model of reading. Other psychological processes support the components when some reading tasks are performed, but not others. For example, to integrate the words in a sentence into single ideas we need to remember the first words that are encountered until they can be related to later words. The early words must be remembered with the aid of some kind of temporary memory system, and so a sensible research question concerns the types of memories that support reading. Another psychological process that has received extensive research attention is speech recoding. Although we can regard understanding as the product of a sequence involving the perception of letters, the recognition of words, and the integration of groups of words into ideas (or propositions), there is evidence to suggest that written words are converted into a spoken representation during the sequence. Questions then arise as to the point (or points) at which these speech codes are generated, and whether they are an essential part of reading or whether they are optional and under the strategical control of the reader. These are the kinds of questions that are to be discussed in this book, and they arise out of the aim of describing the psychological processes necessary for reading.

How should we investigate the skill of reading? The view implicit in most of our discussions is that we can best proceed through laboratory studies in which reading tasks can be determined and in which the materials to be read can be matched against each other. Since our aim is to uncover the psychological processes that operate when we read, the first step is to exclude activities that are not an essential part of reading, or, at least, those activities that are not an essential part of the aspect of reading that interests us. Reading has so many component activities that we have to take care to design tasks that as much as possible are targeted on the component of interest. For example, if we want to know about the process of perceiving letters, it seems obvious that we would not design a task in which words and sentences are to be read and remembered for latter recall. We would present only letters, and devise some task in which individual letters could be shown and perhaps named, or perhaps compared against other letters. We might expect that having our readers search for letters in words and sentences would not give us a clear description of letter perception because their recognition might be influenced by the context in which they are presented. A particular letter might be easier to perceive in some words than others, and in some parts of words more easily than others. We know this to be true; detections of the letter *e* depend upon a number of factors, including whether or not it is pronounced or silent (as in *set* verses *the*). In a similar way, words are identified more easily when they appear in predictive contexts. To avoid these difficulties it is simpler to design a task in which isolated items are to be processed. The criticism that this approach commonly attracts is that it has low 'ecological validity' in that outside the laboratory we spend very little of our time trying to decide on the identity of isolated letters and isolated words. If our aim is to determine the mental processes that underlie reading then this is an irrelevant objection. The task should determine the processes necessary for letter perception whether it is performed inside or outside the laboratory. The processes do not change according to the room in which they are observed. If we are to use reading tasks that are only ever seen outside the lab then we will be severely restricted in choice of research tools, and worse still, our choice of materials will be constrained to the extent that influences from different processes will interact, as in the example of letter perception being influenced by the word in which the letter appears. We have seen that reading can be considered to depend upon a number of component subskills, or component processes. The laboratory approach controls the presentation conditions so that each of these subskills can be investigated in the absence of influences from other subskills. Reading certainly requires letter perception, as well as word identification (or word recognition, as it is also called), word integration, and the construction of a mental model of the ideas in the text that corresponds to understanding the text. Not all reading tasks require all of these processes, however. Words can be identified without being integrated in phrases and sentences, for example, and if we want to know how individual words are identified then we should present individual words. Presenting them in sentences would only add to the confusion. Only when we want to know how the presence of other words influences recognition should words be presented in the context of a sentence. For this reason an enormous amount of research on reading has been concerned with the recognition of individual words, but this is only one of a number of components.

The task of identifying the component processes necessary for reading is not straightforward because they are not directly accessible. We might try to make the readers' mental activities more 'visible' by asking them to read a sentence aloud, but in doing this we are asking them to do more than recover the meanings intended by the writer, and perhaps also asking them to do less. *More* because recognizing meanings does not require the conversion of words from a written form to to an overtly spoken form, and *less* because we can sometimes pronounce words with no knowledge of their meanings. So, converting printed or written material into a spoken representation may or may not require an understanding of the text, but in any case pronunciation is not a prerequisite of reading. Similarly, we cannot investigate reading by simply asking volunteers to tell us what they are thinking about while they read. Thinking about a well-practised activity will often change the performance and interfere with the execution of an automatic action. We are unable to introspect on any cognitive task without changing the activity, and so investigations have to be less direct. While we cannot ask readers what they are doing while they are reading, we can observe them as they read words and sentences that vary in some measurable way. If an increase in measurable difficulty results in an increase in the difficulty of reading, then we can conclude that the mental processes that form our reading skill are sensitive to these changes. Our laboratory method, then, will observe the effects of known changes in the materials that are to be read.

Variations in the difficulty of reading are most simply observed in laboratory tasks, because it is only when we are able to control the potentially important variations that we can isolate and investigate each of them. There are many sources of variation, and if we do not hold all but one of them constant we will be unable to tell where the source of difficulty has come from. For example, one of the most potent sources of variation in the ease with which words are identified or recognized is the frequency of occurrence of the word in the language. In this context 'recognition' is the process by which we come to understand a word's meaning when it is seen. In some experiments recognition is the process by which we know that it is an actual word rather than a jumble of letters, and in others the word may have to be named aloud, and in yet others the reader may have to respond according to whether the word matches a previously shown word. What is common to these tasks is that a written word is presented and the reader makes an immediate response. On the basis of this response we can judge whether the written word has contacted its mental representation. For each word that we know and can recognize, we have a word-memory, by definition. Investigations of word recognition are the simplest studies of the processes necessary for reading, and are investigations of how these memories of known words are accessed. Responses in these experiments are sensitive to word frequency: words that occur often in the language (for example, *back, nothing, people, world*) are recognized more easily than words that are encountered relatively rarely (for example, *bead, netting, podium, waltz*). The speed and accuracy of recognition responses decline as the frequency of the words decrease. The relationship between the frequency of appearance of a word and the ease of its recognition is known, unsurprisingly, as the 'word frequency effect'. This variation in the ease of recognition is of importance for our attempts to model the cognitive processes necessary for word recognition and reading. If there is a change in reading speed as word frequency or word length increase, then the cognitive processes necessary for reading can be said to be sensitive to frequency or length, and so it can be said that these characteristics of words have been processed. The characteristics that are processed are those that are necessary for the activity to progress. A complete description of the mental activity of reading will take into account all of the characteristics that result in variations in the ease of performance. This approach to a cognitive description of reading sees the mental processes as interpreting written or printed language, and in the account that we present here the purpose of reading plays little or no part. We are not concerned here with *why* the reader wants to recover the meaning of the print, so much as *how* the recovery is achieved.

Information and knowledge

Our approach considers that when we read we can be said to process information, and this requires a statement of what this information is that is processed. Descriptions of the processes themselves will form the basis of most of our discussion, but we should first be clear of what is meant by 'information', and how it differs from 'knowledge'. Information is whatever reduces uncertainty, and so when we recognize a letter in a word, recognize an entire word, or realize what a writer was trying to say in a sentence, then uncertainty has been eliminated. Information has been collected. The ideas of information and uncertainty form the basis of an approach to describing what it is that the reader collects from a line of text, and what it is that constrains this process. The reader collects visual information and this process of acquisition is guided by what is already known. If a blot of ink obscures part of the final letter in the sequence *LAW**, then only two possibilities exist to a reader familiar with English words. The hidden letter must be an *N* or an *S*. If the blot of ink fades in the sun and reveals a vertical line, then we can say that information has been acquired. Suppose that the ink blot had been over the second letter, however, to give an appearance of *L **WN*. In this case there is only one legal completion. The fading of the ink blot gives no additional information and even with the second letter obscured we know that the word must be *LAWN*.

If we could extend this analysis of information in terms of the number of alternatives eliminated, we might be able to determine exactly how much information is contained in a sentence simply by counting the number of alternatives. This description is fatally flawed, however, if we attempt to apply it away from guessing games and into a world in which events do not occur with equal probability. If our ink blot appears over the second letter of *Q **AY* we do not need to think about alternatives because there is only one legal possibility. Some letters appear more often in the language than others, and they appear in combinations unequally. The two problems here are that some letters are more redundant than others by virtue of the rules of the language and others are more redundant by virtue of their frequent appearance. The rules of the written form of a language that constrain what letters can appear together with other specific letters are part of the orthography, or the orthographic rules, of the language. The orthography includes the written symbols (letters of the alphabet, in the case of English), the rules that allow them to be combined to form words, together with rules of punctuation and conventions such as the use of capitals.

There is an important distinction to be made here between information and knowledge. A computer playing 'Hangman' without having been given any information about the probabilities of occurrence of letters would be a very poor opponent. It would have no knowledge of the orthography of the words it was attempting, and would have to make random guesses. If an intelligent Hangman program was presented with more and more words, each containing information about the probabilities of letters in certain positions of words and in certain letter contexts, it would make increasingly astute guesses, just like experienced human players. These intelligent guesses can be said to be based on knowledge accumulated through the collection of information. The distinction is that while information is contained in the stimulus and is available for us for gathering, knowledge is information that has been gathered over time and that can guide the collection of future information. In this sense, knowledge corresponds to memories, and experienced users of written words can draw upon their knowledge of orthography to constrain their guesses. It is not just in playing word games that this knowledge is useful, of course, and we can observe the use of orthographic knowledge when readers attempt to interpret semi-intelligible handwriting or read words that are available only very briefly.

The knowledge available to the skilled reader

Orthographic knowledge can help experienced readers anticipate word completions, reducing their dependence upon the visual information available on the page, and other sources of knowledge can also be used in this way. Consider the following incomplete sentence, the final word of which is either partially obscured by our delinquent ink blot, or is perhaps broken by a hyphen at a page break:

> *The captain told the*
> *mate to drop the an-*

How does the *an-* word continue? We could simply turn the page or get the ink blot to fade so that we can extract visual information, or we can use three sources of knowledge available to us. By making use of orthographic knowledge we can declare that the letters *c*, *t* and *a* are more probable in the third position of the word than are the letters *b*, *v* and *x*, although all of these letters are legal continuations. The other two forms of knowledge go beyond the letter probabilities within words, and take account of the sequence of words prior to the incomplete word. Our knowledge of the rules of grammar – syntactic knowledge – also provides constraints, with nouns and noun qualifiers being more probable than verbs and conjunctions, for instance. This restriction on the permissible classes of words will make some particular words more probable than others (*anagram, anchor, antelope* versus *and, announce, antagonize*). We can also make use of semantic knowledge, using the meanings of the other words to make a guess about the scene being described. If we take into account our knowledge of what captains are reputed to instruct mates to drop, then a single candidate offers itself. There is only one realistic candidate unless the previous sentence has set up a conflicting context, of course, in which case our semantic knowledge will allow us to select a different candidate. Suppose the previous sentence had been:

> *The mate was very distractible, and was addicted to word games of all kinds but especially to crossword puzzles.*

The more information we collect about the text, the more constrained will be the guess, and the less we will have to rely upon visual information. Skilled readers will make use of many sources of knowledge to restrict their need to process the information in printed words, anticipating the next word on the basis of what they have already extracted from the page in combination with what they know of the language and of the meaning of the text as it unfolds.

We cannot estimate the information contained in print on the basis of the number of letters in a word, not only because letters have unequal probabilities of occurrence that depend upon their orthographic contexts, but also because different readers have different kinds of knowledge when they see the print. If the sentence about the captain's instruction to the mate was presented to two readers, one of whom knew about this particular mate's enjoyment of crossword puzzles, and one of whom believed it to be taken from a regular description of what captains tell mates to do, then different amounts of information would be available from the incomplete word. Knowing that *anagram* is a likely completion means that when it does appear it contains less information, just as the second letter of $Q*IP$ contains less information than the missing letter of $QUI*$. Information is extracted from printed text, but the quantification is not simple, and indeed has limited uses. Descriptions of the information content focus upon the readability of a text, using measures of the number of words per sentence, the syntactic complexity and the predictability of deleted words, for example. These uses include the determination of whether the text is suitable for readers of different ability, whereas the use of the idea of information here is to indicate the content of the printed letters, words and sentences that the reader extracts and uses. This brings us to the second part of our description of reading, in which we need to declare what happens to the information as it is processed.

The processing of information

As written information is encountered by the reader's eyes, words are recognized, relationships between words are formed into ideas, and a model of the situation or argument is constructed. As the words are recognized they can be pronounced aloud, entailing another kind of processing into speech. The description of reading in the three stages of word recognition, idea formation and model construction will be embellished in Chapter 6. It does, however, require an outline of the kinds of knowledge that the reader can draw upon, of the memory support that is available as we form relationships between words, and also an account of the role of speech recoding in these processes.

As a printed word is first encountered by the reader's eyes it has as little meaning as if it had appeared in an unfamiliar orthography – as a Chinese character, or in Arabic or Hebrew script, perhaps, for most readers of English. At this early stage of processing it is defined as no more than a visual pattern. When a representation or code of the visual pattern makes contact with a pattern recognizer it will be declared as being a specific letter or perhaps a specific word. At this point we can say that the pattern has been processed. A process is a cognitive action that transforms information from one form to another. If a set of marks on a page are recognized as a letter rather than a smudge of ink then information is extracted and a purely visual code is transformed into a letter code. At this point knowledge of the available letters or characters in an orthography has been used. But how do we know what is a letter and what is a smudge? Some general issues in the recognition of familiar patterns are illustrated by a brief consideration of how letters might be processed.

Theories of pattern recognition

When viewing a page of text how do we go about distinguishing letters from each other, or even recognizing them as letters as opposed to commas, full-stops or smudges on the page? Two major theories of pattern recognition have attempted to reply to this problem, namely template matching and feature detection theories. Template matching suggests that we have stored representations in our brain of every pattern that we recognize. Thus the letter T is recognized by comparing the pattern of excitation from the cells in the retina to a template stored in memory. If there is a match then the letter T is perceived. How does such a theory deal with deviant patterns such as T written in a different font, T? Do we have to have a template of the letter T for every other possible type font and handwriting, and size and orientation in which T could appear? This seems unlikely.

$$T_{T_T} T_{T_T} T_{T_T} T_{T_T} T_{T_T} T_{T_T}$$

An alternative account of our ability to recognize patterns with minor deviations such as the type fonts illustrated here, suggests that images are 'cleaned up' before the template matching stage is attempted. This normalization stage eliminates any noise but maintains the important features of the target. However, this is more complex than it may sound. How would we eliminate extra irrelevant lines such as the swirls and curls in a person's signature?

Basically the template model is inefficient. We cannot have the large number of templates we would need in order to recognize the infinite variety of patterns that humans are able to recognize. It is also inflexible, in that it would not be able to recognize upside-down words; but we can:

Although this is upside-down, it is still readable.

An alternative explanation of pattern recognition is the feature detection theory. Imagine you were requested to produce a check-list of what elements a capital letter H should contain. You may report that it had two vertical lines of the same length joined by a central horizontal line of a smaller length. You would have described the essential features of the capital letter H. This is the same approach adopted by the feature detection theory. The initial stage in letter identification is to identify common elements that appear in the letters of the alphabet, such as horizontal and vertical lines, curves and so on. Thus when presented with the letter *T* other letters with the similar feature of a central vertical line will be considered as a response, such as *I* and *J*. Furthermore, letters with the second feature, the upper horizontal line need to be considered, such as *E*, *F*, *J* and *Z*. So far *J* has two features in common with the target *T* whilst *I*, *E*, *F* and *Z* have only one feature in common. However, *J* needs a third feature to be present before it can be selected in response to the target, namely, a bottom curve. This feature is not present and thus the response 'T' is made to the target *T*.

There is a considerable amount of evidence to support the theory of feature detectors. Physiological investigations have suggested that our visual systems contain feature detector cells. Micro-electrodes used to detect the activity of individual cells of the cat's visual cortex indicate that individual cells become active as a function of what the cat is observing. Cortical cells can be found to correspond to line, edge and slit detectors and to more complex patterns. It is plausible that humans also have detectors which correspond to the horizontal, vertical and curved lines, etc. that make up our alphabet.

Support for the feature detector theory from a study of human behaviour has been provided by Neisser (1964, 1967) with a visual search task. He asked subjects to find a target letter, such as a *Z*. embedded in a display of letters. When the display contained very dissimilar letters (*O*, *C*, *B*, etc. in this case) the task was easier than if the display contained letters that were easily confusable with the target (*X*, *Y*, *M*, etc.). This is easily explained as the cells that correspond to the letter *Z* (vertical lines and slanted lines) fire when the confusable letters are also present, but not when the nonconfusable letters make up the display. If there are a lot of cells firing that correspond to the letter *Z* but also to other similarly shaped letters, the visual system needs extra time to distinguish the evidence for the target *Z* from the other 'noise' to ensure that no mistake is made. However, when the display contains dissimilar letters there is no excess noise, since the detectors that fire in response to the curved features (*O*, *B*, etc.) do not interfere with activation of the line detectors.

Whichever theory provides the most satisfactory account of how letters are processed, and feature detection certainly is preferable over template matching, we need to investigate how such a process extends to the recognition of words. Is it that every letter of a word is recognized in serial fashion, which then triggers a word unit in memory (known as the mental dictionary, and often referred to as the mental lexicon)?

Serial or parallel processing of letters?

If we recognized words in a letter-by-letter process then an eight-letter word such as *SKELETON* would take twice as long to recognize as a four-letter word such as *BONE,* but it does not. Long words do take slightly more time to process than shorter ones, but this is a very small effect. The most powerful evidence against this serial letter-by-letter account of reading is provided by the 'word superiority' effect. Letters are sometimes identified more easily when there are several letters to be processed than when they are presented in isolation. If reading were a serial letter recognition process then it would take less time to identify a single letter on a screen than to identify a letter in a specific position within a word. This is not the case. To say that the third letter in a brief presentation of the word *WAGE* is a *G* and not a *D* is easier than saying that a single presentation of the letter *G* is a *G* and not a *D* (e.g. Reicher, 1969). In this experiment, to be described in more detail in Chapter 2, the recognition of an isolated letter is helped when extra letters are provided. If readers recognize letters one after the other then the word context should be a hindrance rather than a help. The word superiority effect suggests that all of the letters in a word are not only recognized at the same time, but that recognition of one letter can help the recognition of its neighbours. The next question to be asked is how sets of letters are processed into a code that corresponds to word recognition.

Accessing the mental lexicon

One of the essential processes in reading involves the recognition of an individual word, with the process resulting in the transformation of one code into another. The resultant code enables us to know that we have seen a word rather than a meaningless string of letters. The 'word code' contains knowledge of the meaning of the word, or it gives access to the equivalent of a dictionary or lexicon where this knowledge is stored. The code that gives access to the mental lexicon may have a purely ortho-graphic or visual form, or alternatively may be similar to the spoken form of the word. The second hypothesis here requires that each set of letters be first transformed into a speech-based code, and that an entry for a word in the lexicon becomes activated by its spoken representation. Although an additional stage of processing is required by this hypothesis, that is, the conversion from an orthographic to a speech-based code, there is some harmony in it because language is first and foremost communicated through speech. We learn our first language by listening and speaking, and so it is reasonable to consider the possibility that our units of language, the words that we know, are recognized and remembered in a code that retains the characteristics of the already-familiar spoken form. When we learn to read there is reason to believe that we learn to map the novel visual forms on to our knowledge of the words we recognize when we hear them. Children who learn these mappings quickly and who show awareness of the significance of variations in the sounds of the spoken language are those who learn to read most easily, as we shall see in Chapter 3.

The suggestion of a speech-based code for accessing the lexicon also comes from early studies using the lexical decision task, a popular tool for investigating word recognition processes. In the lexical decision task (LDT) the reader is presented with a mixture of words and non-words (letter formations that look like real words, for example *ROLT* and *BARP*), which are displayed one at a time on a screen. The task for the subject in an LDT experiment is to decide whether each set of letters forms a word or not and to respond as quickly as possible by pressing one of two keys that are marked 'yes' or 'no'. It takes readers longer to reject non-words such as *ROLT* and *BARP* than it does to say 'yes' to real words in this task, and this yes/no difference itself requires an explanation (see Chapter 2). The lexical decision task is a popular tool for investigating the processes necessary for word recognition because it requires only that the reader checks the existence of the word as an entry in the internal lexicon. If we ask the subject to name a word, and measure the time taken to start pronouncing it, then organization of the response will occupy an additional, unspecified amount of time. Further, words can be pronounced without consulting the internal lexicon – as with words previously unseen, for example. If we are primarily interested in the processes necessary for lexical access, then it is particularly important to avoid using a task that can bypass the lexicon altogether.

The lexical decision task was used by Rubenstein *et al.* (1971) to establish a variation in lexical processing that they called the 'pseudo-homophone' effect. A pseudohomophone is a non-word formed of a string of letters that, if read aloud, would sound like an actual word. So the letter-string *BLUD* is a pseudohomophone of the word *BLOOD*, and *YOO* is a pseudohomophone of *YOU*, *EWE*, and *YEW*. The important result from the Rubenstein *et al.* experiment is that pseudo-homophones have longer decision times than other strings of letters that do not form words. The fact that there is a selective effect for non-words that can be pronounced like words leads to the suggestion that when we make lexical decisions we do need to transform each visual pattern into its spoken, or phonological form. One reason for doing this would be that the units in the lexicon that correspond to words are stored as speech-based codes and that when we are asked whether a string of letters is a word we can only match the string with our lexical memories

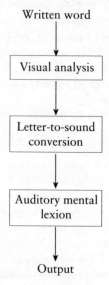

Figure 1.1   Phonological access to the mental lexicon

if a speech-based code is created. The suggestion from the early studies of the pseudohomophone effect is that access to the internal lexicon involves the conversion of print into a phonological code.

The phonological route to the lexicon uses the constituent phonemes of a word to access the mental lexicon (see Figure 1.1). In this simplistic model of word recognition the mental lexicon is taken to be a store of the spoken forms of all known words. It suggests that written words are converted into a speech-based code prior to recognition. The pseudo-homophone *BRANE* would thus be divided into its phonemes /b/, /r/, /eI/, /n/ which together form a code of the non-word that is identical to the phonemic representation of the real word *BRAIN*. This spoken form would be indistinguishable from the spoken form of an actual word stored in the lexicon.

The main problem with this simple version of the pure phonological route is that pseudohomophones should be incorrectly accepted as real words in a LDT. When readers encounter a non-word such as *BURD* they should first convert it into a speech-based code, use this to check whether there is a representation of this code in the lexicon, and when they find that there is, they should respond 'yes', but this is not the case. Pseudohomophones have longer response times and higher error rates associated with them than other non-words but the error rates are not 100 per cent. The simple phonological route would predict that they would be treated as real words, thus *always* incorrectly accepted as real words, and this process will take the same response time as it would for the real word *BIRD*. Rather than using the phonological code alone, the hypothesis suggests that whenever a 'yes' response is indicated by recognition of a speech-based code in the lexicon, readers must first check the spelling. It is this spelling check that takes the extra time in comparison with other non-words that do not have the same phonological representation as real words.

Spelling-to-sound correspondence rules

The written and spoken forms of words are sometimes described in terms of *graphemes* and *phonemes*, and before proceeding with the discussion of the use of speech-based codes in reading a note on this distinction is necessary. Processing the visual form into a speech-based form requires that the graphemes be converted into phonemes. So far we have considered words to be composed of different combinations of the twenty-six letters of the alphabet, but graphemes are not limited to single letters. The graphemes are the units of the writing system, and while they are single letters most of the time, combinations of letters also appear as graphemes, as in the case of the combinations *SH, TH, CH, EE, OO* and *EA*, for example. Thus *PEAR* has four letters, but three graphemes, *P, EA* and *R*. As with the case of single letters, the grapheme correspondence with pronunciation is not always perfect. The words *HAVE* and *GAVE* have the same middle grapheme A, but it is pronounced differently in each word. The two words *BOAT* and *HOE* contain the graphemes *OA* and *OE* respectively but they are pronounced the same in each word. When we come across a letter or a grapheme, how do we know how to recode it into its phonological form? Consider the *EA* combination, which has many possible pronunciations, including those in the words *BEAUTY, BREAD, CLEAR, CREATE, DEAL, GREAT, HEARD, LIKEABLE, REACT, SEANCE*. The letters *EA* sometimes form one grapheme and sometimes two and sometimes they are part of other graphemes. In the same way the letters *SH* usually form a single grapheme, as in *SHIP, SHOE, MASH, WISHED* and so on. The application of the grapheme–phoneme correspondence (GPC) rule that gives the pronunciation of *SH* slips when applied to words such as *MISHAP*, in which the two letters belong to different morphemes or units of meaning. If a model of lexical access is to rely upon application of the GPC rules it has the difficulty of describing how the same pair of letters is converted into the correct phoneme. Not even the immediate orthographic context can help here, because inconsistent pairs like *HAVE/RAVE* have similar forms. It is the word as a whole that determines the appropriate pronunciation, but if the model suggests that the whole word must first be recognized, in order that the pronunciation can be determined, so that in turn the lexicon can be accessed, then that model is in deep trouble!

A phoneme is a separable identifiable unit of sound, and by changing a phoneme within a word we change the meaning of the word. Thus whilst *PEAK* and *PEAR* contained the same central grapheme *EA*, it is pronounced differently in the two words. The grapheme represents different phonemes in these two words, and as we have just seen, there are many other pronunciations of *EA* according to its context. The confusing relationship between graphemes and phonemes arises in part because we have more phonemes in English than we have letters of the alphabet. Some letters and letter combinations therefore represent more than one phoneme. (To make this task of describing the grapheme–phoneme relationship more difficult, we also have multiple ways in which a spoken form can be represented by script, as with *SAW*, *SORE*, *SOAR*, for example). There is an inconsistency in the estimation of the exact number of phonemes that exist in spoken English. Some linguists argue that there are as few as 39 phonemes in use and others as many as 47 phonemes. This inconsistency is due mainly to some analysts including diphthongs (common combinations of phonemes) in their descriptions whilst others do not. A second difficulty comes from variations in pronunciation among users of the same language in different parts of the world; not all dialects contain all of the possible phonemes. For example, many people cannot distinguish between the spoken forms of *PAW* and *POUR* although in some lists of phonemes the vowels in these two words have different pronunciations.

Letters do not have a direct relationship with the pronunciation of the words they spell. The ordering of the letters influences their pronunciation, but not even this is consistent. For example, add a 'silent *e*' to *HAT* and it becomes *HATE* with the *a* vowel lengthened, but the vowel sound of the *a* is pronounced differently in *HAVE*. The 'silent *e*' rule might suggest it be pronounced similarly to *RAVE*, and here we have the inconsistency of the grapheme–phoneme correspondence rules, or spelling-to-sound rules. Word pairs such as *HAVE/RAVE*, *MINT/PINT*, *LOVE/COVE* and *CATCH/WATCH* illustrate inconsistencies when we generate the spoken forms of words. To put this another way, written English is inconsistent in the way in which it represents the sounds of spoken English, using similar spellings for different sounds. These comments do not apply exclusively to the GPC rules necessary for the generation of pronunciations in English, of course, but it is important to note that in some languages there is much less inconsistency in the grapheme–phoneme correspondences (e.g. Finnish and Italian). In these more regular languages knowledge of a few GPC rules is sufficient to

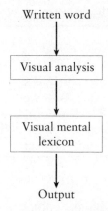

Figure 1.2 Direct visual access to the mental lexicon

generate the correct pronunciation of almost all of the commonly used words. GPC inconsistencies can influence the recognition and pronunciation of words by skilled readers. The difficulty of pronunciation of words varies according to whether they obey the GPC rules. Baron and Strawson (1976) presented lists of words in which all words obeyed the rules (words with regular pronunciations) or did not (irregular or exception words), finding slower responses for the lists formed of irregular words. Inconsistencies in the pronunciation of words with similar spellings pose a difficulty not only for children learning to read, but also for any explanation of the recognition of words that relies upon conversion of print into a speeeh-based code.

An alternative hypothesis of access to the internal lexicon suggests that the graphemic constituents of a word can be used to gain direct access, without using an intervening phonological conversion (see Figure 1.2). This is a simpler model of lexical access than the model in Figure 1.1, in that there are fewer stages of processing necessary: there is now no necessity to perform a letter-to-sound conversion process.

Support for this direct access hypothesis was provided by Kleiman (1975), who asked readers to perform three separate tasks on different occasions whilst they were speaking an irrelevant message aloud. This is known as shadowing, and involves listening to a continuous list of words (in Kleiman's case it was a list of digits), repeating each word as quickly as possible after it is heard. This is a very attention-demanding activity, and in addition it occupies the reader's speech apparatus. In other parts of the experiment the three tasks were performed without shadowing, so that comparisons could be made between performance of the tasks with and without availability of the means of speech recoding.

Table 1.1 Decisions about the characteristics of words

Type of decision	'True' responses	'False' responses	Decision time without shadowing (in msec.)	Decision time with shadowing (in msec.)
Graphemic	HEARD BEARD	GRACE PRICE	970	1,095
Phonemic	TICKLE PICKLE	LEMON DEMON	1,137	1,509
Synonym	MOURN GRIEVE	DEPART COUPLE	1,118	1,238

Source: Kleiman, 1975

In each of the three tasks the readers were requested to respond to pairs of words presented briefly, and their responses were timed. The question was how long the decisions took when the readers looked at two words and made a graphemic decision (do they differ only by the initial letter?), a phonemic decision (do they rhyme?), and finally, a decision on synonymy (do they have the same meaning?). Examples of the pairs of words are given in Table 1.1. The shadowing task was intended to disrupt any speech recoding, and so if subjects have to transform letters into their phonological codes before word recognition can occur it should disrupt performance equally on the phonemic and synonym tasks. The graphemic decision could be considered a pattern-matching task, and so might not suffer when speech recoding was inhibited by shadowing. However, although the shadowing task did disrupt performance for all three decision tasks, it was greatest for the phonemic task (372 msec. increase in decision time), and of similar magnitude for the synonym and graphemic tasks (120 msec. and 125 msec. respectively). The slower responses in the graphemic task can be attributed to the attention-demanding nature of the shadowing task, and a similar interference effect was seen in the synonym task (see Table 1.1). This is a very significant result, as the synonym task required that access be made to the mental lexicon (as the meaning of both words had to be computed), yet shadowing an irrelevant message did not disrupt performance to any greater extent than for the graphemic tasks. This suggests that the phonological coding of words is not a necessary precursor to lexical access.

A further problem for explanations of lexical access that rely upon the phonological route is the explanation of how we recognize homographs. Words that are spelt and pronounced the same but which have different meanings, such as LIGHT, SAW, and MINT, present a difficulty for both GPC and direct access models, but when the homographs are pronounced differently another problem emerges. How could either route distinguish between words that are spelt the same but have different meanings, words such as *READ, INVALID* and *TEAR*? When we pronounce statements such as *He had a tear in his shirt, and a tear in his eye*, the pronunciation must follow recognition of the meaning, but may be assigned on the basis of other factors such as the dominance of one meaning over another. The direct access model, however, allows recognition of the meaning prior to assignment of the pronunciation, and so has no difficulty in accounting for how these words should be pronounced.

Phonological coding may not be a *necessary* preliminary to lexical access, but this does not mean that there is none. We are so well practised at reading words aloud that generating the speech code may be automatic and unavoidable. This might be expected to be especially true with readers of languages in which there is a one-to-one relationship between the printed and spoken forms. With Finnish, for example, the spelling-to-sound rules are regular, and so graphemes represent phonemes consistently. Finnish speakers can rely upon the GPC rules to deliver them the correct pronunciation of a word. Word recognition can therefore rely upon the phonological access route indicated in Figure 1.1. It is not only in phonologically regular scripts that the easy generation of speech-based codes is observed. The influence of phonological codes can be seen with a range of tasks, and three will be mentioned here.

When 'target' words are preceded by another stimulus the first stimulus is said to *prime* the second, and Humphreys *et al.* (1982) found that identification of the target word was enhanced by a preceding word (the prime) when they were homophones. Presenting *SIGHED* immediately before the target *SIDE* made it easier to report the target. An important feature of this experiment is that the priming word was present too briefly to be reported. The experiment suggests that readers made use of the phonological form of the priming word unintentionally and without being aware of it.

A similar result was observed in a lexical decision task in which distracting words were printed to one side of a target word (Underwood and Thwaites, 1982). The distracting word was not reportable, but still caused interference when its spoken form was related to the target. Interestingly, this distraction effect can be observed with children 10–12 years old (Underwood and Briggs, 1984). Presumably after just a few years of reading practice they were automatically accessing the phonological codes of words.

The third piece of evidence comes from a study in which the eye movements of readers were recorded (Pollatsek *et al.*, 1992). Of particular interest was the amount of time spent looking at a target word in a sentence displayed on a computer screen. As a reader's eyes approached the target word it was sometimes changed the moment before it came under scrutiny. With this technique of using a 'contingent display' the words on the screen can be changed according to where the reader is looking. The use of contingent displays is discussed in some detail in Chapter 5. The target word in the Pollatsek *et al.* experiment was sometimes changed from a word very different from the target, and sometimes it was a homophone. For example, as the reader's eyes passed along the words:

|
The generous man gave every sent to charity.
|

the word *sent* would change to the more sensible *cent* at the point marked by the two vertical lines. (These lines were not visible to the readers during the experiment, of course.) The word in the location eventually occupied by *cent* was sometimes unrelated, such as *rack*, and there was a difference in reading according to whether this prior word was a homophone or not. The measure was the amount of time the eyes remained on the target – the fixation duration – and this was shorter if the prior word was a homophone, again suggesting that readers can be influenced by the phonological features of priming words.

These three effects demonstrate that the phonological forms of words are accessed rapidly and automatically, but they do not answer the question of whether the internal lexicon is accessed via the phonological route. They more simply demonstrate that when we see words the phonological code is unavoidably generated. How can these results be reconciled with Kleiman's (1975) conclusion that phonological codes are not necessary for word recognition?

Besner (1987) proposes that a resolution of these apparently contradictory conclusions rests with our understanding of the effects of Kleiman's distraction task. Kleiman used a shadowing task to eliminate the possibility that readers could generate speech-based codes, and similar tasks have been used to demonstrate influences in a range of reading experiments. Shadowing is one form of 'articulatory suppression' and other workers have had their readers repeat 'the, the, the ...' or 'one, two, three, four, five, one ...' while performing word recognition tasks. Sometimes there is a suppression effect with damage to the reading task, as with Kleiman's rhyme judgement task, and sometimes not, as with the synonym judgement task. For example, Baddeley and Lewis (1981) had readers judge whether printed non-words would sound like real words or not, if they were read aloud. The non-word CAYOSS then receives a 'yes' response while *TRID* receives a 'no'. Importantly, there is no effect of articulatory suppression on this decision. Besner (1987) proposed that articulatory suppression influences one form of phonological code, but not another. Phonological codes can be used in lexical access, and are not affected by suppression tasks because they are automatic and unavoidable. They can also be used after lexical access to assemble the components of words in order to make the kind of comparisons necessary in rhyme judgement tasks. Besner concluded that the Kleiman experiments tell us nothing about the role of phonological codes in lexical access and that his suppression effects were located post-access and possibly in articulation.

It can be seen that neither the direct visual route nor the phonological routes alone can explain all of the effects observed in word recognition. One more satisfactory approach that has evolved over the years is to build models that contain both routes that allow parallel use of visual and phonological information and that give access by either form of information. This is the dual route theory of Coltheart *et al.* (1977), and is sometimes called a horse-race model, in that the two routes are in competition with each other, and in which different phenomena can be observed according to which route provides lexical access. These models are described in more detail in Chapters 2 and 4.

Regularize the spelling-to-sound correspondences?

Although we are still unsure about exactly which unit (graphemic or phonemic, or both) is used in natural word recognition, the inconsistencies between spelling and pronunciation lead to the two suggestions that we should take steps to regularize our written language and that children learning to read should be given an artificial alphabet in which there is a regular spelling-to-sound pattern. English has quite an irregular script (consider the example of the ten different pronunciations of the grapheme *EA*, above). One way to regularize it is not to change the pronunciations but to change words spellings so that the graphemes will correspond to the phonemes that they are meant to represent. Thus *tear* (as in the eye) and *tear* (meaning 'rip') would be spelt differently to correspond to their different pronunciations: no more homophones!

The campaign to regularize English spellings has been simmering for many years, and is probably no nearer to success than it has ever been. The inventor of shorthand, Isaac Pitman, was among the more prominant popularizers of the idea of pronunciations consistent with spellings, with a system called Fonotypy, and 150 years ago it was introduced in the UK and the USA as a way of emphasizing phonetics. The necessary introduction of extra symbols, so that each phoneme was represented by its own letter was a problem for the scheme, because in addition to specialized training for reading teachers it also required specialized reading materials. By using the conventional letters of the alphabet the Simplified Spelling Society attempted to revise written English, again to make pronunciation more transparent (see Upward, 1992). Extra letters were introduced into words, other letters replaced or deleted, as in:

> We rekwier dhe langgwej az an instrooment; we maybe aulsoe study its history. Dhe prezens ov unpronoust leterz, three or for different waez ov reprezenting dhe saem sound, three or for uesez ov dhe saem leter: aul dhis detrakts from dhe value ov a langgwej az an instrooment.

This 'Nue Speling' of the mid-1900s did not catch on in spite of good publicity and some very positive reports from teachers who used it with beginning readers. The current change recommended by the Simplified Spelling Society is 'Cut Spelling' or, more accurately, 'Cut Spelng.'

> Cut Spelng exploits th discovry that redundnt letrs cause lernrs th most trubl, and it therfor ataks that dificlty by removing those letrs. Typicl of th resultng spelngs ar: det, iland, burglr, teachr, doctr, neibr, martr, acomodation, dautr, sycolojy.

Perhaps the best known, and most thoroughly evaluated, of the spelling reforms is the Initial Teaching Alphabet (generally abbreviated as i.t.a.). It is intended as a scheme for young readers, with the idea that in the second year of schooling they should make the transition to the traditional alphabet. In i.t.a. every different sound (phoneme) is represented by a different symbol, thereby creating a new alphabet, as did Pitman's Fonotypy. The Initial Teaching Alphabet contains 44 symbols to represent the most common phonemes in English.

The Initial Teaching Alphabet was introduced through the UK in the 1960s, and also in the USA, Canada and Australia on a smaller scale. Its effectiveness was carefully evaluated in an extensive study reported by John Downing (1967). The results were promising, with a considerable advantage gained by children in i.t.a. classrooms over those in traditional classrooms. After one year of schooling, 33 per cent of the i.t.a. children had advanced to Book V of their reading scheme while none of the traditional classroom children had advanced this far. After two years the figure were 66 per cent of the i.t.a. group against 31 per cent of the control group. On specific reading tests similar advantages were apparent. On a test of word recognition and pronunciation (the Schonell Graded Word Reading Test) after one year the i.t.a. group averaged 18 points, against 7 points for the controls taught with the traditional orthography, and on a test of reading accuracy (the Neale Analysis of Reading Ability) the achievements were 25 points against 14 points in favour of the i.t.a. children. One apprehension comes from observations as the i.t.a. children make the transfer to the traditional orthography, usually in the fifth term of schooling. In a silent reading comprehension test (the Standish Test) administered using traditional orthography after transfer, there was a tendency for the control children to outperform the i.t.a. children. Making the transfer lost the gains made by the early use of consistent spelling-to-sound mappings with i.t.a. This tendency for control children to be advantaged was eliminated for children tested after three years of schooling, but the important point is that the i.t.a. children did not have an advantage when tested using traditional orthography.

The failure to make sustainable gains and the difficulty of transferring between orthographies are two reasons that the use of i.t.a. is in decline, but just as significant is the use of unconventional characters that require the printing of specialist reading books, and the training of specialist teachers. A difficulty for the children taught with i.t.a. is that they are essentially bilingual while being exposed to the i.t.a. orthography. They may or may not have received some informal teaching with the traditional orthography at home, or at nursery school, but they would certainly have been exposed to the traditional alphabet around their homes and in the street. Words are ubiquitous and are totally unavoidable – on packages, on television, on clothing, on toys and games, on road signs and on public advertisements. By the time i.t.a. is introduced children will have considerable knowledge of traditional orthography, and will have to put those memories to one side while learning the new symbols. Further, environmental print does not vanish during the two years of i.t.a. teaching. The words that are associated with non-school behaviour are printed in another language, and we might expect to see mutual interference between the reading of two sets of words that have common meanings expressed in different orthographies.

There are a number of reasons for supposing that a regularization of English would not lead only to benefits, and that disadvantages would also exist. Although an English orthography with consistent spelling-to-sound rules would become more regular and may be acquired more quickly (as Downing's study of i.t.a. indicates), we would increase the number of homographs. We already have problems with *SAW* (as the past tense of 'see'), *SAW* (the tool) but such examples are currently rare. However with a regularised orthography, homophones such as *SIGHT/ SITE/CITE, AISLE/I'LL/ISLE, FOR/FORE/FOUR* and *PAW/POUR/ PORE* would become homographs, not only pronounced the same but now spelt the same. And *SAW* would then be joined by *SOAR* and

SORE, all with the same spelling. How would we be able to select the correct meaning with ease? In addition, regularization would reduce the similarities between pairs of words such as *DEMON/DEMONIC, EXPLAIN/EXPLANATION, BOMB/BOMBARD, TELEGRAPH/ TELEGRAPHIST* and *INHIBIT/INHIBITION*. The similar spellings reflect similar morphemic structures: there is a transparency in the similarity in the pairs of meanings, and this transparency may help us to recognize the meanings. Finally, by eliminating redundant letters from words, spelling reforms such as those advocated by the 'Cut Spelng' would not enable easier word recognition, but could well make it more difficult. Our current view of word recognition suggests that skilled readers make use of a variety of sources of information when reading, and by eliminating some of these sources the major gain is likely to be more words on each page, with slower recognition of each word.

Memory support for reading

One of the principal reasons for questioning the suggestion that we recognize words by first converting the print into a speech-based code, is the result from Kleiman's (1975) experiment described earlier. Besner (1987) has questioned whether this result pertains to the question of lexical access at all, and has offered an alternative interpretation based on quite distinct pre-access and post-access uses of speech codes. Independent of the outcome of this dispute is a second important result from Kleiman's experiment concerning the question of what memory support reading requires. In addressing this question it finds a role of speech recoding not inconsistent with Besner's interpretation. It also provides an explanation for the introspective observation that when we read difficult material silently to ourselves, we sometimes have the impression of hearing a spoken form of the material inside our heads.

The internal lexicon is one form of memory support that is essential for reading, of course, for without word memories there can be no word recognition. The meaning of each word would have to be derived from scratch each time we saw it. A more extensive form of support comes from our knowledge of the world, the form of knowledge that is sometimes described as semantic memory. Consider the differences between the following two sentences.

When she saw the possibility of some fun, Elizabeth Bennet winked at her sister Jane, and they disappeared for some time together.

When she saw the possibility of some fun, Mata Hari winked at James Bond and they disappeared for some time together.

The two sentences have similar words and similar syntactic structures and yet they suggest very different scenarios. The first sentence will evoke some very specific possibilities for readers of Jane Austen's novels, and equally specific but very different possibilities will be suggested by the second sentence, which is of course designed to be appreciated by readers of raunchy spy stories. For different possibilities to offer themselves, different memories will be accessed, or to put this another way, different 'scripts' will operate (Schank and Abelson, 1977) to help us organize the incoming information. In Chapter 6 we shall return to the comprehension of text through mental models that rely upon the reader's knowledge of the world, but for the present purposes it is sufficient to note, when we are talking of memory support, that different kinds of memories are used for different purposes. Lexical memories serve the recognition of words, and semantic memories help us to interpret the ideas being described. Kleiman's experiment indicated that temporary or working memories, intermediate between lexical and semantic memories, are necessary for the integration of words in sentences.

As in the first experiment, the task was to make decisions about words while shadowing lists of digits. The shadowing was intended to prevent readers from using speech recoding while they were preparing to make decisions about the visually presented words. Whereas the first experiment asked about individual words, the next experiment required the readers to work with words presented in sentences. There were four tasks, and as before, graphemic, phonemic and semantic decisions were required, with the fourth task requiring the integration of a whole sentence.

In the graphemic task readers decided whether a single word looked like any word in a sentence, for example:

BURY
YESTERDAY THE GRAND JURY ADJOURNED.

For the phonemic task a 'yes' response was required if the single word rhymed with any word in the sentence:

CREAM
HE AWAKENED FROM THE DREAM.

The semantic task involved a categorical word search in which the single word named a category, a member of which might be present in the sentence:

GAMES
EVERYONE AT HOME PLAYED MONOPOLY.

These three tasks produced patterns of interference from shadowing that were consistent with the first experiment. The phonemic task was much more difficult when concurrent shadowing was performed (312 msec. increase in response time), and whereas the graphemic and semantic were slower with shadowing the increases in decision times were much smaller (140 msec. and 78 msec., respectively).

The critical task in this experiment required readers to judge whether a short sentence made sense, for example:

PIZZAS HAVE BEEN EATING JERRY.

This sentence acceptability task was associated with the largest interference effect from shadowing (an increase of 394 msec.), suggesting that while the processing of individual word meanings can proceed with relatively little interference from shadowing, the integration of those meanings cannot.

There are two possibilities here, in accordance with two effects of shadowing. Kleiman intended the shadowing to inhibit the conversion of the words in the decision tasks from their visual form to their spoken form. While the readers were shadowing they could not easily articulate the printed words or generate a subvocal version of their spoken form. Accordingly, any task damaged by concurrent shadowing may depend upon generation of a speech code. The interference to the phonemic comparison tasks in both experiments confirms this suggestion. These tasks require the comparison of the sounds of words, and performance is damaged while shadowing.

The second possibility is that shadowing has simply reduced the amount of attention that can be dedicated to the task. Shadowing has long been used in experiments as a means of directing a listener's attention to a spoken message, often to determine the extent to which some other message can be understood, and is accepted as an activity that demands concentration. The tasks in Kleiman's experiments that were most vulnerable to shadowing could simply be those that require most attention, but this fails to account for the considerable interference suffered by the phonemic tasks. The other tasks were affected slightly, and this may be attributable to the general loss of attentional capacity caused by the need to shadow the digits, but the phonemic tasks were damaged over and above this level. This suggests that shadowing has affected the need to recode words into the speech code that is essential for the decision. In the second experiment the sentence acceptability task also suffered extensive damage, again suggesting that speech recoding supports reading. Kleiman's suggestion is that the integration of words in this task requires the use of working memory, which is served by the retention of individual words using the speech code.

Working memory is a cognitive system proposed by Baddeley and Hitch

(1974) to account for limitations in the temporary storage and processing of information. There are three interacting subsystems in the model, with the core being the central executive which has responsibility for controlling the flow of information and for storing the products of processing. This component has limited capacity, and is supported by two subordinate subsystems, or slave systems, that have memory capacities of their own. These are the articulatory loop, used for maintaining verbal information through subvocal maintenance rehearsal, and the visuo-spatial scratchpad, which retains visually presented information. The working memory model, and its account of significant events in the acquisition of reading skills, is described further in Chapter 3.

Daneman and Carpenter (1980) and Just and Carpenter (1992) have demonstrated the usefulness of the working memory model in solving a difficulty for traditional models of human memory that relied upon the distinction between short-term memory (STM) and long-term memory (LTM). The difficulty is that an individual's reading comprehension ability is not predicted particularly well by his or her STM capacity. Comprehension must involve the temporary storage of words during sentence comprehension, so that words and phrases early in a sentence can be integrated with words presented later in the sentence. Repeated attempts with various measures of STM capacity have failed to find consistently predictive relationships between short-term storage and reading comprehension (e.g. Farnham-Diggory and Gregg, 1975; Guyer and Friedman, 1975; Perfetti and Goldman, 1976). Poor readers appear to have no more limited a STM system than skilled readers. Daneman and Carpenter (1980) looked at the relationship between storage and comprehension using the idea of working memory, criticizing the traditional approach as emphasizing the structural limits to memory. Models of STM envisaged a fixed number of memory slots into which incoming information is placed, and once the slots are all filled STM is said to have reached capacity. In contrast, working memory gives emphasis to the functions of memory, with readers being seen as having an information processing task to perform with the assistance of temporary storage. The comprehension task will occupy varying amounts of capacity in the various working memory systems, and as comprehension difficulty increases, so the amount of residual capacity will decrease. Also, readers with more effective comprehension strategies will have greater storage capacity left over after processing of the reading task. More efficient readers will therefore appear to have greater functional storage capacity, even though their short-term memory spans may be similar to those of poor readers.

In the Daneman and Carpenter task readers performed a comprehension task with a simultaneous storage task. The storage task assessed the number of words readers could remember while they comprehended a series of sentences. Individuals in the experiment read aloud sets of unrelated sentences, and then reported the last word of each sentence in the set. After each recall of terminal words, the number of sentences in the set was increased, and for each individual reader the number of successfully recalled words noted. This measure of memory span did predict reading comprehension, with some readers remembering only one or two of the final words, and others remembering four or five. As the number of recalled words increased, so did a number of measures of comprehension, including a test of the integration of ideas between sentences, in a further study that required the comprehension of paragraphs. An interesting result from the experiment with paragraphs was that the integration task (deciding who the pronoun 'it' referred to in an earlier sentence) was performed differently by different kinds of reader. A varying number of sentences could be presented between the pronoun and its referent. Individuals with small memory spans were less likely to be successful in deciding on the referent of the pronoun when six or seven sentences intervened, and were generally less successful than readers with larger spans. Daneman and Carpenter concluded that the task of associating a pronoun with its referent noun – an essential component when we comprehend passages – is easier when the referent is still present in working memory. The availability of information will therefore depend upon the individual's working memory capacity, with more effective readers being better able to keep ideas in memory until they have to be integrated. More recent evidence presented by Just and Carpenter (1992) suggests that individuals with larger working memory capacity are better able to integrate semantic and syntactic information, and better able to maintain and consider alternative syntactic interpretations of ambiguous sentences.

Skilled information processing

As we learn to perform an action and practise it, the activity becomes skilful. The relationship between practice and skill is most apparent in the case of physical activities such as tying shoelaces, riding a bicycle, writing with a pen or driving a car. It also applies to cognitive activities such as performing mental arithmetic, recalling simple facts and reading.

The change from unskilled to skilled action is accompanied by faster, smoother performance, in which we no longer need to give careful attention to the stimulus environment in which we are operating. Our minds are released from the need to perform detailed examinations of the information that we need to operate upon. The information being considered here includes the position of the shoelaces in our fingers, our grip on the gear lever in the case of physical activities, or the values and operators in arithmetic and the details of the words to be recognized when reading. This change from attention-intense to attention-free or automatized behaviour can be described as being accompanied by a change in the mode of control. When we perform an unfamiliar action we need to take careful account of the information that we operate upon, and of the small changes that are associated with our action. Feedback from the effects of our actions upon the state of the environment is valuable in telling us whether the task is being performed appropriately, and attention to feedback allows us to make continuous corrections during performance of the action. When we become skilled performers we no longer need to take account of the feedback loop: our actions are guided directly by the stimulus and do not need to be corrected. When tying shoelaces, for example, there is no necessity to inspect the state of completion after performing each component action, and when answering simple mental arithmetic questions such as 'What is 15 divided by 3?' there is neither detailed consideration of alternative answers nor attention given to the meanings of individual words. In both cases the presentation of the problem, equivalent to presentation of a stimulus, is sufficient to guide us to a completed action. There is no introspection about intervening states. Performance of these physical and cognitive actions is sometimes described as being under open loop control when feedback is not given consideration, whereas unfamiliar actions are completed only with closed loop control (Reason, 1979; Underwood, 1982).

The distinction here is between actions that require attention, and those that are automatized or controlled, to use the terms used by Schneider and Shiffrin (1977) in their demonstrations of the relationship between practice and the automatic performance of complex perceptual analyses. When we are sufficiently practised to be regarded as skilled our behaviour is automatized and is under the direct control of the stimulus. Our attention is free for other activities and is called upon only when our over-learned mental structures do not include a procedure for dealing with the stimulus. Only with novel stimuli do we need to attend closely or to select the appropriate response. Attention is necessary for cognitive actions that are not in regular use, such as the recall of information ('What is the name of the President of the USA prior to Bill Clinton?' or 'What is the name of the capital city of the Netherlands?'), or the calculation of recognizable but infrequently performed arithmetic problems ('What is 11 multiplied by 15?''), or, and this is the point to be made here, the integration of words during reading. Sentences usually contain novel combinations of words, and attention is necessary for the integration of these words: to identify the referents, to reconstruct the ideas, and to create a mental model of the story or argument.

For the skilled reader letter recognition and word recognition are well practised cognitive actions, and do not require the detailed attention that a beginning reader will give them. The recognition of words in regular use may be as automatic as answering questions such as 'What is the name of the capital city of France?' or 'What's the name of the current British Prime Minister?' in which the questions themselves serve as the direct stimulus for the answer. LaBerge and Samuels (1974) suggested a model of reading development in which word decoding skills become increasingly automatic. Only when letter and word recognition is automatic can readers think about the meanings of sentences.

Automatic word recognition: Stroop tasks

One of the principal sources of evidence that support the idea of automatic word recognition has come from Stroop-like tasks. In the original form of the Stroop test subjects name the colours of patches of ink. The patches form printed words, but the words are to be ignored, and the colours named as quickly as possible. So a word might be printed in red ink, and the response would be 'red' regardless of what word was formed. When the word formed the name of another colour, slower responses are observed. The word GREEN, printed in red ink and requiring a spoken 'red' response, would get a slower response than a non-colour word printed in red ink. The meaning of the actual word being formed is irrelevant to the subject's task, but it cannot be ignored. Although the subjects can perform the task by processing only the colour of the ink, they cannot easily avoid reading the word.

One variant of this task is illustrated below. Imagine that a single word appears on a screen, and your task is to say whether the letters are printed with large or small letters. It is the physical size of the print that is important, and the word that is spelled by the letters is irrelevant. The word may be irrelevant, but it interferes with the size judgement. In this case the interference or variation in the response is an inhibition effect in that the response is slower and less accurate. The two words on the top row, where the word agrees with the size, give easier judgements than the two words on the bottom row, where the word conflicts with the required response.

SMALL   LARGE

SMALL   LARGE

In this case it is important that the word spells a member of the 'response set', the set of words which together form all of the words used as responses. Stroop-like interference is most likely a product of interference in the selection of the appropriate response, and when the word spells a plausible but incorrect response interference occurs. This is not the only source of interference in Stroop, however, and variants of the task have found interference from words that are not part of the response set, but are associates of the stimulus that is to be the subject of the response.

Variants of this task that allow the use of a greater range of words have used the same 'interference' argument to observe the effects of distracting words upon other words, and upon pictures, using a number of reading and naming tasks. A study using a picture-naming variant of Stroop demonstrated that words that are not given attention can cause interference in the time taken to start producing the name of a picture, and the presence of interference indicates that the words were recognized automatically (Underwood, 1976). The picture-word stimuli were displayed for 60 msec. in this experiment, a duration long enough for the subjects to identify the picture, but not long enough for them to move their eyes to the word. Each time a picture was displayed, it was shown in the centre of the screen, where the subjects were instructed to direct their eyes. Subjects were told that distracting words would appear, but that they were to ignore them. Pictures that were accompanied by words that were semantic associates, as in the bread–butter example shown, had slower naming times than pictures that either had no distracting words, or had meaningless strings of letters by the side of them, or had unassociated words with them. Interference from the meaning of an associated word indicates that the word is recognized without attention.

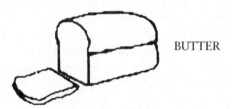

BUTTER

Picture-word interference has been used to record the developmental course of the acquisition of automatic word recognition. During the first six months of schooling, for example, Guttentag and Haith (1979) found an increase in the amount of interference caused by distracter words in a picture-naming task. During the period reading became a practised activity and word recognition became automatized. Towards the end of the children's elementary education, after five or six years of reading instruction, a number of reading processes could be seen to be automatized.

Automatic word recognition: access to meanings

A second source of evidence leading to the conclusion that the meanings of words are recognized automatically comes from priming tasks, in which one word is shortly followed by a second word. The reader is asked to perform some task in response to the second word (sometimes called the 'target word') and the response is influenced by the first word (the 'prime'). So, the priming word *BREAD* might appear on a screen shortly before the target word *BUTTER* and the task for the subject might be to name the target or to make a decision about it, such as a lexical decision. In this case the associated prime would be expected to result in a faster response to the target than if an unassociated or neutral prime had been presented. The neutral priming condition, usually a string of letters that do not form a word, is important in assessing the different effects of associates and non-associates. Interference effects are assessed as the difference between the response time with the neutral prime and the response time with either an associated or non-associated prime. We have already encountered an example of a priming task, in the Humphreys *et al.* (1982) experiment, in which a priming word aided the recognition of a homophonic target (*SIGHED → SIDE*).

In experiments with sequential presentations of words, the effect of the prime upon the target varies according to the time interval between them. Short intervals – in the order of a quarter of a second – give rise to facilitation effects with associates. With long intervals (in the order of two seconds) the pattern changes. Facilitation from associates is still observed, but there is now an inhibition effect from non-associates (Meyer and Schvaneveldt, 1971; Neely, 1977). These effects are described in more detail in Chapters 2 and 3, in the framework of Posner and Snyder's (1975) two-process model of recognition. At short priming intervals only one process can operate: a fast automatic process in which the recognition of one word influences the recognition of its associates without attention playing any role. At long priming intervals, however, the reader has time to think about the priming word, and to use it to generate a set of words that could follow. The process of generating expectancies is slow and requires attention. If the expectancies are incorrect, as they would be if a prime was not an associate of the target (e.g. *CANARY → DOCTOR*), there would be no match between the target and the anticipated target, and only after attention has been directed away from the expected word can the processing of the actual target proceed. The Stroop experiments demonstrate that words themselves can be recognized automatically, and demonstrations of priming indicate that the processing of one word can automatically influence the processing of another. Meanings of words are not only accessed automatically, but they can also influence the processing of other word meanings automatically. These are two effects that are observable independently of the reader attending to the processing of words.

When the priming word is presented subliminally, then these two effects are combined in a single demonstration. Marcel (1983) presented primes below the threshold for conscious report, following by targets that required lexical decision responses, and found a facilitation effect for associated primes that was similar to the effect observed when the primes were fully reportable. Demonstrations of subliminal processing of words are not strictly the same as demonstrations of unattended processing, in that in the case of subliminal displays the processing is *data limited* and in the case of unattended displays the processing is *resource limited* (Norman and Bobrow, 1975). The effects of unattended and subliminal words are often very similar, however (cf. Philpott and Wilding, 1979, and Underwood, 1976), and when a subliminal word has an effect upon behaviour it follows from processing without the reader choosing to apply processes to the word.

The priming of one word by another is not restricted to a single meaning of a word. When a word with a number of meanings is processed, each of its meanings can influence the processing of a target. Swinney (1979) presented subjects with two tasks simultaneously. While they listened to a short narrative they watched a screen for the appearance of a string of letters, ready to make a lexical decision response. Immediately prior to the visually presented word a priming word was presented as part of the story. The prime influenced the target in this experiment, as would be expected from the priming experiments of Meyer and Schvaneveldt (1971) and Neely (1977). For example, one of Swinney's narratives contained the following:

The man was not surprised when he found several spiders, roaches and other bugs in the corner of the room.

In this the lexically ambiguous *bugs* has been provided with an interpretative context. In this sentence *bugs* refers to insects rather than hidden microphones used by spies, but both of these meanings influenced the lexical decision to a word presented immediately afterwards. A word such as *sky* gained slower responses than words such as *ant* and *spy*, and this pattern was obtained whether or not the context of the story biased the interpretation of the prime or not. The lexical decision times from this study are shown in Table 1.2; it shows the priming effect from an

Table 1.2 Both meanings of ambiguous primes influence lexical decisions to targets

	Same meaning as the context (ant)	Other meaning (spy)	Non-associated meaning (sky)
Ambiguous prime (*bugs*):			
Interpretative context	890 msec.	910 msec.	960 msec.
No context	916 msec.	925 msec.	974 msec.
Unambiguous prime (*insects*):			
Interpretavie context	887 msec.	958 msec.	963 msec.
No context	914 msec.	967 msec.	972 msec.

Source: Swinney, 1979

ambiguous word and from equivalent responses when the ambiguous word was replaced by an unambiguous equivalent.

When the ambiguous prime is replaced by another word that fits the context of the narrative the pattern of facilitation changes, such that a target associated with the other meaning of the ambiguous prime no longer gains facilitation. This is to be expected, since the target (*spy*) is no longer associated with either meaning of the prime (*insect*). A striking result from this experiment is that the context has no effect upon the availability of the meanings of the prime. Both meanings are effective in facilitating the lexical decision response to the target. This result only holds if the target is presented immediately after the prime, however, and if it is delayed by as little as one second, then facilitation is only seen if the target is congruent with the context. This suggests that both meanings of an ambiguous word are available shortly after it is perceived, and both meanings will automatically influence the processing of other words during this time, but that very soon after presentation the ambiguity is resolved and only one meaning can be effective.

Attention and reading

Individual words are recognized without the skilled reader having to attend to them. The processing of the meanings of words is also influenced by the context provided by immediately preceding words. Reading is not an activity for which attention is unnecessary, of course, and when we do find ourselves 'reading' without attention the meanings of sentences and paragraphs will be lost to us. Moving our eyes skilfully over a page, while daydreaming or worrying about some problem unrelated to the text, resembles reading only in its outward appearances. The ideas represented in the sentences may not be recognized, and a mental model of the text will not be constructed.

If we fail to attend to a sequence of words, they cannot be integrated into a personal representation that will allow us to make predictions. This is the conclusion from a study of the use of sentence contexts in a listening task, in which an unattended string of words was heard at the same time as subjects shadowed an attended message (Underwood, 1977). The shadowing task was similar to that used by Kleiman (1975), except that the words being shadowed were not digits. The final word of each set of words was a target word, in that the shadowing latency to this word was measured. The shadowed words sometimes formed a sentence such as

The angler returned the fish to the trout stream.

and sometimes were unrelated, as with

Antelope cover income hat collect stream.

In other cases just the words at the end of the sentence were congruent with the target:

Antelope cover the fish to the trout stream.

The interval between presentation of the target *stream* and the listener repeating it was measured in each case, and was found to vary according to the amount of congruent context provided. The more the words formed a sentence, the faster was the shadowing response, suggesting that the listeners had used the context to help predict the target word. On some of the trials where non-sentences were shadowed the context was provided in the unattended message. In these cases the context did not help the shadowing of the final target word, suggesting that attention is necessary if we are to integrate the meanings of words in such a way that we can understand a sentence well enough to predict how it will finish.

This conclusion about the use of attention in the integration of word meanings comes from a study of listening, and we must be cautious about extrapolating to the use of context when reading. Kleiman's (1975) results can be used to support the conclusion, however, for when his readers had their attention captured by a shadowing task they were able to perform simple reading tasks involving the comparison of single words, but unable to integrate the meanings of words in order to judge whether they formed a sentence. An attention-demanding shadowing task caused considerable difficulty for readers attempting to decide whether the words *Pizzas have been eating Jerry* formed a sentence. While this task required attention, making decisions about the visual, phonological and semantic similarities of pairs of words did not. Attention is not necessary for the first level of activity that involves word recognition, but it is required for the second level, in which the propositional structure of a text is identified, and for the third level, in which the reader creates a personal mental account of an interpreted text.

This introductory chapter has set out the assumptions of an approach that sees reading as information processing. Information, as has been said, is whatever reduces uncertainty, and when we are reading we use visual information in combination with psycholinguistic knowledge as we build our own mental model of the ideas intended for us by the writer of the text. We use our knowledge of the orthographic rules that determine which letters are likely to appear next, knowledge of the probabilities of individual words on the basis of their general frequencies of occurrence and on the basis of the semantic context provided by earlier words in the sentence. In addition, our knowledge of the rules of grammar will lead us to expect certain syntactic classes of words in certain locations in sentences. This syntactic expectancy is dependent again upon what has gone before. The information-processing approach requires us to identify the information that the reader uses, and to identify the stages of processing that are applied in order for the reader to come to an understanding of the text. An example of a stage of processing is the conversion of information on the page in a purely visual form into a form that corresponds to its spoken form. This transformation from a visual code into a speech-based (or phonological) code is central to an ongoing controversy in reading research. Is it necessary to convert a printed word into its phonological code before it can access the internal lexicon? The answer to this question has consequences for the way in which children are taught to read, because if phonological coding is essential, then surely we must teach children to appreciate the relationships between graphemes and phonemes as early as possible. This particular debate will be taken up in Chapter 3, after we have first used evidence concerning the sources of variation in the ease of recognition to evaluate the different types of cognitive models of reading that are available.

2

Cognitive Processes in Word Recognition

What determines how long it takes us to read? There are variations in the skill of different readers and there are variations between texts. A 10-year-old reader will be expected to read a given text more slowly than a 20-year-old undergraduate, and the undergraduate will read a text expounding the thoughts of a twentieth-century philosopher more slowly than a description of the exploits of James Bond. Not only will the philosophy text contain more difficult concepts than the Bond novel, but there will also be differences in the vocabularies used by the two writers. Some words will be more difficult to process than others, and this variation between words is the subject of the present chapter. The componential model supported in our discussions see reading enabled by identifiable processes that deliver different representations to the reader. The three levels of representation involve (i) the identification of the words in a sentence, (ii) the extraction of the essential ideas or propositions in the sentence, and (iii) the formation of a mental model from these words and ideas in which existing knowledge is used to elaborate on the information actually presented and to develop causal links. Most of our discussions will concern the first level of representation, in which the reader accesses the meanings of individual words, and this is the specific focus of the present chapter. The extraction of the essential ideas formed by these words, and the formation of the reader's mental model, are processes described in Chapter 6.

One of the most powerful predictors of the amount of time taken to read a sentence is the number of words it contains. If a skilled reader reads relatively straightforward text at a rate of 300 words a minute this gives us an average of 200 msec. per word. However, not all of the words will be inspected, and some may be inspected longer than others. This depends on many factors such as word length, frequency and context. These inspections, or eye fixations, are described in Chapter 5. The first purpose of the present chapter is to describe the time-consuming processes that determine our reading rate. Not all of the reading time will be spent in recognizing words, of course. In addition to the time taken to move the eyes from one word to another and from the end of one line to the beginning of another, there are the time-consuming processes associated with inter-word and inter-sentence integration. Before we can start to extract the ideas within a sentence, of course, we must first identify the meaning that is represented by each visual pattern that corresponds to a word.

For every word that a reader can recognize we can say that a memory must exist. This word-memory becomes activated whenever a printed sequence of letters is inspected. The sum total of a reader's word-memories can be thought of as his or her mental dictionary or internal lexicon, and the process of activating a specific entry in this lexicon is described as lexical access. If you can recognize letter-strings such as *CHUKKA*, *FOSSULATE*, *TRIPTYCH*, and *UMBLES* as words then you can be said to have an entry for them in your internal lexicon. These words are interesting because they are uncommon, and so it is likely that for at least one of them you will be able to say that you know that it is a word, but that you cannot say what it means. The entry in the internal lexicon is present, but associative connections to other words and to event memories are not accessible. Unlike a conventional printed dictionary, the lexicon may be a store of nothing more than the spellings of words known to that reader, with meanings, mental images, pronunciations and syntactic knowledge stored separately. This operational separation has implications for the ways in which we access and use the different kinds of information that exist for a word.

When readers recognize a word they can be said to have achieved lexical access, and the word becomes available for further processing such as pronunciation, accessing the meaning, or integration with other words in order to comprehend a sentence. Whether the internal lexicon contains words or the morphemic components of words is a matter which we shall set aside until the reasons for the variations in lexical access time have been outlined.

Sources of variation in lexical access

What causes variations in the time taken to recognize words, and what can we conclude about the underlying cognitive processes from the regularities in these variations? Some of the characteristics of words which are associated with variations in recognition time will be described here before we consider the models which have been established which attempt to explain these findings.

Word frequency

Consider the following simple sentence:

When the rhinoceros saw the gnu it was running very fast.

Although it is not a difficult sentence, there are a number of sources of processing delays which perhaps become apparent by comparison with a grammatically similar sentence in which one or two key words have been replaced:

When the supervisor saw the rat it was running very fast.

The words *rhinoceros* and *gnu* are both uncommon relative to some other words of similar length, such as *supervisor* and *rat*, and one of the most reliable factors associated with the speed of word recognition is the frequency with which a word is encountered. This *word frequency effect* is the observation that common or high frequency words are associated with faster responses than are uncommon or low frequency words (Rubenstein *et al.*, 1970).

This effect is demonstrated not only in sentence processing tasks but by a variety of other methods. One of the most popular of these methods has been the lexical decision task, in which readers respond positively by pressing one button if a letter-string spells a word, and negatively by pressing another button if it does not spell a word. There are advantages and disadvantages in using this task, and they will be discussed presently, but when it is used we must not only select a set of words to be used in the experiment, but also a set of non-words. The composition of the non-words has been found to affect their speed of rejection.

Non-word legality effect

Non-words which resemble words (*FLINK*) in some way (*FLING*, *BLINK*, etc.) have slower response times than non-words which are not word-like (*FKINL*), and these effects are informative about the features of words which are used during recognition. This is known as the *non-word legality effect* (Rubenstein *et al.*, 1970). This non-word legality effect is the equivalent of an effect seen for actual words in which words containing frequent letter bigrams such as *EA* and *TH* or frequent trigrams such as *STR* and *ION* are themselves recognized more easily than other words. For these sequences of letters to help word and non-word processing they must appear in the parts of the letter-strings where they appear most often. For example, in the words *HEALTH* and *STRAP* these letter combinations are in common locations, whereas in *EAST*, *OTHER* and *ASTRAY* they are in relatively unfamiliar word positions.

Lexical status effect

There is an overall difference in response times to words and non-words in favour of words. Positive responses are generally faster in the lexical decision task. A word such as *PARTY* gains a faster 'yes' response than does a non-word such as *CARTY* gaining a 'no' response. This difference is in the order of several hundred milliseconds, a substantial difference in lexical decision tasks.

Pseudohomophones

As non-words increasingly resemble words they become more difficult to categorize. One aspect of this concerns the similarity in pronunciation between a non-word and a real word. Non-words which would sound like words if read aloud, but which are spelt differently are homophones of actual words, and give rise to what is termed the *pseudohomophone effect*, an effect already encountered in Chapter 1. While a homophone is a word which sounds like another word (for example, *HALL* and *HAUL*, or *PEAR* and *PAIR*), a pseudohomophone is a printed non-word that would sound like an actual word if read aloud. Letter-strings such as *BURD*, *GRENE* and *GROE* are non-words because they do not correspond to the spellings of any English words, but they are orthographically similar to words, and if pronounced they can sound like frequently occurring words. Rubenstein *et al.* (1971) found that strings of letters forming words such as *GIFT* and *WALL* gained responses that averaged 760 msec. in their lexical decision experiment, whereas non-words formed of legal sequences of letters, such as *ROLT* and *BARP*, required decisions lasting 1,013 msec. However, a special type of non-word that *sounds* like a real word posed a bigger problem for the reader making lexical decisions. These letter-strings known as pseudohomophones take longer to reject than other non-words, with decisions lasting an average 1,076 msec. Thus pseudohomophones such as *BURD* and *GROE* take longer to reject than the non-words *ROLT* and *BARP*. It appears that they require further processing because they *sound* like the real words *BIRD* and *GROW*. An important feature of the lexical decision task is that it is conducted in silence; words and non-words are shown on a screen, and the only response made by the reader is to press one of two keys marked 'word' and 'non-word'. The task itself does not require the reader to produce a speech-based code of a pseudohomophone that matches a real word stored in the lexicon. This effect has been used as evidence for a role of speech recoding during lexical access, although questions have been raised about the locus of this code (before or after lexical access?). There have been questions about the orthographic similarity of the pseudohomophones to the words with which they are homophonic (see Martin, 1982; Taft, 1991). The pseudohomophone *GROE* shares three of its four letters with its base word *GROW*, and so the slow response may be a result of orthographic rather than phonological interference. Control conditions are necessary to observe the extent of orthographic interference, and when they are used the pseudohomophone effect survives. Although the pseudohomophone effect has had a mixed history it is now regarded as genuine, and is among the phenomena to be taken into account by our description of word processing (Dennis *et al.*, 1985; Underwood, Roberts and Thomasson, 1988).

Word superiority effect

The word superiority effect is important in its own right, and appears in a task in which the subject is asked to judge which of two briefly presented stimuli have previously been presented. The interest is in the difference between two main experimental conditions. In one of them a single letter is presented and the subject is asked to judge which of two letters have just been displayed, and in the other condition a whole word is presented and the subject is asked to judge which of two letters has been presented in a specific position of the word. Suppose that in the first condition the target letter was a *D*, and the subject is asked to say whether it was a *D* or a *G*. We can now determine the exposure duration necessary for subjects to be correct on, say, 75 per cent of occasions. In the second condition we present the target word *WADE* together with a

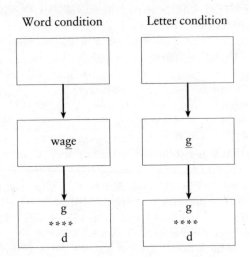

Figure 2.1   The word superiority effect

The task in this example of the experiment is to decide whether a specific letter is a *d* or a *g*. In the 'Word condition' the letter is embedded in a word, and in the 'Letter condition' it appears in isolation. In each condition the position of the target letter is indicated by underlining. The display presenting the target letter (either in a word or in isolation) is shown very briefly, and in some experiments it is 'masked' by the display of 'visual noise' such as fragments of letters immediately after the target display. Detection of the target letter is not perfect, and is easier when it appears in the context of a word than when it appears in isolation.

signal to say that it is the letter in the third position which is of interest (for example, a short line printed beneath the critical letter when the full word appears). A choice then has to be made between the letters *D* and *G* as the letter in the third position. Note that both *WADE* and *WAGE* are viable competitors as lexical units, and so the extra three letters provide little lexical information. What happens in this experiment is that if we keep the exposure duration constant in both conditions, then subjects are more often correct when a full word is presented: hence the word superiority effect (see Figure 2.1). A letter presented in the context of a word is recognized more easily than a letter presented in isolation (Reicher, 1969; Wheeler, 1970).

Context

Just as unusual structures within a sentence can result in slower recognition, processing can be seen to be faster in the case of contexts which predict specific words. When words appear at the end of highly constraining sentences they tend to be recognized more rapidly than otherwise. For example,

The eskimos were frightened by the walrus.

takes less time to process than

The bankers were frightened by the walrus.

Similarly, when a word is to be recognized in isolation, it will be recognized more slowly than when a word presented shortly before it is a semantic associate (Meyer and Schvaneveldt, 1971). This is the case of word recognition being aided not by an entire sentence but by a single word. If we had presented *RHINOCEROS* as the first word (the 'priming' word) and *HORN* as a word to be responded to (the 'target' word), then the response to the target would have been faster than if there had been no priming word, or if the prime had been an unassociated word. This *semantic priming effect* is observable with single words presented one after the other when the two words share features by virtue of being from the same semantic categories. When one member of a category has been processed, then the processing of other members becomes easier for a short while. There is some argument about the generality of these context effects during sentence comprehension (Fischler and Bloom, 1979; Stanovich and West, 1981), and they are certainly more robust when isolated words are to be recognized. The use of context in the identification of words varies according to the ability of the reader, and this relationship is described in detail in Chapter 3. Context has an effect upon our patterns of eye fixations, with predictable words being more likely to be skipped or to receive short inspections, as we shall see in Chapter 5.

Repetition priming

A special case of this priming effect is seen when a word primes itself, and this is the repetition priming effect (Scarborough *et al.*, 1977). If a relatively unusual word like *RHINOCEROS* is recognized, and then followed by the same word again, the second presentation is recognized somewhat more readily than the first. In this case the target shares all of the semantic features of the priming word, and a substantial facilitation effect can be observed.

Word similarity

It has already been noted that non-words similar to real words take longer to reject on a lexical decision task than non-words dissimilar to real words. An additional factor to consider is the number of real words that the non-word is similar to. The non-word *WOOK* is just one letter different from many real words: *LOOK, COOK, BOOK, WOOL*, etc. The exact number of words which are one letter different from a target whilst preserving letter positions is known as a word's *neighbourhood*. A large neighbourhood is detrimental for non-words as it slows down response times compared to a non-word such as *WOLN* which has a small neighbourhood: *WORN, WOLF* (Coltheart *et al.*, 1977). However, for real words the opposite effect has been observed. The word *LOOK* is similar to many other words: *COOK, BOOK, LOOT, LOOM*, etc., but this facilitates response times compared to a real word with a small neighbourhood (Andrews, 1992). To complicate matters further this neighbourhood effect, which is reported by Andrews, is observed only for low frequency words; response times for high frequency words are not influenced by neighbourhood size. It is important to note that, although the non-word neighbourhood effect is an extremely reliable one, finding the real word neighbourhood effect reported by Andrews is not. There is a great deal of research currently being conducted into this area and contradictory effects are being reported. This research will be mentioned later. Thus the predictions made by a word recognition model about word similarity effects are of great interest within this area.

Ambiguity

Many words have more than one meaning. Homographs, for instance, are words that are spelt the same but have different meanings (and often pronunciations) depending on the surrounding context. For example, the word *TEAR* can refer to a rip in a piece of cloth or a water drop from the eye. The number of word meanings available to any pattern of letters is a predictor of recognition time, with more meanings being associated with faster recognition (Jastrzembski, 1981). Semantic and syntactic context generally eliminate all but one meaning, and it is only when two meanings are equally viable that we become aware of this economy in our language. If we had separate words for each meaning, we would need a vast increase in the number of words in circulation.

Models of word recognition: word detection with lexical units

The purpose of any model is to capture the essential features of the object or system under consideration. In the case of word recognition, the model describes the cognitive processes necessary for the task of recognizing words and, more recently, of rejecting non-words in lexical decision tasks. A model is deemed successful when it meets criteria of acceptability. In the case of a model railway it must possess certain essential physical features such as a track and an engine and operating features such as the engine running along the track. Other features are less important for some model enthusiasts but perhaps not for others. What will be regarded as non-essential are, for example, the scaled speed of the engine, the details of paintwork on the carriages, or the means of propulsion. The same can be said of models of word recognition, with models being designed to explain specific phenomena while neglecting others. Most models have been designed to account for particular difficulties in word recognition, and have been subsequently modified to take other effects on board.

The criteria of acceptability for word recognition models are explanations of the word and non-word recognition effects which have been outlined above. The ideal model will explain all of these phenomena, and anticipate as yet undiscovered ones, but as yet no model has provided an explanation of all of them. Some models account for certain phenomena, and some for others, but it remains to be seen whether the explanations can be consolidated into one general model of word recognition. This section will not attempt to describe every model of word recognition which has been proposed, but will focus upon the three main classes of models. To explain why certain classes of words are recognized more slowly than others these models have proposed word detectors, search processes and verification processes.

One approach to the modelling of word recognition processes is to propose the existence of word-specific memories which serve to detect the existence of words in the printed environment. These memories are often called 'logogens', the term introduced with the most influential model of word detectors (Morton, 1969). These are essentially passive recognition models, with mental activity being prompted by the different features of the input. The life of a detection system is determined by what the input features have caused to occur in a pre-set cognitive organization. One of the intuitively appealing characteristics of word detection models is their account of why it is that unfamiliar foreign languages sound so much like an undifferentiated babble, while familiar languages such as one's mother tongue sound like a sequence of well-differentiated words. The difference is that no detectors have been formed for foreign words, whereas listening to a familiar language is a passive process of allowing detectors to pick out the successive words. With no detectors we can hear only speech sounds, while for a familiar language we hear categorized clusters of sounds which have activated our word detectors.

There are three main refinements to the basic detector model: first those concerning the number of logogen systems in the word detection and output organization, second the specification of the relationships between feature, letter and word detection, and finally the description of more general word processing routes, which allow for the generation of pronunciations and semantics from printed words. The word detection system and its subsequent refinements will be described in separate sections here, although the idea of recognition through the collection of word-specific evidence is the central feature of each model.

The logogen model

One of the most widely used models of word recognition proposes that the internal lexicon is composed of word detectors or collectors of printed evidence. This is the logogen model suggested by John Morton (1969), although it has a clear antecedent in Ann Treisman's (1960) model of the influence of inattention upon word recognition.

Treisman was concerned with the occasional recognition of unattended words, and the essentials of her model are an informative starting point, even though she was specifically accounting for attentional variations in the data collected in experiments using spoken messages. The model proposed that while unattended messages are not precluded from access to the internal dictionary altogether, words gain access in a degraded or attenuated form. The notion of an 'internal dictionary' finds one of its earliest proponents in Treisman's description, as shown in Figure 2.2. Attended words gain access to the internal dictionary after separation of the two messages on the basis of physical characteristics such as spatial location or loudness or pitch of voice, and this access is unrestricted. Unattended words gain attenuated access, and this means that a weaker signal is available. Only certain words will reach the threshold required for recognition once they have been attenuated, and Treisman's account takes care of important words such as one's own name (equivalent to highly frequent words for that particular listener), and contextually probable words predicted by the preceding sentence. Unattended words are recognized when the threshold can be reached either by the attenuated information reaching a low

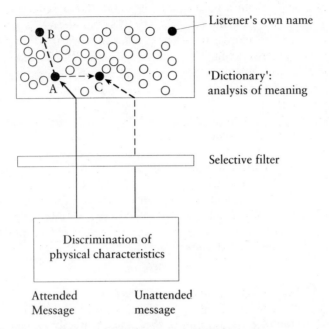

Listener's own name

'Dictionary':
analysis of meaning

Selective filter

Discrimination of
physical characteristics

Attended   Unattended
Message   message

Figure 2.2 Word recognition in Treisman's theory of attention

Treisman's (1960) model of the effects of inattention, in which a word recognition mechanism was proposed. The 'dictionary' is a collection of lexical entries, each one corresponding to a known word. The model proposed thresholds for the activation of these dictionary units, and the listener's name (together with other important words) were considered to have a lower threshold for activation.

Three other words are indicated by the letters *A*, *B* and *C* in the figure. As word *A* is recognized (part of the intended message), it is considered to lower the threshold of recognition of words *B* and *C*, by virtue of contextual constraint. Word *C* is also partially activated by its presentation in an unattended message, accounting for the occasional report of contextually probable words even when attention is directed away from them.

threshold (very common words such as the listener's own name) or by the preceding context lowering the threshold immediately prior to the word's presentation. Although it was not suggested specifically as a model of word recognition, Treisman's internal dictionary accounts very well for two of our basic phenomena: the word frequency effect and the sentence context effect. Morton addressed the question of visual word recognition using the notion of the internal dictionary, and explained the mechanisms by which word detectors reach the threshold for firing.

In Morton's (1969) model of word recognition, the detectors collect information from print and speech and are triggered when enough information has been collected. Each detector, or logogen, has a threshold for firing, and as activation builds up during the collection of

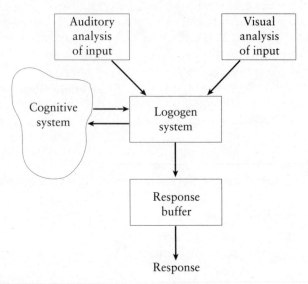

Figure 2.3   Morton's (1969) early version of the logogen system

evidence so the threshold is approached and eventually exceeded, giving rise to recognition. When a word is inspected a number of logogens may become activated, especially if the word has a large number of ortho- graphic neighbours. A word such as *HAND*, for instance, will activate the logogens for a number of other words through multiple parallel processes, including *HANG*, *HARD*, *HIND* and *LAND*, each of which differ by just one letter. The logogens for these other words will become activated, but only the logogen for *HAND* will be able to collect enough information to reach its threshold for firing. When the logogen fires the word becomes available to other processes such as those responsible for generating its pronunciation. The 1969 version of Morton's model is shown schematically in Figure 2.3.

The threshold for firing (or the logogen's resting level) is set according to the likelihood of encountering any word, and the likelihood is a statement of frequency of use. Readers are more likely to come across the word *POCKET* than the word *PICKET* because of their relative frequencies. The ratio of frequencies of these words, unless affected by their special significance for some individuals, is approximately 5:1. A word's threshold (or baseline) is set by the number of times it has previously been encountered, therefore the threshold for *POCKET* would probably be set lower so that the logogen fires earlier (alterna- tively the baseline setting could be higher) than that of *PICKET*. Consequently, a high frequency word will be recognized earlier, or with less visual evidence having been accumulated, than a low frequency word. Word recognition can then be seen to proceed through a form of sophisticated guessing by the logogen system, by which logogens are triggered when the best guess can be made on the basis of the available evidence. The amount of evidence necessary for firing will vary according to the probability of encountering the word, and for a very low frequency word such as *AARDVARK* the reader may need a long hard look at it before it is recognized. The model thus provides a clear description of the *word frequency effect*.

Factors other than frequency of occurrence can influence the logogen thresholds in Morton's model. While the probability of encountering a word will remain relatively stable over time, the preceding events can have short-lived effects on the threshold. Once a logogen has fired it returns to its resting value, but only after a recovery period. If the word is presented a second time, during recovery, then firing will be faster than it was the first time. This is because the logogen is already in a state of partial activation, not having returned fully to the resting value. This assumption of a slow return to the initial value is equivalent to less evidence being necessary in order for the threshold to fire upon a second presentation of the word, and provides an account of the family of context effects – the *word repetition effect* being the simplest.

When the word *BUTTER* is presented twice within a short interval, the same logogen is being activated, but other priming affects can also come under this umbrella. An associated word will also have an effect if the logogens are able to collect information from what Morton termed the 'cognitive system'. Information about words related to *BUTTER* will be presented via this semantic system, if currently available, because they have been recently presented to the logogen system. Therefore, the logogen system collects information from both the current sensory input and from a semantic input triggered by the cognitive system. The prior presentation of the word *BREAD* can then facilitate the processing of the word *BUTTER* by the semantic features they share being co-activated. This explanation of the semantic priming effect assumes that the logogen system is a store of known letter-strings or lexical entries, and that the cognitive system stores everything that the reader knows about the meanings of those words.

However, if semantic features are stored within the lexicon rather than in a separate cognitive system along with information about the word's spelling, then the word repetition effect is explained as before, but the locus of the semantic priming effect is now restricted to the logogen system. Not only would logogens collect physical features about the printed words, but semantic features could also be accumulated as evidence to be used to reach the threshold. The semantic features of

BREAD are triggered in the cognitive system and then are collected by this word's logogen, and also by the logogen for *BUTTER*; thus when *BUTTER* is subsequently presented it is already in a state of partial activation.

Morton needed to propose a separate logogen and cognitive system in order to account for the third type of context effect, the *sentence context effect*. This is also explained by assuming that logogens are influenced by information that is collected from semantic sources. So, when reading the incomplete sentence

The zookeeper responsible for ant-eaters fed the young . . .

the presentation of the final word *AARDVARK* results in easier recognition than if no prior context had been presented, because the detector for *AARDVARK* had already been partially activated by relevant information. Of course, the fact that you have probably recently seen this word in an earlier paragraph may also help with its recognition (namely the word repetition effect). For Morton the influence of the sentence upon the final word comes from the cognitive system having processed the sentence's underlying meaning. For the unified model the semantic features of *ZOOKEEPER* and *ANT-EATERS* would be shared with *AARDVARK* and would partially activate it, leading to an explanation similar to that used for the semantic priming effect. The unified model only works if the sentence contains semantically associated words, but sentences can have facilitating effects even when strong associates are absent (Stanovich and West, 1981). For these sentence priming effects the unified model has to resort to an effect mediated by a cognitive system. As we shall see later (Chapter 3), there are good reasons for supposing that there are two types of sentence priming effect, one of them being feature-based and automatic, and the other being of a predictive, problem-solving nature and under conscious control.

So far as the lexical ambiguity effect is concerned, there are a number of possible explanations available. Jastrzembski (1981) favoured a probabilistic explanation which points out that a word with two or more lexical entries has a better chance of having a high frequency than does a word with only one entry. The ambiguity effect then becomes a variant of the frequency effect.

Word detector models such as the logogen system provide satisfactory explanations of the variations in processing time observed when words are read, but how can the logogen system make any response to non-words such as *BDUL*? Furthermore, why should this particular letter-string be any easier to reject as a word than *BULD*, or for that matter *BLUD*? When any of these letter-strings are presented there should be no level of activation in any of the logogens in the lexicon sufficient to reach the threshold for firing. But the subject in a lexical decision experiment does not sit looking at the screen waiting for a logogen to fire! Such decisions are made quite easily and quite quickly. A letter-string such as *BDUL* would gain the required 'no' response with a response time of well under a second. Coltheart *et al.* (1977) suggested that a negative decision is triggered if lexical access has not been made after some pre-set interval has elapsed. If no logogen reaches the threshold level of activation then a deadline will expire, and the negative response executed. Non-words should therefore always receive longer decisions than words (*lexical status effect*) otherwise the deadline might expire before all of the word detectors have finished collecting the available information. The individual readers must set their own deadlines on the basis of their knowledge of their own word recognition skills. A reader with particularly fast lexical access would be able to set a deadline more severely than a reader with slow letter and word decoding skills. The notion of the decision deadline is very simple, and gives the logogen model a good lever on the effects involving non-words.

When the orthographically illegal letter-string *EBLD* is presented there will be a minimal level of activation in the word detectors, and this will be less than when *BELD* is presented. *BELD* has more similarities with existing lexical entries, and will partially activate *BALD*, *BEND*, *WELD*, amongst others. This partial activation will be insufficient to reach the threshold for any of the logogens corresponding to these words, but it can have the effect of delaying the lexical decision. A deadline is set so that a decision can be made about non-words, but if there is some activation in the lexicon, then the deadline may be extended to allow more time for evidence of word status to be collected. If partial activation below the threshold for firing causes an extension to the deadline, then any non-word which has word-like properties will receive a longer decision time than non-words which do not resemble words. This account of the *non-word legality effect*, using an extended deadline caused by partial activation of at least one real word, has also been used to explain the non-word neighbourhood effect.

Non-words that have many real-word neighbours will partially activate all those neighbours when presented in a lexical decision task. This activation in the system will result in increasing the deadline time compared to a non-word that has a small neighbourhood and thus creates less activation in the system. Therefore the model correctly predicts inhibitory effects for non-words with large real word neighbourhoods. The system cannot so easily explain the facilitatory effects for real words with large neighbourhoods (Andrews, 1989, 1992). The response time to real words is based on their frequency, not the system's general activation level. Therefore words matched on frequency but varying in neighbourhood size should have similar processing times, according to the logogen model. This prediction is supported by the analysis of response times to high frequency words with different sized neighbourhoods (none, small and large), where there is no reliable effect of neighbourhood size. For low frequency words a large neighbourhood is beneficial in its processing. If the real word neighbourhood effects reported by Andrews prove to be reliable this finding will be extremely problematic for the logogen model.

The non-word *BLUD* has a longer decision time than *CLUD*, and this has been attributed to a shared pronunciation with a word (*BLOOD*). When Morton modified his model in 1979 he separated the orthographic and phonological input systems, because of reports of an absence of cross modality priming (Winnick and Daniel, 1970). This results in a difficulty in explaining the pseudohomophone effect as it is only the orthographic features that are used when accessing the visual input logogens. Phonological codes are not produced until the target reaches the output logogens, and this would not occur for a non-word since no entry would be found in the visual input logogen system, so causing the target to be rejected. Therefore pseudohomophones would not be rejected any more slowly than other legal non-words.

How many logogen systems are necessary?

A number of refinements of the detector model of word recognition are worth mentioning. The first has been made by Morton's team in response to new data involving priming effects. The original model had a single logogen for each word. Whether the word was to be spoken or written it would access the same entry in the logogen system. The study that caused a development of this original model was one in which cross-modal facilitation in recognition could not be found, and was reported by Winnick and Daniel (1970). In their experiment subjects were presented with a picture of a butterfly, which they might have to name, followed by the visual presentation of the word *BUTTERFLY* to which they had to make a lexical decision response. Winnick and Daniel found no facilitation from the first presentation to the second when using pictures prior to test words, and no facilitation either when dictionary definitions were used in the first stage. Only words were found to facilitate the recognition of words, and further experiments considered by Morton and Patterson (1980) found little evidence for auditory to visual facilitation (subjects hear 'butterfly' and then see the word). Their proposal for a model with separate logogen systems is shown in Figure 2.4. (This model also accounts for the pronunciation of non-words,

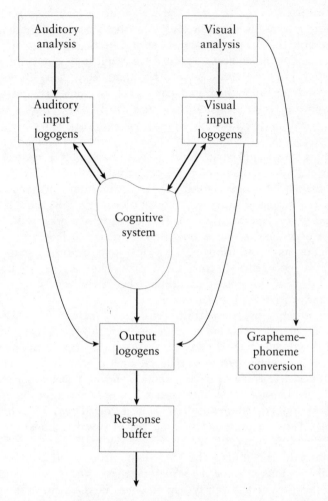

Figure 2.4   Morton and Patterson's (1980) later version of the logogen system

through grapheme–phoneme conversion, a processing route which will be discussed further when we consider the possibility of dual routes to the internal lexicon.)

Separate input logogens for spoken and written words get over the difficulty that arises when we encounter non-facilitation effects, but when cross-modal priming effects do appear (Swinney, 1979), the original single logogen system looks attractive once more. A criticism of the experiments discussed by Morton and Patterson is that the intervals between the priming stimulus and the target stimulus were up to 45 minutes, and this may not have provided the best estimate of a priming effect restricted to the lexicon. The lexical items may have returned to their resting level during these long intervals; when very short intervals are used cross-modal priming can be seen. Effects of printed words upon picture naming have been reported for sequential presentations (e.g. Irwin and Lupker, 1983) and for simultaneous presentations (e.g. Underwood, 1976) with related pairs of items such as a picture of a horse and the visual presentation of the word *COW*. Studies in which printed words and pictures have interfered with each other are reviewed by Lupker (1985). Swinney (1979) has furthermore demonstrated an effect of a word spoken in continuous speech upon a related printed word in a lexical decision to a printed word that was presented at the same time as the spoken word. This is an important demonstration of cross-modal priming. In these demonstrations – and these are the tip of a literature iceberg awaiting the titanic logogen model – the interval between prime and target is brief or nonexistent. These data argue for single logogens for all forms of the lexical item, if priming is to have its effect by temporarily affecting the activation of the lexical item. The alternative is to propose that priming has an effect in the cognitive system rather than the logogen system.

It is entirely possible that the effects considered by Morton and Patterson that support the idea of multiple logogens are themselves based in the cognitive system, and result from sophisticated guessing based upon recent experiences. The short-term priming effects between pictures and words, and between spoken and printed words, could not result from the same mechanism because the response in these tasks is immediate rather than considered and reconsidered. One important difference between these tasks is the use of timed responses to clearly visible stimuli in one case, and the use of the measure of probability of recognition in the other. The short-term priming effects result from reflex-like responses, while the recognition tasks allow the consideration of alternatives. The logogen system may well be the locus of the priming effects while the cognitive system is the locus of the recognition effects used to build the logogen model.

What constitutes a logogen unit?

The question of the size of the units stored in the logogen system has also been addressed using priming experiments. Do we need a separate lexical entry for *LINE*, *LINES*, *LINED*, and *LINEAR* and where would *UNLINED*, *OUTLINE*, *OUTLINES*, *UNDERLINE*, and *UNDER-LININGS* fit into this family (and *ALIGN*, which is also from the same root meaning but which has undergone a spelling change)? This family of words is derived from the single morpheme word *LINE*, which can be described as a free morpheme: it is a morpheme which can appear freely as a simple word on its own. A morpheme is an indivisible unit of meaning which is either a single word or a group of letters which modify a word. *LINE* has a meaning which cannot be further reduced but which can be modified in a number of interesting ways. In comparison, the word *LINES* contains two morphemes: the free morpheme *LINE* and the plural inflection which is itself described as a bound morpheme, and which only appears in conjunction with at least one other morpheme. New words have been added to the language not only by modifying simple words with inflections that change their syntactic role and imply negation, but simple words have also been joined with other simple words to form compounds of two free morphemes. Hence we have *LINESMAN* and *PIPELINE*, as well as their own inflections.

Families of inflected and derived words may be represented as separate entries in the lexicon, or they may be stored as variants of a single morphemic entry. If these suffixed and prefixed forms each required a separate entry then not only would we need many more entries, but the relationship between the words would also be lost. Murrell and Morton (1974) found support for the notion of morphemic storage by first having subjects learn a set of words and then observing the effects of this learning upon a subsequent tachistoscopic recognition task. The question was whether prior exposure to a word helps the recognition of another word which contains the same morpheme. The results were that prior experience with *BORING* facilitated recognition of *BORED*, suggesting that the first word had been remembered as a variant of *BORE* and the second word was also recognized as an inflected variant. Although the two words share three letters this facilitation effect was not visual in nature. Learning the morphemically unrelated word *BORN* had no effect upon the recognition of *BORED*. The morpheme issue will be discussed in more depth later, starting with a series of experiments by Taft and Forster (1975), which will be described in some detail as part of the discussion on search models of word recognition.

Dual routes to the internal lexicon

The lexical status and non-word legality effects were accounted for in the logogen model by adding the notion of an extendible deadline. This has resulted in the possible addition of a second route which bypasses the lexicon. We have assumed that a logogen can become at least partially activated by the collection of phonological evidence, with access to the lexicon now being possible through a direct visual/orthographic route, and through a separate phonological route. Coltheart (1978) suggested that the phonological route was travelled using grapheme–phoneme correspondence (GPC) rules, more simply described as the spelling-to-sound rules. By the application of these rules to a printed letter-string we can generate the pronunciation of words existing in our lexicons, new words and orthographically legal non-words. At least, those words that obey the rules can be pronounced, and in Figure 2.4 this is achieved by a GPC route which bypasses the logogen system, transforms the output of the visual analysis and presents it to the response buffer. It is worth noting that there is an alternative theory involving a phonological route which works on similar principles, but it passes through the cognitive system and so has a greater influential effect. This was mentioned in Chapter 1 in the description of Kleiman's (1975) experiments using articulatory suppression.

The application of the GPC rules to the non-obedient words – exception or irregular words – will either fail to produce a recognizable pronunciation (as with *HAVE*, *PINT* and *BISCUIT* for example) or will produce a pronunciation of another word altogether (for example *SOOT* may be pronounced like the word *SUIT*). In word naming tasks it takes longer to start pronouncing irregular words than regular words; this is known as the *regularity effect*, and the class of models which employ word detectors can account for this with the notion of dual routes through the lexicon. The orthographic route can be travelled by any known word, regardless of its phonological consistency, whereas the GPC or phonological route will attempt to process any letter-string but will provide an acceptable pronunciation only for regular words. An irregular word will fail to gain a pronunciation that resembles its correct pronunciation as defined by its lexical entry. Suppose now that each route is attempted by each word or non-word as it is presented, and that the processes necessary for travelling the routes can be applied in parallel (with the direct visual route being faster for regular words). On some occasions the orthographic route might result in faster lexical access and consequent pronunciation and on others (novel or non-words) the GPC route might produce the faster pronunciation. For regular words the pronunciation can be generated following whichever process has been first to finish, but for irregular words the GPC-generated pronunciation will be inconsistent with the pronunciation produced via the direct visual route and thus conflict will arise at the output buffer and a possible rechecking procedure may have to be implemented.

This explanation is the most favourable account of the regularity effect, because irregular words will experience conflict at the response buffer, which will slow down responses compared to regular words, which experience no conflict. However if subjects are encouraged to respond as quickly as possible, thus responding as soon as the output has reached the response buffer, and prior to the GPC's output reaching the buffer the regularity effect disappears (Stanovich and Bauer, 1978). There are a number of subsidiary questions remaining for this description of the pronunciation of regular and irregular words, but in general, with modifications, the word detector model can now provide a picture of the basic phenomena to be taken into account by any model of word recognition.

Models of word recognition: word detection through connectionist networks

The second major development to the notion of word recognition through word detectors has been to specify the nature of the inputs to the detectors and the nature of their interactions. The popular interactive-activation model proposed by McClelland and Rumelhart (1981) and Rumelhart and McClelland (1982) does just this and is an early example of the connectionist networks that have achieved widespread attention since the 1980s. This interactive-activation network can be seen as a refinement of the approach adopted by Morton, and in addition to accounting for the same phenomena as the logogen model it provides a good explanation of the word superiority effect.

Before delving into a description of the McClelland and Rumelhart network we shall give a brief overview of how connectionist networks work and why they have become so popular since the 1970s. Connectionist models, also known as parallel distributed processing (PDP) models and neural networks, are a radically different conception of the basic processing system of the mind, which is inspired by our knowledge of the nervous system. The basic idea is that there is a network of simple units, each of which has some degree of activation. These units are connected to each other so that active units excite or inhibit other units and these excitations and inhibitions are spread amongst the system. There is no fixed number of units that a system has to contain; some have thousands of units, but even those with only a few units can behave with surprising complexity and subtlety. This is because processing is occurring in parallel and interactively. When researchers develop a connectionist network they test it using a limited set of input units, and thus they are directly able to access their network's ability at modelling human behaviour.

The four most salient components of a network system have been defined by Bechtel and Abrahamsen (1993) as: (i) simple elements called units; (ii) equations that determine an activation value for each unit at each point in time; (iii) weighted connections between units, which permit the activity of one unit to influence the activity of other units;

and (iv) learning rules which change the network's behaviour by changing the weights of the connections. In the McClelland and Rumelhart network system the researchers themselves set the equations that determined unit activation, and the weightings of the units. The challenge for current researchers is to have the network figure out the appropriate changes in weights without the aid of an external programmer. The weights within a system partly determine the state a network reaches as a result of its processing, so changes in weights result in changing the overall characteristics of the system. The basic goal is to provide a way of changing weights that increases the ability of the network to achieve a desired output in the future. Naturally, if the system is able to adjust its own weights in response to partial information it becomes much more powerful and more human-like. To appreciate the character of these networks it is necessary to observe them in operation and we shall do just that with McClelland and Rumelhart's interactive-activation (IA) model.

The interactive-activation model

This model illustrates how a multilayered network can recognize visual patterns, specifically, four-letter words presented in a particular type font. An interactive network was constructed which consisted of an input layer of features (e.g. a top horizontal bar), a middle layer of letters (e.g. *F*) and an output layer of four-letter words (e.g. *FINE*). There are 14 visual feature units which become active when the feature is present, and 14 for when the feature is not present. These visual features are detected at the lowest level of the detection hierarchy and activate all the letter units that possess those features (and inhibit those they do not). So, if a horizontal mid-height bar is detected, the capitals *A, E, F, H* and possibly also *B* and *R* are activated. ('Possibly' in this context means that the exact typographic font will be important, and also that activation may not be as complete as for the clear exemplars.) If a visual feature is also detected which corresponds to a low-height bar then the capitals *E, L* and possibly *D* will be activated. Each of the feature detectors can operate at the same time, and so by totalling the amount of activation received by each letter detector unit (26 in total) it is able to identify the letter which has been presented as being the one receiving the most activation from the feature detectors.

In addition to the connections with the feature units the letter units are positively connected to those word units (1,179 units) that contain that letter, and negatively connected for those word units that do not. It should be noted that the system is designed to deal with words of four letters, so four copies of the feature and letter sets are used (one set for the first letter or feature of the word, one for the second, and so on). Finally, all word units and letter units are negatively connected to all competitors within the system. For example, when the word *SEND* is presented the letter units for *S, E, N* and *D* become active, and this activation is passed up to all of the words which share these letters, and not just to the word detector for *SEND*. The units for *BEND, SAND, SEED, SENT*, among others, will also become activated. In addition to the excitation received from the letter units, the word units also receive inhibition from letter units which signify the absence of particular units, thus *BEND* will receive excitation from letter units *E, N, D* but inhibition from the letter unit *B* since the feature unit which detects the absence of vertical lines in the first letter of the input string states that it cannot be a *B* (or an *D*, or *F*, or *H* and so on). As the activation for the word unit *SEND* increases above those of its competitors it starts to inhibit its competitors. Thus competitor word units receive excitation and inhibition from the letter units and feature units (via the letter units), and also from the word units. Unlike the logogen system this is truly an interactive network.

The word superiority effect can be explained with particular ease by the interactive-activation network, where the notion of variable activation plays a major part. The task for the subject is to guess which of two letters was previously briefly presented, and the direction of the result is for superior performance when the letter is part of a word rather than presented in isolation. The two letters presented for the choice are both viable completions in the experimental condition in which words are presented. Thus if the subject is to recognize the third letter of *WAGE*, then the two letters in the choice stage might be *G* and *D*. Why should the presence of *W, A* and *E* help in the recognition of the *G*? (See Figure 2.1 for an illustration of the sequence of events in this experiment.)

The interactive-activation model states that as letter detectors become activated, through the visual feature detectors, this activation is passed on to all words containing that letter. So, when *WAGE* is shown, the letter detectors will help with this word, but also with words like *SAGE*, *WADE* and *WAGS*. But *WAGE* will be activated the most, and this may help inhibit the other candidate words, and in turn this inhibition will itself act to inhibit certain letters. The letter *D* initially receives some facilitation from the feature detectors, but once the *G* has superior activation *D* will receive inhibition from *G*, the activation level of *WAGE* will be greater than the activation level for *WADE* and thus *WADE* will be inhibited and feedback will inhibit the letter detectors. Thus, *D* receives inhibition from both the letter level and the word level, and *G* receives facilitation from both. A single letter on the screen only

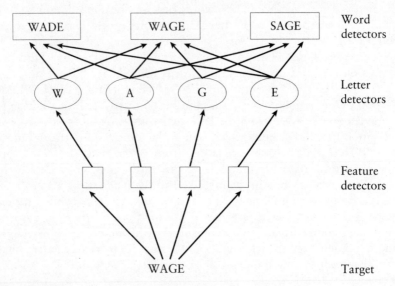

Figure 2.5   The interactive-activation model
Source: McClelland and Rumelhart, 1981; Rumelhart and McClelland, 1982

receives facilitation and inhibition from the letter level and has less input and will take longer to reject or accept than a word. (See Figure 2.5.)

One of the key explanations for the word superiority effect is that orthographic information reduces the number of alternatives by providing letter contexts. For example, take the simple situation of guessing the identity of a two-letter word when you have reduced each candidate letter to two possibilities. Suppose that you are sure that the first letter is either *O* or *U* (your visual feature detectors have found a convex bottom edge), and that the second letter is either *F* or *P* (your feature detectors have found a left-side vertical with upper protrusion, say). Your letter detectors by themselves cannot distinguish between the two pairs of alternatives, but your word detectors will be activated for only two words. If the letter combinations *OP* and *UF* were both words then there would be no advantage in knowing that the target was a word. As it is, orthographic redundancy can be used to help identify the word even though the component letters are unidentified. In this particular case the four logical possibilities have been reduced to the two lexical candidates *OF* and *UP*. In the same way orthographic information can restrict the number of candidates in the word superiority task and improve guessing performance when letter-specific information is poor.

Thus it appears that the interactive-activation model is at an advantage in comparison to the logogen model owing to its ease at explaining the word superiority effect. It also has been stated that it is able to predict the neighbourhood size effect, particularly the reason why it is only reported for low frequency words. Words that are visually similar can help the processing of each other in terms of what McClelland and Rumelhart (1981) call the 'gang effect'. Thus the presentation of *LOOK* will activate detectors for *BOOK, COOK, TOOK*, etc. which all feedback to the letter level and strengthen the *O, O, K* detectors. If the target has few neighbours this facilitatory feedback system will be weaker than if it has many. It also would predict that this benefit from members of the 'gang' will be greater for low frequency than high frequency words, as the high frequency targets will easily reach activation without the aid from the facilitatory system (Andrews, 1989). It can be seen that the interaction activation model can explain the interaction of neighbourhood size with target frequency as reported by Andrews.

As the research stands at the moment the interaction-activation model is the most convincing of the models cited above. However, evidence by Grainger (1990) suggests that neighbourhood size is not important; it is the mere existence of at least one higher frequency neighbour that is the main predictor of response time, and this is in the opposite direction from that suggested by Andrews's data. Thus the existence of a higher frequency neighbour results in a large inhibitory influence for real words in lexical decision (Grainger *et al.*, 1992). Grainger's argument is that when low frequency words are processed using a LDT, if they have at least one higher frequency neighbour this slows down decision times in comparison with low frequency targets with no neighbours. Similar effects are also reported from preliminary investigations in our laboratories, although they are dependent on many variables such as the size of the non-word neighbourhood, and the magnitude of the higher frequency neighbour. Would such contradictory evidence be problematic for the model? Grainger's interpretation of the IA model differs from that of Andrews and they both use this model to account for their patterns of data. Grainger *et al.* (1992) concentrate on the inhibitory processes within the IA model whilst Andrews relies on the facilitatory effects. The different interpretations that can be formed from the model makes it highly flexible, but also unfalsifiable, as the nodes and weightings can be rewritten to produce whatever output is required. This in itself makes it an interesting 'model' of findings, but a poor predictor.

Obviously, a network model which sets its own weights would overcome such criticisms, and such a network is described in the dual-route cascaded (DRC) network proposed by Coltheart *et al.* (1993). The DRC network is a dual-route model of reading that is formalized computationally and that can learn about new letter-strings. It is still in the process of being developed, and only the nonlexical route is implemented in the Coltheart *et al.* description. Its ability to pronounce non-words and irregular words matches the behavioural data with human readers, including some of the acquired dyslexia subgroups. The DRC network model is described in some detail in Chapter 4 (see, for example Figure 4.4), together with other connectionist models proposed by Seidenberg and McClelland (1989) and by Hinton and Shallice (1991), in the context of attempts to build models of acquired reading disorders.

We have described how the logogen model's structure was revised into the interactive-activation model, a connectionist network whose key feature is its ease in accounting for the word superiority effect observed in the reading literature. A further modification of the logogen model which contrasts sharply with the connectionist approach is the concept of alternative routes through the lexicon. This comparison is described in Chapter 4.

Models of word recognition: word recognition with lexical search

The third class of model to attempt to account for the set of word recognition effects proposes that when a letter-string is presented the lexicon is searched one item after another until a match is found. Whereas the word detector models propose that word features access all detectors or logogens simultaneously, search models propose a serial, but selective, search through the lexicon. The notion of recognition through a serial search gained early support in the descriptions of Rubenstein *et al.* (1970) and Stanners and Forbach (1973) and is an integral part of the extensive models proposed by Kenneth Forster (1976) and Marcus Taft (1979a, 1985, 1991).

These models propose that the sensory input is matched against the items in the lexicon, but it would not be economic to search all items. A critical idea here is that the matching process is restricted to selected items, and these items form what we can call a search set. If the incoming letter-string spells *DOT* then it is unnecessarily time-consuming to check this input against entries such as *ADMINISTRATION*, *SENTIMEN-TAL* and *VOLCANO*. In this particular case the search might be restricted to just those words which have approximately three letters and which begin with the letter *D*. This would cut down very considerably the number of items in the search set and at the cost of increasing the time taken to create the search set there is a benefit of having a much smaller number of items to be compared. The likely criteria for selecting candidates for the word set are initial letter and word length, but other criteria could be imported under special circumstances. In an experiment where all the words are of very high frequency, for example, it would be pointless to include low frequency words when forming the search set. These would never result in matches and their inclusion could only ever incur time costs and never produce time benefits. In the case of printed words the access code, which is derived from the stimulus and which defines the characteristics of the search set, is likely to be described in terms of a subset of the letters of the word.

In Forster's (1976) version of the search model a central lexicon or 'master file' is consulted through orthographic or phonological access files, according to whether the word has been seen or heard. Words in the access files are ordered according to their frequency of occurrence in natural language, and when a match is found between the input and a word in the access file this points to the correct entry in the master file, where the full information about the word is stored. A final check occurs between the original input and the output from the master file; if the letter-strings do not match the search resumes. An important question is concerned with what form of representation is used for items in the access file. This is a critical question, because it will determine the code by which words access the internal lexicon. Much of Marcus Taft's work on developments of the search model has been concerned with the nature of this access code, and is summarized in Taft (1985, 1991).

The access code

As in the case of the Murrell and Morton (1974) analysis of lexical constituents, Taft has found support for the proposal that the lexicon is accessed through morphemes. Each entry in the lexicon is considered to be accessed using the stem morphemes as their access codes. When a morphemically complex word is presented its stem must be identified before any attempt is made to consult the access file and then the master file. This implies a process of stem identification in which any prefixes and suffixes are removed so that the access code can be isolated. We need to establish the plausibility of these processes by looking at the evidence in support of the notion of stem identification prior to search.

One of the attractive features of the search model is that the notion of an access code can be used to describe the processing of morphemically complex words which are built by adding prefixes and suffixes to the stem morpheme. For example, the words UNLUCKY, LUCKY, LUCK-LESS, and LUCKILY are derived from the same simple word LUCK, and the same access code could be used for recognizing any word within the whole family. Taft and Forster (1975) found evidence of the storage of stem morphemes which did not themselves form words (MIT from

ADMIT, SUBMIT, PERMIT), and evidence of prefix stripping in a lexical decision task in which stems were presented as parts of non-words (*JUVENATE* from *REJUVENATE*).

Words like *REJUVENATE* and *REPERTOIRE* have different morphemic structures, in that the letters *JUVENATE* form a stem while the letters *PERTOIRE* do not. The *RE* of *REJUVENATE* means 'to repeat', as in *REVIVE* and *RECOUNT*, and so *JUVENATE* can be considered as a real stem although it is bound in that it does not appear as a separate word in its own right. This is not the case with *PERTOIRE*, where the *RE* does not form a prefix any more than it does with *READING* or *RELATIVE* or *REVERENCE*. The letters forming *PERTOIRE* can be described as forming a 'pseudostem' and Taft and Forster found that when bound stems (*JUVENATE*) were presented as non-words in a lexical decision task they were more difficult to reject than pseudostems (*PERTOIRE*), decisions took longer and more errors were made, suggesting that they were seen as being more word-like. Taft and Forster concluded that bound stems are stored as lexical representations.

Another experiment described in the same paper added weight to the conclusion that the trading currency of word recognition should be described in terms of morphemes rather than whole words. This was a lexical decision task again, with the non-words created by taking real stems and pseudostems from words (for example, *SIST* and *SCUE* respectively taken from *RESIST* and *RESCUE*), and then adding inappropriate prefixes to them. From *SIST* we can create *BESIST* and from *SCUE* comes the non-word *BESCUE*, each time by the addition of a legitimate prefix to the stem or pseudostem. As in the first experiment, the same set of initial letters have been removed from each member of a pair of words, where one word contains a genuine prefix such as *RE-*, *PRE-*, *CON-* or *DIS-* and where the other member of the pair contains these letters in a non-prefix form. Once the prefix (or pseudoprefix) has been removed it is replaced by another group of letters which can act as a legitimate prefix, to create a non-word with a real stem or a non-word with a pseudostem. These newly formed non-words then appeared in a lexical decision task, together with words which acted as filler items.

The results were very clear from this experiment. Non-words which had prefixes inappropriately attached to real stems had both longer decision times and higher error rates than non-words formed from pseudostems. This was interpreted to mean that when attempting to gain lexical access a letter-string is first broken into its morphological components by stripping the stem of any prefixes and suffixes, and the underlying stem is used as the access code. When the stem correctly matches an existing entry in the lexicon a check must be performed to ensure that the combination of prefix and stem is plausible before the

Table 2.1 A step-by-step guide to affix stripping

Step 1	All potential affixes (*re*) are detected by the prelexical affix stripper and removed.
Step 2	The residual stem (*pertoire*) is compared with orthographic descriptions of stems in the lexicon.
Step 3a	If the stem if found, the lexical entry is unpacked to determine if the combination is possible, and an affirmative lexical decision is made. (In the case of *pertoire* no entry will be found).
Step 3b	If the stem is not found, further searches are conducted for further stem entries.
Step 4	If no stems are found then the whole word is assembled (*repertoire*).
Step 5	A lexical search continues for the whole word; if found, an affirmative lexical decision is made for the free form.

letter-string is declared as a word. In the Taft and Forster experiment the slow responses to prefixed real-stem non-words can be attributed to the access code matching a lexical entry and thereby necessitating the checking procedure. When there is no match a rejection decision can be made immediately. The high error rate could be due to uncertainty as to whether certain stems can be combined with certain prefixes.

Further evidence of the existence of prefix stripping in lexical decision tasks and word naming comes from Taft (1981), who reported that real words which look as if they are prefixed (for example, *RELISH* and *UNIQUE*) take longer to accept or to name than words which are genuinely prefixed (for comparison, *REVIVE* and *UNABLE*). The suggestion here is that pseudoprefixed words are sometimes mistakenly stripped of the letters which elsewhere form prefixes. This results in the wrong access code being used to consult the lexicon, and this in turn produces a delay until the correct code is selected; this is further displayed in Table 2.1.

Some readers may query the definition of *REJUVENATE* as an example of a prefixed form. Taft's definition of affixed forms has been questioned by other researchers, resulting in a more stringent definition in many studies. For instance, Rubin *et al.* (1979) define a prefixed word as one having a stem which can stand alone (or free). Using this criteria *IMPRESS* was defined as prefixed; this would be considered by some (e.g. Henderson, 1985; Smith and Sterling, 1982) as a very dubious definition because although *PRESS* is a word its meaning is altered when combined with the prefix *IM-*. Andrews (1986) used a very tight definition that very few theorists (with the possible exception of Marcus Taft) would argue with. A suffixed item was defined as a word with a real stem, a pseudosuffixed item was a word with a real word stem that did not relate to the meaning of the whole word, and a control item was a monomorphemic word. Using such a definition evidence for suffix stripping has been provided, but little support has been collected for prefix stripping (Batt, 1993; Batt *et al.*, 1995).

Having considered the evidence for the stem morpheme as the access code in the process of lexical access, and having established the plausibility of Taft's framework, we can now turn to the account given by the search model of the range of phenomena that are being used to test models of word recognition. More details of the access code and of the morphemic structure of the lexicon are described in Taft (1985), together with an outline of a refinement of his position, in which it is argued that it may not be the whole stem that acts as the access code. The refined position is that it is the first syllable of the stem that is the access code, where the syllable is defined in terms of its orthographic and morphological structure (the BOSS, or basic orthographic syllabic structure) rather than its pronunciation (Taft, 1979b).

Accounting for the data with a lexical search model

The data to be accounted for are those concerning word frequency, priming, ambiguity, lexical status and so on. These have the effect of slower responses or more erroneous responses being made to certain classes of words and non-words and can be used as evidence when speculating on the structure of the internal lexicon and on the cognitive processes used to access lexical entries.

Search models provide a straightforward account of the word frequency effect by proposing a serial search that is frequency-ordered. A target word is matched against each item in the access file, starting with the most frequent items. If the target happens to be a very common word (e.g. *DOOR, ENOUGH, ACTION*) then it will be matched successfully earlier than if it has a low frequency (e.g. *FIFE, SLEUTH, MELLOW*) as this is further down the list in the file.

The context in which words are presented can also influence their matching time. The search time for a high frequency word will depend upon the other words in the experiment, with a longer search time for the same word if the other words have a range of frequencies rather than all being high frequency words themselves (see, for example, Glanzer and Ehrenreich, 1979). This finding that words in an experiment that have a similar frequency are accessed faster leads to the suggestion that searches can be directed to a subset of words in the lexicon that are themselves defined by the demands of the experiment.

To account for repetition priming effects the search model suggests that when a word is first presented it has a temporary special status in that it is moved to the head of a reordered list of words in the search set/ access file. On the word's repetition there will be a fast decision or fast naming since the target is at the front of the search set. A strong prediction of the search model concerns the relative size of the repetition priming effect for high frequency words and low frequency words. If the effect is due to the reordering of words, with a recently presented word being moved near the head of the subset of words to be searched, then there should be a larger priming effect for low frequency words. This is because a high frequency word needs to be moved a shorter distance to get it to the top of the stack, in comparison with a low frequency word. If a word is already near the top of the stack, by virtue of being a high frequency word, then there will not be much of a benefit in moving it right to the top of the stack. In contrast, when a word is moved from near the bottom of the search set up to the top, then a large advantage is gained. Scarborough *et al.* (1977) observed exactly this advantage, with larger priming effects for low frequency words.

With the search model the semantic priming effect can be described separately from repetition priming, by assuming that words in the lexicon are linked according to their natural associations of meaning. If a word has links to a set of other words including *KENNEL, COLLAR, PUPPY, CAT, COLLIE, MONGREL*, etc., then the meaning of this unspecified word is constrained, and it is even guessable. When one word in the network is recognized a spread of activation is triggered along the links, and this can determine the items in a separate semantic search set, which is searched at the same time as the access file. Semantic priming, like repetition priming, serves to reduce the size of the word frequency effect (Becker, 1979), as a match will probably occur between the target and an item in the semantic search set rather than the access file. The semantic set is organized in terms of the degree of relatedness with the prime not frequency, therefore there will be no difference in the access times for low and high frequency words found in this semantic set.

Word frequency is also implicated in the search model's account of the ambiguity effect, in that words with more than one meaning have more than one chance of appearing near the head of the search set. The ambiguity effect then becomes a special case of the frequency effect, and dependent upon the frequency ordering of the search.

The search model has extreme difficulty explaining the pseudohomophone and neighbourhood effects. It is able correctly to predict differences between legal and illegal non-words, and the lexical status effect, but legal non-words which sound word-like could only take longer to process than other legal non-words if their phonology is computed at the same time as the search is conducted in the access file. It would therefore conclude that *BRANE* is a real word with a pointer to *BRAIN* in the master file and only on the final check when the output is compared with the input will the decision be rejected. This raises the question of whether the access files are defined in terms of orthography, phonology or frequency.

Like the logogen model the search model can explain the neighbourhood effects for non-words. Non-words with lots of real-word neighbours will trigger a large access file which would have to be more exhaustively searched than a non-word with a small neighbourhood, small access file and thus shorter search time. However, the prediction concerning real words with large neighbourhoods is incorrect. Large neighbourhoods result in large access files and low frequency words would have to wait for a longer duration until accessed than a low frequency word with a small neighbourhood and small access file. The prediction is correct in that high frequency words do not show an influence of neighbourhood size, since they are always near the beginning of the search set (Andrews, 1992; Grainger *et al.*, 1992) but the low frequency prediction is in the wrong direction, that is, it is one of inhibition rather than facilitation from a large neighbourhood. The model's inability to predict Andrew's neighbourhood effects for real words is not too disabling, owing to the inconsistency of findings in this new area of research.

One of the most replicable results in lexical decision tasks is the word/non-word difference, and it is this lexical status effect which first resulted in the suggestion of a serial search (Rubenstein *et al.*, 1970; Stanners and Forbach, 1973). Non-words attract long rejection times, by this model, because they require an exhaustive search of a lexical set, whereas when a word is found the search can be halted and a decision executed. Furthermore, a non-word that is not word-like (*LKFIN*) will not trigger a search of any access files and therefore will be rejected faster than a legal non-word (*FLINK*) which does trigger an exhaustive search of an access file.

The accounts of frequency and lexical status effects, and their variants, stand out as the strengths of the search model, but there are also difficulties associated with the suggestion that the lexicon is searched in a serial fashion. A search of the entire lexicon, every time a word is presented, does not seem plausible given the number of items in store and given the number of times we need to access the store. This difficulty was recognized by search theorists, and led to a refined model which incorporated restricted search sets. The difficulty then becomes one of deciding how to select the words which are to be searched. On the basis of what characteristics are words admitted to the set? A combination of word length and initial and terminal letters seems to be a good possibility, but searches can also be influenced by the likelihood of encountering a word of given frequency (Scarborough *et al.*, 1977). The selection of words for the search set is under strategic influence, and this opens the possibility that lexical searches are a product of the kinds of tasks used in psychology experiments. A serial search may be the optimal alternative available to a subject in a lexical decision task, but as with so many of our experiments, they only demonstrate that subjects can behave in a certain way under encouragement from the constraints applied by stimulus selection. The problem of selecting items for the search set also arises in a major variant of the search model that is to be considered here, the verification model.

Word recognition with a verification process

This variant of the search model has the advantage of some of the features of word detector models. Its most attractive feature is its account of context effects, although by adapting itself to make use of features from the other classes of models the verification model takes on considerable explanatory power. The verification model will also be discussed in Chapter 3, when the use of context by young readers will be examined.

The verification model is associated principally with the work of Curtis Becker (e.g. 1976, 1979, 1980, 1985; Becker and Killion, 1977), and starts the process of word recognition with a primitive representation of the stimulus. This sensory trace consisting of line features is used to activate word detectors (as in the logogen model), and when a reasonable number of detectors are activated these are used to generate a search set. The items in the search set are candidates drawn from the lexicon on the basis of similarity to the sensory trace. These candidates are good guesses as to the identity of the stimulus, using only the line features extracted from the primitive representation. The second stage is the verification process. Here the candidates in the search set are compared to the representation of the sensory trace of the input. These comparisons are made serially and are frequency ordered, as in the search model.

Therefore the verification model explains the frequency effect in a similar way to the search model, with a frequency-ordered search through a possible set of stimulus items. The non-word effects are also explained in a similar fashion to the search model. Illegal non-words do not activate any word detectors and therefore no verification set will be created; this results in a quick rejection of an illegal non-word compared to a legal non-word. The legal non-word on the other hand would activate some word detectors and a verification set will be generated and searched, eventually leading to the rejection of the non-word. The prediction concerning the non-word neighbourhood effect would be that large neighbourhoods will exert an inhibitory influence, and this is supported by the experimental findings. Another similarity with the search model is that the wrong prediction is made for real words with large neighbourhoods, concerning the appearance of inhibition for low frequency words. As with the search models, supporters of search and verification processes will closely be watching the neighbourhood size and frequency studies, for reliable findings will prove either valuable or disastrous for their favourite models.

The semantic priming effect is explained by marking lexical entries that are semantically related to the prime and these semantically defined targets are searched first in the 'semantically defined' set prior to the 'sensory defined' items in the verification set (this is the main deviation from the search model's explanation in which the two sets are searched in parallel). Thus the primed target will usually be one of the semantically defined set that is not frequency specific and thus shows equivalent processing times for high and low frequency items. This is the verification model's main advantage over the other models, since it can not only explain facilitatory priming effects that are dependent on the size of the semantic set, but also correctly predicts inhibitory effects from unrelated primes.

Size of the search set

The size of the search set is the basis of Becker's (1980) two-strategy approach, in which subjects are assumed to be selecting one of two semantic strategies for using the context. If the semantic set is small (*PUPPY* priming *DOG*) the subjects use the *prediction strategy* correctly to predict a target stimulus, and recognition is aided more than it is with a no-prime condition. However, if the target is unrelated and therefore not in the search set, the set is quickly rejected because the set size is small, and thus little or no inhibition is observed. There is little time wasted on an unproductive search. Becker contrasts this strategy with one for large semantic sets, the *general expectancy strategy*. Here a context stimulus is used to generate a rather large set of candidates for a related target word. When the target is presented it is this large set that is searched, and one effect is that this increases the time needed to find a related target within the set. The second effect is that this large set delays the processing of unrelated targets (which are in the sensory set that cannot be verified until the semantic set is searched). Thus unrelated targets will experience large inhibition effects. And small facilitation effects will be recorded for related targets, together with large inhibition effects for unrelated targets.

These predictions were supported by Becker (1980), who found larger facilitation and fewer inhibition effects the smaller the semantic set (e.g. *DOG* received great facilitation from the prime *BONE* but little inhibition from the prime *MOUSE*). If the prime is not very specific (*ANIMATE*) this will generate a large semantic set in which small facilitation, but large inhibition effects are noted.

This approach has been criticized because of the finding that some subjects appear to select the prediction strategy in response to demands of the task, while others select the expectancy strategy (Eisenberg and Becker, 1982). The use of different strategies by readers of different ages and abilities is discussed in more detail in Chapter 3, which describes individual differences. The verification model makes good predictions about the use of context by good and poor readers.

Locus of the frequency effect

One of the problems for the verification model is the uncertainty over the origins of the frequency effect. It has been stated that, similarly to the search model, the frequency effect arises from the ordering of the verification set. Therefore the information is stored in the logogens that determine the positioning of the possible targets in the search set. The verification model would predict that when a word is repeated the activation stage is affected and the logogen for that word would be at a higher resting level than before, and so will all logogens similar to the target word, since they would also have been partially activated by the word's first presentation. Thus the verification set will be created faster than on the first presentation. Once the verification set is created the target is compared with all entries in order of frequency. Thus an additive account of frequency and repetition is predicted, where both high and low frequency words gain equally from its repetition. This prediction is supported by Forster and Davis (1984) but contrasts with the predictions of the other models and the research conducted by Scarborough *et al.* (1977). Forster and Davis's additive effect for repetition and frequency is only observed when the first presentation is masked so that there is no conscious recognition of the prime. This in itself is not problematic for the verification model, but the reported interactive effects when the prime is consciously recognized (Scarborough *et al.*, 1977) is a challenge. One attempt to explain this is that the verification process starts as soon as a possible target enters the verification set, and as a high frequency target will enter first, regardless of whether it has been presented before or not, little advantage would be gained. A low frequency word would usually enter the verification set last or near the end, however; if it has been previously presented its activation level would be higher than normal and its entry into the set would be faster, and thus a large gain would be observed for the repetition of low frequency targets. This suggests that the frequency effect is not located in the ordering of the verification set but in the activation stage, which starts to resemble its original framework of the logogen model.

Assessing models of word recognition

It can be seen that the models vary in their ability to explain the reasons for the main sources of variation. The logogen model was designed to explain findings from experiments using tachistoscopic displays, not lexical decision tasks, and therefore originally had difficulty explaining findings such as the lexical status effect. The search model was designed to approach the word/non-word difference, but has difficulty with effects such as neighbourhood size. The verification model deals specifically with the semantic priming effect and experiences difficulties when faced with issues such as neighbourhood size and pseudohomophones. All of these models have been modified to try to account for the reported sources of variation and one of the better contenders is the interactive-activation model which was briefly discussed. Its main advantage is that it can explain facilitatory and inhibitory influences, owing to its inter- and intra-level feedback system. However, even this model has its critics, who state that it is unfalsifiable, and that by hidden units whose weightings can be altered whenever necessary it is possible to fiddle with the parameters to produce simulations that are consistent with the major research findings.

For a model to be truly successful, it must not only be able to explain findings from the experimental word recognition literature which has predominantly used the lexical decision task (a task that has been criticized by Balota and Chumbley, 1984, and defended by Taft, 1991), but also the neuropsychological findings from case studies such as acquired and developmental dyslexics. Chapter 4 reviews several of the above models in greater depth, taking into account this literature. The following chapter deals with the issues surrounding the development of reading skills. We have seen how the main models explain such effects as semantic priming of targets presented on a screen, but do people generally make use of such information, and are there any individual differences in the use of this expectation device?

3

Reading Development and Reading Difficulties

Individual Differences in Acquisition and Skill

Having established what it is that the skilled reader must do in recognizing printed words, and having outlined some of the character- istics of words that are associated with variations in the ease of recognition, we turn now to developing readers. We have seen that some characteristics of words lead to recognition difficulties: words of low frequency, words in inappropriate contexts, and words with irregular orthographies, for instance, take longer to recognize than high frequency, contextually well-placed, regular words. Do young readers show this same pattern of difficulties? In identifying the kinds of words that present particular difficulties for children who are in the process of acquiring reading skills we will not only provide evidence for our theoretical models of reading but, more important, we will also be able to advise on teaching methods. By knowing what children are and are not capable of doing, and by knowing where difficulties will occur we can recommend teaching methods that play to children's strengths.

There is a well-established tradition of psychological investigation and theory being used to inform educational practice, and the so-called 'great debate' between phonics and whole-word approaches has had no shortage of fuel from this source. Should children be taught to read by decoding words into their components, and encouraged to develop an awareness of the relationship between these components and their corresponding sounds, or should the emphasis be on the shape, sound and meaning of the whole word? The importance of decoding skills and of phonological awareness is currently receiving attention, but the debate is not settled, and after watching skilled readers some educationalists have advised caution in applying any assumptions to the classroom setting before firm conclusions are reached. The early emphasis on decoding skills received a severe jolt from the introduction of a psycholinguistic approach to reading advocated by Kenneth Goodman (1967, 1969) and Frank Smith (1971, 1973). Before we evaluate the Goodman–Smith position on the importance of the meanings of words, it is appropriate to retrace our steps and describe what is meant by instruction through phonics, and why it might be rejected.

Written language is a visible form of what we speak. This is not a trivial definition, because it states the direction of the relationship. Spoken language is acquired first, both by civilizations and by children within those civilizations. Writing is an attempt to capture spoken language, and so we might expect the form of written language – the orthography – to reflect variations that occur in speech. Some alphabetic languages succeed in this quite well. Finnish and Italian, for example, have relatively regular relationships between written letters and their corresponding sounds. They have few irregular words, those that do not follow standard grapheme–phoneme correspondence (GPC) rules. Some languages do not use alphabetic components, and cannot be described in terms of their GPC rules. In languages with logographic scripts such as Chinese, the written characters represent the whole word, and it makes little sense to attempt to identify the components of these 'words' except to look for graphic features shared by logographs with related meanings. The logographs do not represent the spoken language, however, in the way that the alphabetic languages do to varying degrees. We have seen in Chapter 1, that whereas Finnish and Italian can be pronounced by readers having little knowledge of the language other than the rules of pronunciation, English is notoriously infested with exceptional, or irregular, spellings. It is this degree of irregularity that leads us to question the dominant use of phonics in reading instruction in English.

Phonics and the use of spelling-to-sound rules

The phonics method of teaching reading attempts to use the child's existing knowledge of spoken language as a bridge between sight and meaning. A word that is known in its spoken form, but unfamiliar when written, can be recognized by first converting the letters into sounds. Once the written word has been 'decoded' with letter-to-sound rules, these individual sounds are then blended together into the spoken form of the whole word. It is the meaning of the spoken form that is then recognized, by a process of phonic mediation. Through repeated decoding of the same word the mediation will eventually become unnecessary, and when a word is recognized directly from its visual form without the need to decode the sounds of the letters, it can be said to have been added to the young reader's 'sight vocabulary' of known words. The skill of phonic decoding is then not necessary for recognition of the meaning of this now familiar word, but the general rules of pronunciation will continue to be useful when other new words are encountered. Consider *MOSSIANT*, for instance. In all probability you know how to pronounce it, by using well-learnt and well-used spelling-to-sound rules. It could be a word, but it does not actually have a meaning. If it *had* been a genuine word rather than an example of a string of letters that obey the orthographic rules of English, then you would have been able to generate its spoken form, and perhaps even say it out loud to yourself in an attempt to remember its meaning. The spoken form of a new word may be able to access the internal lexicon, and the word's meaning discovered by this indirect route through recognition of the word's pronounced form. The rules of pronunciation that are emphasized by phonics methods are of undoubted value when we puzzle over the meanings of words that appear in an unfamiliar written form.

Whereas phonics methods may work very well when we are learning to read languages with regular orthographies, they stumble with English. The first problem is with the number of rules that would have to be learned. Rule-governed systems may work well if the language obeys the rules, but English does not. A much loved rule in reading classrooms is the 'magic *e*' at the end of a word, a letter that is not pronounced itself but which changes the pronunciation of the preceding vowel. So when *HAT* becomes *HATE*, the vowel is lengthened, but what about a word like *HAVE*? To follow the rules it would have to be pronounced to rhyme with *CAVE*.

The rules not only have exceptions, but they are also inconsistent. The *LOVE, MOVE, COVE* . . . orthographic family provides one example of this inconsistency. If following the *GPC* rules the word *LOVE* should be pronounced to rhyme with *COVE* and *STOVE*. But *LOVE* is an orthographically irregular word, like *HAVE*, and similar to those that we have previously encountered (see Chapter 2) in that they have pronunciation rules that apply only to a small section of the orthographic family. Some of these irregular words are joined by other outcasts from the family (e.g. *DOVE*). Others have quite idiosyncratic pronunciations (e.g. *MOVE*). How should the 'magic *e*' pronunciation rule be applied here? It will certainly not result in the correct spoken form that can be used to mediate recognition of the word's meaning. In this and in many other cases, the GPC rules will not take the reader from a visual form of the word to a spoken form that will be recognized by the internal lexicon, or they may present the reader with the wrong entry (e.g. *MOVE* → 'mauve').

Learning the sounds that correspond to letters is one problem, of course, because spoken English uses between 39 and 47 phonemes (depending in part on how the phonemes are defined). When we consider groups of letters that form the phonemes the problem of inconsistency becomes intimidating. How should the *TH* at the beginning of word be pronounced (as in *THIS* or as in *THINK*?), or the *EA* in the centre of a word (consider *HEAL*, *HEAR*, *HEALTH* and *HEART*)? Some of the rules are specific to single words (e.g. pronunciation of the *F* in *OF*), or are used with a small set of words (e.g. the 'unfriendly' or 'strange' words such as *BISCUIT*, *YACHT*, *DWARF* and *UGLY* that we have previously described as being orthographically and phonologically irregular (or OIPI) words: Parkin and Underwood (1983), Schlapp and Underwood (1988).

There are more than two hundred GPC rules needed to pronounce correctly the most common 6,000 words used by 9-year-old children (Smith, 1971), and the vowels alone account for 79 rules. Each word requires the correct letter-to-sound rules in a set order. The rules themselves are abstract, of course, in that they have little relationship with the readers' natural environment or other non-scholastic experiences. There is therefore little opportunity for scaffolding their learning processes, and on this basis alone we have to ask whether young learners would be better spending their time developing their sight vocabularies rather than learning the combinations of rules that apply to each combination of written letters. Smith points to additional problems for phonics that question whether we can rely upon pronunciations when attempting to recover meanings. Spellings give us little information about stress (compare *ACORN* with *ADORN*), again suggesting that a unique rule is required in these cases of inconsistency. Furthermore, pronunciation often depends upon the syntactic class of the word (*PERMIT*, along with a large number of other words, is pronounced differently according to whether it is a noun or a verb). Together these problems lead Smith to suggest that phonological mediation is untenable as a route to the meaning of a word, and phonics on its own cannot be a sensible way to teach children to read. We sometimes know how to pronounce a word only after discovering its meaning; pronunciation of the *TH* in *FATHEAD* is only apparent after recognizing the whole word as a compound with two morphemes, compared to the monomorphemic word *FATHER*. If we need to use the sound of a word at all, says Smith, it will become available only after recognition of its meaning.

There is also experimental evidence to support the suggestion that some children do not use the phonological code for a word when reading. In a study of the word recognition skills of 9-year-old London children all readers were found to use the visual, direct access route to the lexicon, but only the better readers used the GPC rules (Coltheart *et al.*, 1986). Furthermore, some suggest that beginning readers will experience greater success if they are encouraged to think about the meanings of the words they are encountering rather than the phonemic representation of the targets. This proposal is described in the following discussion of the major alternative to reading by phonic decoding.

Reading as a psycholinguistic guessing game

If phonics methods do not provide the best basis of teaching reading, then what are the alternatives? The traditional competitor is the much-parodied 'flash-card' being waved at rows of children who wait to see what single word is written on the card before calling out its name in unison. We hope that this is a scene of the imagination rather than a classroom reality, but the essence of this 'look–say' method has its supporters in those who advocate the development of a sight vocabulary that is not dependent upon fine-grained decoding of the components of words. A variant of this emphasis on the recognition of the whole word comes from Goodman's (1969) discussion of errors, or miscues, made by children reading aloud. Goodman prefers the term 'miscues', as being in accordance with his argument that skilled reading is rarely error-free and that 'perfect' reading should be regarded as inefficient. This is because the proficient reader must be continuously using many sources of information to anticipate what words are likely to appear next. In this model of reading, skill is indicated by the type of information that a reader uses, with relatively unskilled readers relying more on graphical information extracted directly from the word being inspected, and accomplished readers relying more on the underlying meaning of the sentence:

> As he strives to recreate the message, the reader utilises his experiential conceptual background to create a meaning context. (Goodman, 1969)

One of his earlier statements of this position described reading, somewhat famously, as 'a psycholinguistic guessing game' in which advanced readers are viewed as using minimal graphical information, and instead relying upon predictions based upon syntactic and semantic information

(Goodman, 1967). Miscues that preserve the meaning of the text are therefore indicative of skilled reading, and can indeed be seen in the oral readings of young children (Seymour and Elder, 1986; Wells, 1906). When the printed word *YACHT* is read aloud as 'boat' it appears that the appropriate meaning has been recognized, from the context of the sentence perhaps, and the specific representation of this meaning substituted by a word with a very similar meaning.

Miscues of this kind can be used as a valuable diagnostic. Goodman (1969) suggests a scheme that can tell us whether the young reader is relying upon graphical information (e.g. *BATTER* is read as 'butter'), or has some awareness of the morphemic structure of the text (e.g. *TELEVISED* is read as 'television'), or appreciates the syntax of the sentence (e.g. *HOW HE WANTED TO GO BACK* ... is read as 'How he wants to go back ...') to the level of semantic substitution (e.g. *THE LADY'S WIG WAS* ... is read as 'The lady's fake hair was ...'). This analysis suggests that if the miscues of skilled readers indicate an attempt to anticipate the next word so as to minimize the use of printed information, then perhaps beginning readers should be encouraged to think about the meanings of words and phrases rather than learning letter-to-sound decoding skills.

The Goodman–Smith model of reading as 'a psycholinguistic guessing game' makes the straightforward prediction that increased reading skill is associated with increased use of the context in which a word appears. Smith (1972) points out that skilled readers will rarely, if ever, make a reversal confusion between *WAS* and *SAW*, or a visual confusion between *DOG* and *BOG*, because only one of these words will make sense in its context. The skilled reader will require little visual information in order to identify the actual word presented, but some unskilled readers typically confuse these word pairs on a regular basis. Or at least they do when the words are presented in isolation – on 'flash-cards' for example. Smith recommends that children who are prone to these reversals should read them in meaningful contexts, again emphasizing that limitations on the ability to extract visual information from the page can be compensated by the use of syntactic and semantic context. We now have good evidence of the use of contextual information by skilled and unskilled readers, and this will be discussed in some detail in this chapter.

Reading skill and the use of context

When skilled and less-skilled readers are given the task of naming printed words, the Goodman–Smith model predicts that the more skilled readers will make greater use of the sentence context. This is the prediction tested in a study reported by Richard West and Keith Stanovich (1978), and because this study has results of great importance for the influential 'guessing game' theory of reading it will be described in some detail. Three groups of readers were observed: 48 fourth graders (averaging 9 years, 9 months old), 48 sixth graders (averaging 11 years, 6 months), and 48 college students (averaging 20 years, 5 months), and the reading ability of each participant was estimated using the reading subtest, a standardized psychometric test (the Wide Range Achievement Test, or WRAT). The laboratory task was to read out loud a single word as quickly as possible, and the interval between presentation and pronunciation onset was timed. This 'target' word was presented on a screen as the subjects came to the end of reading an incomplete sentence such as

The dog ran after the __

with the target word being either congruent with the context (*cat*) or incongruent (*chair*). The target was presented about half a second after the subject read out the final word of context, which was always the word 'the'. To be sure that any effects between these presentations were the product of the effects of context, rather than differences in the difficulty of recognizing specific words, West and Stanovich presented each target word in a congruous context and in an incongruous context. So, the words *cat* and *chair* each also appeared shortly after the subjects had read out *The girl sat on the* —', in which they were now incongruous and congruous.

To obtain a baseline against which these two conditions can be compared, West and Stanovich (1978) also included a neutral context condition, in which only the word 'the' preceded the target. Without the baseline it would be difficult to interpret any differences between the other two conditions. A difference could be due to facilitation from the congruous context, or inhibition from the incongruous context, and these two patterns of influence were observed in West and Stanovich's results. For the youngest readers the neutral condition resulted in an average naming time of approximately 600 msec., with the congruous context providing facilitation (approximately 550 msec.), and the incongruous context providing inhibition (approximately 640 msec.) – a pattern of *facilitation-with-inhibition*. (The reading times for words presented here are approximate because they are estimates taken from a diagram in West and Stanovich's paper.) The oldest readers named words faster overall, of course, and the neutral condition (approximately 430 msec.) indicated a facilitation effect for the congruous context (approximately 400 msec.), but no effect at all for the incongruous context (approximately 430 msec.). This is a pattern of *facilitation-without-inhibition* and these different patterns of interference will appear in the explanation of the effects of context on recognition. By calculating the difference between each reader's word-naming time in the neutral condition and that in the congruous context condition a 'facilitation score' can be found. Similarly, the difference between an individual's neutral naming time and his or her incongruous naming time gives an 'inhibition score'. These two scores were calculated for each reader, and correlated with their reading ability as indicated by their score on the WRAT subtest. There were significant negative correlations between both scores and the reading ability score: the better readers showed smaller effects of both congruous and incongruous context.

Suffice it to say, for the present, that the results do not support the idea that as we become more skilled we make greater use of context. In a study of children's oral reading of coherent paragraphs and of lists of words in which no contextual help was available, Nicholson (1991) also found that context was of more benefit to poorer readers and to younger readers. Context had a greater affect on the recognition of words by younger readers, a pattern confirmed in another study using materials taken from children's books (West *et al.*, 1983), and this is inconsistent with Yuill and Oakhill's (1988) findings with skilled and less-skilled comprehenders. In the studies of context that follow this initial investigation it is demonstrated that the effects of context only occur when word recognition is slow enough to allow them to be effective. A model of cognition that specifically predicts when we should observe facilitation and when we should see inhibition is described below, together with some of the evidence that gives it support.

The two-process model of context effects

Posner and Snyder's (1975) two-process model of recognition provides a framework for understanding the relationship between skill and our responses to familiar stimuli such as letters and words. The two processes can operate simultaneously, but the critical feature involves the speed of operation. The first of these processes involves *automatic pathway activation* and it does not require attention. This process is a characteristic of skilled operations and it is fast acting. In the case of word recognition it allows the recognition of one word to influence another by facilitation only. The mechanism to account for this facilitation-without-inhibition is spreading activation, by which the activation generated by the recognition of one word will permeate an associative network of words. When one word is recognized, all associated words will become partially activated. In terms of the logogen model of word recognition discussed in Chapter 2 all associated words would have their thresholds temporarily lowered by the activation spreading from the word recently recognized. If one of the associated words is presented before the activation has dissipated completely, then less stimulus evidence will be required before the word's threshold is reached. Associated words can therefore provide each other with facilitation through Posner and Snyder's fast acting automatic process. Meyer and Schvaneveldt (1971) proposed that spreading activation could account for the facilitation observed when two associated words such as *DOCTOR* and *NURSE* are recognized at the same time. There are no costs incurred by the processing of unrelated words, because the mechanism only allows for spreading activation to lower the recognition thresholds of some items. Words that are not associated are unaffected by this mechanism, and so it predicts a pattern of facilitation-without-inhibition. When this pattern is seen, we can conclude that the automatic spreading activation pathway is responsible.

The second of Posner and Snyder's processes involves *conscious pathway activation* in that it requires attention. Whenever we engage attention then costs are incurred. We have to decide what to think about, and as well as not being able to think about other things, the decision takes time. This may only take a few hundred milliseconds, but differences in the speed of word recognition in these experiments are small enough for this to be a large factor. The benefit associated with this pathway follows from this characteristic of choice. We can think about whatever aspects of the word we choose, and actively generate our expectations rather than relying upon our over-learned automatic associations. These expectations require our limited attentional resources, and are selective. If we allocate these resources to the generation of expectations that eventually turn out to be correct, then there will be a facilitation effect. On the other hand if we are misled, by incongruous context for example, then the unexpected word will be recognized more slowly than otherwise. Attention then has to be redirected from the anticipated word to the word that actually appears, and this process costs us time. The conscious activation pathway can therefore give facilitation *or* inhibition, resulting in a characteristic pattern of *facilitation-with-inhibition*. When this pattern is seen, the resource-consuming attentional pathway is implicated.

When there is a short interval in which context can have its effect facilitation-without-inhibition should result because only the automatic pathway will have time to operate, and as the interval increases then facilitation-with-inhibition will result, as the attentional mechanism now has the opportunity to generate expectations. These two mechanisms operate in ways similar to those proposed by Meyer and Schvaneveldt

(1971), who described them as the spreading activation (equivalent to automatic pathway activation) and the location shifting (equivalent to conscious pathway activation) models. The predictions of the two-process model have been confirmed in series of studies on word-upon-word interference patterns described by Neely (1977) and many other investigators.

Neely's primed lexical decisions

A version of the lexical decision task was used by Neely (1977) in which subjects classified strings of letters as words or non-words by quickly pressing one of two response buttons. The letter-strings were preceded by a category name (e.g. *BIRD*) or by a neutral stimulus (a row of *x*s). When a category name appeared as the first event, or prime, a word indicating a member of that category usually followed as the target, after a short interval. This interval, between the first appearance of the priming word and the first appearance of the target, is usually called the stimulus onset asynchrony (SOA). So, a typical sequence involved a prime word (*BIRD* in upper-case letters) followed by a target word (*robin* in lower-case letters) to which the subject would press the 'yes' button. The priming category name accurately predicted the target category on two-thirds of all trials in the experiment, and the subjects were encouraged to expect a target that was a member of the priming category. On the other trials the target was a member of another category that was being used in the experiment. The prime was always presented briefly (140 msec.), but the SOA interval between onset of each word was varied between 250 msec. and 2 sec. The response time in the neutral condition was taken as the baseline, and each of the other conditions were compared to this. When the priming category was valid (*BIRD* → *robin*) there was a facilitation effect (relative to the neutral condition) of 33 msec. with a 250 msec. SOA, and of 14 msec. with a 2 sec. SOA. With an invalid category prime (*BIRD* → *arm*) there was no difference between conditions, with a 250 msec. SOA, and a 70 msec. inhibition effect with the 2 sec. SOA. (There were a number of groups in Neely's experiment, with different groups receiving different combinations of prime–target intervals. These figures are taken from the group receiving a mix of 250 msec. and 2 sec. intervals. Other groups received 400 msec./2sec., 700 msec./2sec. or 2 sec. only intervals. The facilitation effect for the 2 sec. group was 47 msec., and their inhibition effect was 72 msec.)

There is a difficulty here in explaining the very small facilitation effect with a 2 sec. prime–target SOA interval, but otherwise the two-process model accounts for the patterns of influence upon the processing of the target very well. The difficulty is that with a long SOA the two-process model predicts that there is enough time for both the automatic pathway and the attentional pathway to be effective, and both pathways provide facilitation for congruent targets. The facilitation effect with a 2 sec. SOA should certainly not be smaller than that observed with a 250 msec. SOA. If anything it should be larger, as the facilitation from one process adds to the facilitation from the second process. When subjects only performed the task with long SOAs there was indeed the largest facilitation effect of all, and so we should conclude that the small facilitation effect shown by the mixed-SOA groups is a product of strategies induced by the uncertainty over the SOA from trial to trial.

The two-process model predicts a pattern of facilitation-without-inhibition at short SOAs, and facilitation-with-inhibition at long SOAs, and this is the general pattern that was observed in Neely's rather elaborate experiment. The two-process model accounts for the patterns by invoking an automatic process of word recognition that operates very quickly, and an attentional process that operates slowly. These processes can be used to explain the pattern in the West and Stanovich (1978) experiment.

There were a number of other manipulations in the experiment that do not directly concern the present discussion, but one in particular deserves a mention. On some experimental trials the subjects were required to shift attention away from the category of the prime word: they were instructed that if the prime *BODY* was presented, then they should expect a target in one of the other categories (in this case, *BUILDINGS*). If the target then happened to be a member of this non-attended category (e.g. *heart*), then at the 2 sec. SOA an *inhibition effect* (63 msec. with the group receiving the 250 msec./2 sec. mix of SOAs) was found, even though prime and target were related. With *BODY* → *heart* at the 250 msec. SOA, however, a facilitation effect (20 msec.) was found, as expected. This indicates that at the short SOA attention could not be shifted to the category appropriate to the experimental instructions, and the facilitation effect is a product of the structure of the associative links in the subjects' semantic memories. When given the longer SOAs, however, they had sufficient time to move attention away from the prime word and to start generating expectancies of words in another semantic category. When sufficient time is given attention can be deployed, but with very brief intervals only well-learned associations will be effective. This pattern again fits the predictions of the two-process model in which the context can be used to create expectancies volitionally only if time is available.

Two processes in West and Stanovich's experiments

The two-process model predicts that context can only provide inhibition if there is sufficient time for the priming word to be used to generate inappropriate expectancies. Deploying attention requires time, and if readers have enough time they can think about the words that might appear on the screen. In Neely's (1977) experiment the inappropriate expectancies were targets from the 'wrong' categories, either because the category and target did not match when they were expected to (*BIRD* → *arm*), or because they did match when they were not expected to (*BODY* → *heart*). With little time in which actively to generate expectancies only the automatic pathway will be influential (facilitation-without-inhibition). West and Stanovich (1978) used this model in an ingenious account of the differences in the use of context by skilled and less-skilled readers. As well as being faster overall in the task that measured the onset of their naming aloud of a single word that completed a simple sentence, the college students showed facilitation-without-inhibition. West and Stanovich accounted for this pattern by suggesting that the students were reading the target words too quickly for the conscious activation pathway to take effect. The word appeared on the screen and was recognized before their attention could be deployed to generate expectancies. The fast recognition of words could only be influenced by a faster process, and the automatic activation pathway did allow facilitation from congruent sentences.

For the younger readers a pattern of facilitation-with-inhibition was observed, suggesting that they were recognizing the targets so slowly that the conscious activation pathway was responsible for the effects of context. The fourth and sixth grade schoolchildren were making use of the sentence context to predict possible target words, and their word recognition processes were slow enough to allow these predictions to have both facilitating effects with congruent targets and inhibitory effects with incongruent words. This explanation of the differences in the use of context casts serious doubts on the Goodman–Smith description of reading development. It suggests, instead, that less skilled readers do make use of context but have relatively slow word recognition processes that are assisted by correct guesses or disabled by incorrect guesses based on the preceding context. Skilled readers on the other hand also make use of context but do so very efficiently and are not disabled by inappropriate guesses.

This model of development has been described in detail as an *interactive-compensatory model* (Stanovich, 1980) in which poor decoding skills are compensated as necessary by whatever other information is available. If the semantic context allows a prediction, then it can assist the slow recognition of the word, and as inappropriate words rarely appear in heavily contextual text, poor readers would benefit from guessing. Morton's (1979) logogen model specifically allows for the interaction of sensory and contextual information during word recognition, as we have already seen, and Stanovich incorporated the notion of recognition units as collectors of evidence about words in his description of skill acquisition. The model allows for the use of context in word recognition, but contrary to the predictions of the Goodman–Smith model, Stanovich proposes that context is most likely to be used when visual word recognition is poorly developed. As reading skills develop so recognition becomes more automatic and less influenced by anticipations. Congruent words may still be facilitated by the automatic pathway, but incorrect anticipations will have no adverse effects because by the time the anticipations have been generated the word will have been recognized on the basis of the visual information contained in its letters.

The two-process model of context provides a good account of the West and Stanovich (1978) result, and they went on to test specific predictions on the time-course of the effects of context in a series of studies. West and Stanovich raised a criticism of their original study over the ease of task for the adult readers. The sentences and the target words were designed for use with 8- and 9-year-old children, and were therefore simple for the adults. The materials may have exaggerated the influences of automatic recognition processes, and they predicted that adults would be observed to use context when more difficult tasks were used. A variety of tasks have now been used to test this prediction, and not only is it upheld, but the two-process model continues to provide a good account of the use of context being dependent on the skill of the reader and the difficulty of the task.

Reducing a reader's level of skill

If skilled readers make little use of context because their reading is so fast and efficient, what if we slow down their reading? Will they then make use of any available context? Word recognition can be made difficult in any number of ways, and West and Stanovich seem to have used most of them in their attempts to turn competent adult readers into slow plodders. Their prediction is that if we can slow down the word recognition process, then context will have an opportunity to have an effect. This effect, predicted by the two-process model, should be for the pattern of interference to change from facilitation-without-inhibition (automatic pathway) to one of facilitation-with-inhibition (attentional pathway). One well-established method of slowing the process is to make the letters forming the word less distinctive. Meyer *et al.* (1974) added 'visual noise' (randomly placed dots) to the words in a lexical decision task, and found that slower responses were accompanied by larger priming effects of associated words. This technique was extended by Stanovich and West (1979) to investigate their customary congruous/neutral/incongruous sentence contexts with and without degradation. If degradation slows word recognition, then adults should show inhibition effects, and they do. With normal displays adults showed a small facilitation effect (15 msec.) and no inhibition, but by adding visual noise to the target recognition was slowed by more than a fifth of a second, and the facilitation effect became large (49 msec.) and the inhibition effect even larger (88 msec.). The further demonstration of how readers could be encouraged to use context is provided in the West and Stanovich studies. The target word in these experiments is displayed immediately after the subject pronounces the final part of the pre-target sentence, but by delaying the onset of the target the reader will have an opportunity to generate some anticipations. This would result in facilitation and inhibition patterns and this prediction by the two-process model was confirmed. Without a delay facilitation-without inhibition was observed, and with a delay both facilitation (43 msec.) and inhibition (31 msec.) were observed.

One possible difficulty with these sentence context experiments is that the subjects may have avoided their usual reading habits in response to the large number of unpredictable words, as it is unusual to find highly incongruent words embedded within a text. If skilled readers can vary their use of different sources of information then the presence of the incongruous trials may have led to a more passive reading strategy in which expectancies were not generated and in which visual information alone was used. Stanovich and West (1981) dispensed with this possible objection by varying the proportions of congruous and incongruous trials. Each adult reader responded to 60 sentences, and in 40 of them the target was congruous, thereby inducing a reliance upon context. The other 20 trials were distributed between the neutral and incongruous conditions. There was a strong facilitation effect in this experiment, and no inhibition effect. The final demonstration of the generality of the two-process explanation of the effects of sentence contexts addressed the question of the simplicity of the task for adults. The dominance of the automatic pathway in the early experiment may have resulted from the ease of recognition of words used, and so Stanovich and West (1981) varied the targets. The sentence

The accountant balanced the ___

was completed either by *books* (easy condition) or by *ledger* (difficult condition). Targets in the easy condition were both shorter and more

Table 3.1   Context effects with matched groups of readers

	Congruous context	Neutral context	Incongruous context
More skilled readers (reading age 10–11 yrs)	693 msec.	687 msec.	761 msec.
Less skilled readers (reading age 8–9 yrs)	692 msec.	800 msec.	917 msec.

Source: Briggs, Austin and Underwood, 1984

frequent than the difficult words, and in a separate free completion task they were offered as completions four times as often as the difficult words. The difficult words obtained more facilitation (95 msec.) than the easy words (39 msec.), and inhibition was seen with neither type of word. The lack of inhibition effects shows that facilitation-without-inhibition is observed even for difficult tasks. These experiments present a coherent account of the influence of context by two processes in word recognition, and of how less skilled readers may rely upon context to compensate for their poorer word recognition processes.

However, not all of the evidence is consistent with this account, and by way of introducing an alternative model of the influence of context in word recognition, we shall present an experiment that set out to replicate the West and Stanovich (1978) pattern of interference in young readers. The comparisons made by West and Stanovich were between adults, young readers and even younger readers, and so Briggs *et al.* (1984) sought to extend the comparison to young skilled and less skilled readers. We first matched pairs of 10- and 11-year-old children on the basis of their chronological and mental ages, but arranged that they differed within a pair on a standardized reading test by at least 2 years in their reading ages. The intention was to observe the use of context in two groups of children who differed only in their reading ability. The design of the study was otherwise similar to that of West and Stanovich, and the reading times of the children were as shown in Table 3.1.

These results do not follow the same pattern as that reported by West and Stanovich, and are not easily accommodated by the two-process model of contextual interference. Incongruous context provided inhibition for both groups of children, although the less skilled readers did have slower naming times in this condition. The main problem for the previous account is that for Briggs *et al.* it was only the less skilled readers who showed any sign of a facilitation effect from the congruous sentences – exactly the opposite result from that expected on the basis of the West and Stanovich result. Using the descriptions used previously, we can say that the less skilled children showed facilitation-with-inhibition, a pattern that the two-process model explains with the conscious activation pathway, while the more skilled children showed inhibition-without-facilitation, a pattern that the two-process model does not admit. Facilitation should always be present when the context predicts the target, and it is not displayed by these skilled readers, and inhibition should arise from incongruous contexts demonstrating that context has been used, but it should not appear without facilitation. The two-process model fails to explain this pattern of *inhibition-dominance*, and we will have to turn to an alternative account.

The alternative considered by Briggs *et al.* (1984) was based upon an observation of inhibition-dominance reported by Fischler and Bloom (1980), who varied the rate of presentation of the words in a sentence. At slow rates of presentation (4 words per second) they found facilitation-with-inhibition, but when the presentation was speeded (28 words per second), the pattern changed to inhibition-dominance. Fischler and Bloom regarded facilitation effects to be under voluntary control, being a product of an attentional process that required the context to be available for sufficient time for effects to develop. This attentional process might be avoided by skilled readers on account of the time-costs associated with the generation of expectations, and this might account for differences in the patterns seen with more skilled and less skilled readers. It does not account for the appearance of inhibition-dominance. These studies suggest that more skilled readers are influenced by context but only in a disabling way. It should be noted that the more skilled readers referred to in the Briggs *et al.* paper were 11-year-old children, and therefore were more similar to West and Stanovich's 'less skilled' readers. Fortunately, Becker's (1980, 1985) model is very specific in predicting when we should see each of the patterns described by the two-process model as well as the conditions for inhibition-dominance.

Additive and interactive effects and Becker's verification model

The verification model of word recognition that was introduced in Chapter 2 was proposed as an attempt to account for results from a series of single word priming experiments (Becker, 1976, 1980; Becker and Killion, 1977; Schvaneveldt *et al.* 1976). Before using the verification model to explain the appearance of inhibition-dominance in sentence context experiments we need first to describe the model and outline its account of existing results.

We have seen that recognition is sensitive to word features such as frequency, orthographic regularity and so on, and also to display features such as the contextual environment or stimulus degradation. When two of these factors are combined in a single presentation, their effects can be additive or they can be interactive.

Additive effects simply mean that the recognition delay attributable to one factor (say, x msec.) is added to the delay attributable to the second factor (y msec.), and that when the two factors are present then the total delay is the sum of the two delays (i.e. $x + y$ msec.). An example of an additive effect is presented by Becker and Killion (1977), when using stimulus intensity and word frequency. In one of their lexical decision experiments the difference in response times between high and low frequency words was approximately 150 msec. whether high or low intensity conditions were used. Intensity also had an effect of approximately 25 msec. In other words, each factor had a fixed effect. When the low frequency, low intensity words were presented then the delay (175 msecs.) compared to high frequency, high intensity was equivalent to these two differences (150 + 25 msec.) added together (see Figure 3.1).

Becker and Killion also demonstrated that single word priming contexts (*NURSE → DOCTOR*) and stimulus intensity do not have additive effects. These factors interact. With low intensities pairs of related words resulted in decisions that were 70 msec. faster than those for unrelated words, but with high intensities the difference was only 30 msec. (see Figure 3.2). Additive factors suggest that they influence different stages in the processing of the stimulus, with delays at one stage being carried to a subsequent stage. In contrast the presence of interactive factors suggests that they have their influence at the same stage of processing. Using this 'additive factors logic' in the interpretation of Becker and Killion's results we should conclude that stimulus intensity and word frequency have their effects at different stages, and that single word priming has its effect at the same stage as stimulus intensity. As stimulus intensity must have its effect during the extraction of visual information from the display, during encoding operations, we can conclude that single word context also affects encoding. The visual feature analyser that is impaired by low intensity may be affected by context by having the first word allow a directed search of the features of the second word, for instance. The visual features can be used to identify a stimulus for a word detector such as Morton's (1969) logogen system, where the frequency of word may then influence the difficulty of recognition.

The verification model explains the appearance of additive and interactive factors by suggesting that there are visual feature analysis and word detector components at work. The feature analysis provides a primitive description of the word, in terms of segments of lines, curves,

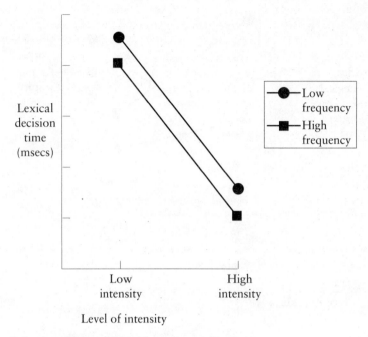

Figure 3.1   An additive effect of frequency and intensity
Source: Becker and Killion, 1977

and so on, but does not result in recognition of the word so much as the delivery of a subset of candidate words. This list of candidates words is described as the *stimulus set* (sometimes Becker also calls this the *sensory set*), and each candidate will possess the visual features of the stimulus that was actually presented. For example, if the stimulus is the word *LAND*, the stimulus set based upon the presented visual features might include *LAND*, plus *HAND*, *LEND*, *LAID* and *LANE*, as well as all of its other orthographic neighbours. The members of the stimulus set are words that have some visual features in common with the stimulus. The primitive features of the incoming stimulus activate a number of word detectors (logogens) that possess these features, and any word can enter the stimulus set on these basis of its visual similarity to the actual stimulus. An important assumption here, necessary to account for Becker and Killion's results, is that the stimulus intensity will affect the rate at which visual features are extracted.

When the stimulus set has been generated the verification process is necessary. This process samples items from the stimulus set and compares them with the image of the stimulus available in visual memory. If a comparison fails to match the relational features of an item selected

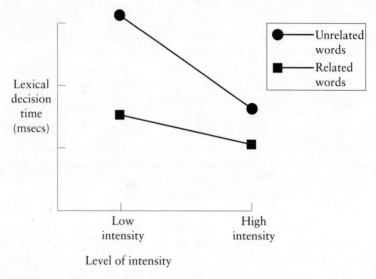

Figure 3.2   An interactive effect of context and intensity
Source: Becker and Killion, 1977

with the features of the stimulus, then another word is sampled. The process of verification continues, one word at a time, until a match is made and at this point we can say that the stimulus has been recognized and that a response will be available.

When the stimulus is preceded by context the process changes slightly. The context, or priming word in the case of a single-word priming experiment, acts on the lexicon before the target stimulus appears. The context activates a set of logogens that are semantically related, and this is described as the *semantic set* (or sometimes the *expectancy set*). The verification process can use the features of the words in the semantic set as soon as the target stimulus is presented, eliminating the need for a stimulus set that is compared on the basis of its visual features. The context is used to generate the candidates, and verification compares each of them with the stimulus until a match is found. For example, if the stimulus to be identified is again the word *LAND* preceded by a priming word such as *EARTH*, then as soon as the prime is recognized a semantic set of words such as *LAND, MOON, DIRT, PLANET* and *SOIL* would be generated. If the priming word is not related to the target the semantic set would be sampled completely without a match being found, and only when this happens does verification proceed to sample the stimulus set.

Becker's (1976, 1980) model can explain how stimulus intensity and context can interact by describing their effects upon the generation of the set of candidates. The verification process compares the features of the stimulus with contents of either the stimulus set or the semantic set, and each of these sets can be influenced by factors operating prior to verification. Common words are selected for verification prior to rare words, and this is sufficient to explain differences in the speed of response. When the target is a low frequency word it will be selected for verification later than if it is a common word.

If a semantic set is available through the early presentation of a prime, then the search is determined by semantic factors rather than by word frequency. Becker (1979) uses this difference in the order of searching the stimulus set and the semantic set to account for an interaction between context and frequency. Frequency does not have a constant effect upon related and unrelated pairs of words (as a simple logogen model suggests that it should), but there is a reduction in the size of the frequency effect for primed words. When the target word is a member of the semantic set generated by the prime, the verification model predicts that word frequency should have minimal effects upon recognition, and this is what is found.

This summary of the verification model of word recognition is incomplete, and the model is described in more detail in Chapter 2. It is important to note that not all of the model's strong predictions have been confirmed, and more detailed evaluations are presented by Neely (1991) and Taft (1991). The model has some power in describing the appearance of additive and interactive effects, however, and it is also successful in accounting for different patterns of facilitation and inhibition in contextual priming experiments.

When incomplete sentences are used to provide context we can observe facilitation with congruent targets and, if encoding is not simple, inhibition with incongruent targets (Stanovich and West, 1979, 1981; West and Stanovich, 1978). The two-process model provides a good account of these effects provided that the pattern of results is either facilitation-without-inhibition or facilitation-with-inhibition. It has trouble with inhibition-without-facilitation, the pattern of contextual interference found by Briggs *et al.* (1984), and the difficulty is also exemplified in two studies of adults reading sentences reported by Schuberth and Eimas (1977) and Fischler and Bloom (1979). In the Schuberth and Eimas study congruous targets were words that were strongly predicted by the contexts, and a pattern of facilitation-dominance was found, while Fischler and Bloom used congruent but less strongly related contexts and targets and found a pattern of inhibition-dominance. Becker (1980) explained this difference in terms of the size of the semantic set that could be generated by the context.

The verification model allows for faster responses if the context preceding a target is used to generate a set of words that can be sampled for comparison with the stimulus. If the set of candidates is small then the verification process will take less time than if it is large. If the context generates a semantic set that happens to be unrelated to the stimulus, then a small set will incur a small delay before the stimulus set is searched, in comparison with the costs associated with an unproductive search of a large semantic set. This account predicts that the size of the semantic set will determine the pattern of facilitation and inhibition, and the prediction was tested in Becker's (1980) study of single-word priming with adults. Words in a lexical decision task were preceded by related or unrelated words or by a neutral context (a string of *x*s, as in Neely's experiment), and for related words the nature of the relationship was varied. In one experiment pairs of antonyms were used (e.g. *UP* → *down*) and in another a target was preceded by its category name (e.g. *BIRD* → *crow*). In both experiments the subjects were told about the relationships between prime and target and that they should think about the meaning of the priming word. The subjects in the antonym exper-iment would be able to generate fewer expectancies than subjects in the category experiment, and in terms of the verification model, antonyms would result in a smaller semantic set than would category names. This difference had an effect on the pattern of influence of prime upon target. With antonyms there was a 52 msec. facilitation effect and no inhibition, and with category names there was a 62 msec. inhibition effect and no facilitation. The effectiveness of context depends upon the extent of the constraint it imposes upon the generation of expectancies. If it is very constraining, as with antonym priming, then facilitation-dominance will be observed because the small number of items in the semantic set can be searched quickly. If the verification process finds the target in the set then it will do so after a small number of comparisons, and if it does not find the target then it can move to a search of the stimulus set with minimal delay. In contrast, a less constraining context will generate a large semantic set that will require a larger number of comparisons to be made before either a match is found or the process abandoned in favour of a search of the stimulus set. Unlike the two-process model, the verification model predicts the appearance of inhibition-without-facili-tation according to the number of expected words that could be generated for the semantic set.

The pattern of facilitation-dominance with antonyms and inhibition-dominance with category primes has been confirmed in a number of studies, including one that observed schoolchildren making lexical decisions (Becker, 1982). This experiment again demonstrates the importance of being able to predict a set of items on the basis of the context. The children were third grade (approximately 8 to 9 years old) and fifth grade children (approximately 10 to 11 years old) and the pattern of results initially did not confirm Becker's predictions perfectly. The younger children showed facilitation-dominance with antonyms and inhibition-dominance with category primes, but the older children showed facilitation-dominance with both sets of materials. On close inspection of the materials the reason becomes clear. The target words in the category priming task were all high frequency words that were very typical of their categories (*FURNITURE* → *bed*, *ANIMALS* → *cat*, *TOYS* → *ball*, and so on), and so a small semantic set could be generated. The categories were declared before the experiment started, and the targets were very predictable. When the older children were re-tested with restrictive categories and less predictable targets the pattern of inhibition-dominance returned (*BIRD* → *goose*, *TREE* → *maple*, *FRUIT* → *lime*, and so on).

We previously mentioned that Briggs *et al.* (1984) found that children varied in their use of sentence contexts depending upon their reading ability, in a study that was intended as an investigation of the two-process model used in West and Stanovich's account of context effects. Briggs *et al.* found that young good readers were inhibited by incongruent contexts and not helped by congruent contexts, a pattern of inhibition-dominance. Posner and Snyder's (1976) two-process model cannot explain inhibition-dominance, but Becker's verification model does provide a good explanation. The young good readers read sentences that were very simple for them, in the sense that they were able to make a large number of predictions about the completing word. They generated a large semantic set. The poorer readers showed both facilitation from congruous contexts and inhibition from incongruous contexts. A pattern of facilitation-with-inhibition follows from the generation of a small semantic set. If the poorer readers can generate only a small number of predictions, then congruous words that are in the semantic set will receive early verification and incongruous words will be delayed only a short time while the semantic set is searched and then rejected in favour of the stimulus set.

One of the implications of the verification model explanation of our differences between young good and poor readers is that it emphasizes the number of words that can be predicted. The good readers do not receive help from the context because they have a greater knowledge of language, or perhaps just the time available, to generate a large number of alternative completions. The poorer readers receive help as a consequence of generating a smaller number of alternatives with sentences that have somewhat predictable completions (for example, *the dog ate the* ... BONE). The model accounts for the pattern of interference by assuming that all readers attempt to generate predictions on the basis of the context available, and that good readers are better at using the context than the poor readers. The Goodman–Smith model of reading development makes a similar statement, and if we are to accept the verification model we cannot reject the notion of using the context to generate predictions about words that are about to be read.

We can conclude at this stage that highly skilled readers will make use of context if their reading is slowed down, otherwise it is automatic and no facilitation or inhibition effects are observed. Young skilled readers, or 'middle' readers will make use of context because their reading is not fully automated. If highly congruent text is presented facilitation effects will be observed; if incongruent text is used, a large semantic set will be generated and no facilitation but large inhibition effects will be observed. Poor, less skilled readers make use of context, but produce smaller semantic sets and smaller facilitation and inhibition effects are observed. Therefore, the appearance of inhibitory and facilitatory effects are dependent on the skill of the reader, the congruency of the text, the time available to make the decision and the difficulty of the text. It suggests that poor readers should be encouraged to make use of congruent text to build up a large semantic set, until the stage at which their reading becomes fully automated and such a process is not activated.

Phonological awareness and phonological memory

When reading becomes difficult, children undoubtedly make use of the context when reading, although it is unclear how this helps to identify each word. One possibility suggested by the verification model is that the anticipated words that form Becker's (1976, 1980, 1982) semantic set are used to identify the specific word on the page. A second possibility, suggested by the differences in the number of anticipated words that can be generated, is that context is used after word recognition has been achieved, to develop associations between words. Context could then enrich the reader's understanding of the sentence schema, and help integrate the ideas or propositions by accessing a rich meaning of each word. As each word is recognized the meaning that is taken can be restricted to a small set of semantic features and associations, or enriched by the development of a large number of associations. Context can help in the generation of a rich text meaning, and perhaps better readers not only access the meanings of individual words more quickly than poorer readers, as suggested by the West and Stanovich (1978) study, but perhaps they are also able to use the context of a sentence to generate more associations between words, as suggested by the Becker (1982) and Briggs *et al.* (1984) studies. The Goodman–Smith model has better readers avoiding the detailed decoding of the visual stimulus and instead has them making use of the context to facilitate recognition. Frank Smith (1973) specifically argues against the use of decoding rules based upon phonics, and instead advocates that when children are having difficulty identifying a word then they should be encouraged to make an informed guess. The recent evidence of the significance of spelling-to-sound correspondences suggests that this recommendation may have been made too strongly, and that efficient use of context is what defines a skilled reader, not necessarily what makes a skilled reader, and that an appreciation of phonology is an important part of normal reading development. We turn now to a consideration of this evidence.

The Goodman–Smith model of reading development – what might be characterized as the guessing model – has received inconsistent support from the evidence of the use of context, but during recent years the importance of phonics has become very clear. At the same time as the unsupportive evidence was being reported a number of other studies indicated that phonological processing and awareness of phonology were good predictors of successful reading development (e.g. Gathercole *et al.* 1991a). Before we can delve into studies of phonological awareness, a few words about definitions are necessary.

Syllables, phonemes or intra-syllabic units?

There are three common ways of breaking a word down into its constituent sounds: syllables, phonemes and intra-syllable units. For example, the spoken form of *CAT* is monosyllabic, whilst *CATKIN* has two syllables corresponding to *CAT* and *KIN*. The spoken *CAT* contains three phonemes corresponding to *C*, *A* and *T*. and consists of two intra-syllables, known as the onset and rime. The onset is *C* and the rime is *AT*. So when we suggest that children are phonologically aware, are they aware of all of these units or just some, and at what stage in a child's reading development do they become aware?

As children learn to read monosyllabic words initially, the question of whether they can determine if a word consists of one or more syllables has little use at this stage, as they tend to be capable of reading only single syllable targets. Numerous studies, however, have attempted to determine if children can detect phonemes, and to determine the cognitive processes necessary for such an operation.

If reading were dependent on phonemic awareness children would have to be able to identify phonemes within their language prior to learning to read. On the other hand, if reading causes phonological

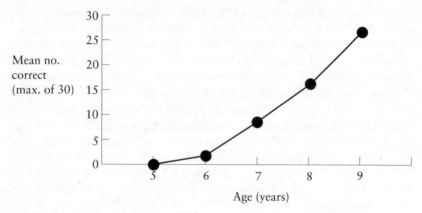

Figure 3.3.   Performance on the deletion and elision of phonemes tasks
Source: Bruce, 1964

awareness then beginning readers will not be aware of the phonemic components within a word. These predictions also are formed concerning intra-syllabic units. Bruce (1964) originally devised a simple task for determining phonemic awareness. Children aged 5 to 9 years were given three tasks in which a word was spoken and were to repeat it with one component sound removed. The tasks required deletion of the initial sound (*JAM* → *AM*), deletion of the final sound (*FORK* → *FOR*), or elision of the middle sound (*STAND* → *SAND*) within a set of words. The 5-year-olds could not do this task, getting no deletions correct, the 7-year-olds did slightly better, scoring 8.75 out of 30, and the 9-year-olds performed very well, with 26.7 correct out of 30 (see Figure 3.3). This suggests that phonemic awareness does not precede reading development because young readers were unable to perform the task well. As they became more competent readers, their deletion/elision performance improved.

A second common technique used to detect phonemic awareness which has produced a similar finding, is the tapping task; in this a child is asked first to repeat a spoken word and then to tap out the number of units of sound it contains. Liberman *et al.* (1974) found a direct relationship with reading ability and performance on the tapping task. Segmentation by phonemes (*CAT* should receive 3 taps) was more difficult than segmentation by syllables (*SUPERMARKET* should receive 4 taps), but as children progressed from nursery school into the first year of formal schooling (from 4 years old to 7 years old), their success with the phoneme trials on the tapping task improved. There is a difficulty with this study, of course, in that the reading ages of the children varied as well as other abilities such as their experiences of written and spoken words, in addition to their mental and chronological ages. A further problem is that it is relatively easy to tap out syllables as tapping is a rhythmic activity and the rhythm of a word is captured in its syllables. This hypothesis was tested by Treiman and Baron (1981) by changing the style of the task. Rather than tapping out syllables and phonemes, the children had to lay down on the table the number of tokens that each word contained. As with the Liberman *et al.* study, the syllable task was easier than the phoneme task, and even 5-year-olds performed with some accuracy.

Matching the experiences and abilities of groups of subjects is a recurring problem in reading research, and was addressed neatly in a study of phonological awareness reported by Morais *et al.* (1979). The task they used involved the addition or removal of a segment of a spoken word. The first phoneme was to be added to some words and deleted from others, and the readers in their experiment were Portuguese adults who were classified either as illiterates or as ex-illiterates. The ex-illiterates had attended adult literacy classes and could now read, but were otherwise indistinguishable from the illiterates. Whereas the illiterates performed with around 20 per cent success, the ex-illiterates performed at around 70 per cent, suggesting again that acquisition of reading skills is associated with knowledge of the phonological components of words.

These studies are striking examples of how reading precedes phonemic awareness. How about intra-syllabic awareness? Returning back to the phoneme deletion task we can interpret the findings in a different way. Calfee (1977) trained children to delete the initial sound of several targets. After the initial training phase they had to attempt this task on a new set of targets. The 5- and 6-year-old children performed at an 80 per cent accuracy rate. This shows that children may be able to delete the initial phoneme or the onset of a word. Treiman (1985) played a game with 4- to 6.5-year-old children, showing them a puppet which she said had a favourite sound, for example *s*. The children had to identify the words that contained this favourite sound. They found it easier to identify targets where the favourite sound was the onset (as in *SA* and *SAN*) rather than when it was part of the onset (as in *SNA*), suggesting that onset deletion is easier than initial phoneme deletion.

Kirtley *et al.* (1989) tested the hypothesis that children can detect onset and rimes with ease by asking them to detect which of three words is the odd one out. When the two similar words shared the same onset (*DOLL, DEAF, CAN*) 5-year-old children performed the task extremely well; if the onset also shared the same vowel sound (*DOLL, DOG, CAP*) the task was no easier. Again it appears that it is the onset that the children are using in conducting this task, not the initial phoneme. When presented with targets which shared the same rime (*TOP, RAIL, HOP*) children found this task much easier than when the similar targets merely shared the same final phoneme (*WHIP, MOP, LEAD*). This suggests that children also can easily detect the rime within a word, more easily than its final phoneme.

We have reported a few studies that show that children are able to hear onsets and rimes within words, and these suggest that young readers are able to detect which words rhyme and which are alliterative, prior to being able to detect whether a word contains a certain phoneme, or number of phonemes. That is, onset and rime awareness comes before phonemic awareness. This leads to the question of whether children who are unable to read can detect onset and rimes. Rhymes are a common feature of children's activities and they frequently make up rhymes when playing. Lenel and Cantor (1981) showed that pre-school children are well aware of rimes prior to learning to read. The experimenter read a word aloud and the child had to chose which of two other words rhymed with the first one, for example, *CHAIR, PEAR* and *FLAG*. Sometimes the word to be rejected also contained one of the same sounds as the rhyming words, as with *SUN, BUN* and *PIN*. Children did better when the word to be rejected did not share a sound with the one to be matched, but even the pre-schoolers performed above chance on both conditions of the task.

Phonological awareness training

If children's reading development matches the development of their phonological awareness, then we should ask whether training on this meta-component can enhance reading. This question has been asked in a number of studies in which groups of children have received different 'interventions' or training regimes. Bradley and Bryant's (1983) large-scale intervention study started with the assertion that sensitivity to rhyme and alliteration is associated with reading ability. Indeed, an earlier report by Bradley and Bryant (1978) found that backward readers were generally worse than other children at detecting rhymes in sets of words, and also in a task requiring the production of rhyme. The large-scale study incorporated two methodologies, looking at the relationship between phonological awareness and reading ability over a three year period, and at the effects of different types of training on groups of children with poor scores on the sound categorization tasks.

Bradley and Bryant's (1983) longitudinal study observed a total of 403 4- and 5-year-olds who had no measurable reading ability at the start of the project. (The number in the project had decreased to 368 after three years.) They were first assessed on their ability to categorize sounds by identifying a word that did not fit in a set of three or four words. So, in the group *HILL, PIG, PIN* the word *HILL* is the oddity, and with *BUD, BUN, BUS, RUG* the word *RUG* was to be identified. The older children were given a set of four words to remember, and the 4-year-olds were given three words. After three years Bradley and Bryant returned to the classroom and assessed reading and spelling using standardized tests. Performance on the sound categorization task prior to formal schooling correlated well with both reading (r = +0.57) and spelling (r = +0.48) after three years. This demonstrates a relationship; but it is not a causal relationship, of course, for it may have been some third unknown factor (e.g. phonological memory, which will be discussed in the next section) that was responsible for performance on both the categorization task and the reading task. Exposure to print or to word games at home would be candidates if we were to look for underlying factors. Similarly, in a study by Bond and Dykstra (1967) knowledge of letter names in pre-school children predicted reading performance after a year of formal reading teaching. The Bradley and Bryant result is suggestive, but it does not establish a cause and effect relationship, and they were well aware of this problem. The second part of their study addressed this issue directly.

After the longitudinal study had started, Bradley and Bryant (1983) selected 65 of the children who had low scores on the sound categorization task (their scores were at least two standard deviations below the overall group mean). These children were selected for specialized training, or were allocated to control groups. There were four groups in all:

Group 1: categorization training using coloured pictures of familiar objects, with names that shared common beginning, middle or final letters (e.g. *HEN/HAT, HEN/PET* and *HEN/MAN*);
Group 2: categorization training, as for Group 1, but they were also shown plastic letters and how the common sound was represented in the alphabet;
Group 3: control group using categorization tasks involving concepts (e.g. *HEN/PIG* as farm animals);
Group 4: control group receiving no training at all.

The training consisted of 40 individual sessions spread over two years, lasting until the end of the project. The two training groups outperformed the two control groups on both reading and spelling tests, with gains of between 4 and 14 months in reading age, and between 4 and 23 months in spelling age. The largest gains were made by Group 2, who received sound categorization plus training in letter–sound relationships, when compared with Group 4 who had normal schooling but no specialized training. There were only small differences between the two training groups except on the spelling test, at which Group 2 excelled.

Reading development greatly benefited from the combination of training in sound categorization and in the relationships between letters and sounds, and this establishes a causal link between phonological awareness and reading. A similar conclusion may be drawn from two other intervention studies. Lundberg *et al.* (1988) developed the phonological awareness of Danish pre-school children with a range of rhyming games that were designed to emphasize the components of speech. Initially the games and exercises helped the children to identify words in sentences, and progressed during the pre-school year to differentiate between syllables and then phonemes. Two years after the training programme had been completed the reading and spelling abilities of these children were considerably superior to a control group. Cunningham's (1990) intervention study with two experimental groups also allows us to conclude that training in phonological awareness directly helps the development of reading skills. The training involved the segmentation and blending of sounds in real and nonsense words. Her two experimental groups differed in the extent to which the phonological training was explicitly related to reading, and while both of these groups outperformed a control group who were given listening exercises, the experimental group who were shown the links between phonemes and their printed forms enjoyed the greatest gains. This supports Bradley and Bryant's (1983) result, in that phonological training alone is of benefit, but can be enhanced with further training that helps to develop the relationships between the written and spoken forms of letters (assembled phonology).

Phonological awareness for beginning readers

Although skilled readers show awareness of phonetic structure of words, this knowledge does not precede reading development. Pre-schoolers do have some knowledge of the sound of words and these are the intra-syllabic forms of words, commonly known as onset and rimes. Training children to be more aware of these units improves their reading considerably.

Seymour and Elder (1986) studied the errors made by a group of first grade school children who had been taught the whole word method (look and say). There was hardly any evidence of phonological errors, and most errors were semantic (*WHITE* read as 'green'). They concluded that these children did not use any method of spelling-to-sound (GPC) translation.

The suggestion that beginning readers do not use phonological codes also comes from Uta Frith's (1985) influential model of the relationship between reading and spelling. There is little or no involvement of assembled phonology in the first stage. This comes later, after readers have developed through a logographic stage that makes use of their visual discrimination and visual memory abilities. It is only in the second, alphabetic, stage that children start to recognise the relationships between letters and their pronunciations, and to use the spelling-to-sound rules to generate sounds as a way of addressing new words. In this way unfamiliar words are added to the sight vocabulary. In the third stage of reading development, the orthographic stage, words can be identified as having familiar components. These are the regularly occurring orthographic segments that correspond to morphemes, and a reader at this stage of development will not require phonological mediation but will recognise words by their orthographic features alone. Frith suggested that both reading and spelling can be described as passing through these stages of development, but that at any one time a child could be at different stages with these two activities. Indeed, proficiency with one strategy (logographic, alphabetic or orthographic) will drive the development of the use of this strategy for the other activity. Specifically, the proficient use of a logographic reading strategy will motivate the development of a logographic spelling strategy, and alphabetic spelling will help the development of the use of spelling-to-sound rules in reading. Finally, the acquisition of an orthographic reading strategy will prompt the use of orthographic spelling. Phonological codes are of use at a restricted stage in this model, after the initial use of visual codes, and before the higher-order orthographic codes have become familiar. Less experienced readers may make use of an assembled phonology because of a relatively inefficient visual recognition process for reading (Backman *et al.*, 1984). Only when these processes become more efficient will the use of assembled phonology be discontinued (except for unusual and low frequency words). However, in the initial stages of learning to read there is a reliance on a very limited word recognition device; it is not until the second stage that there is a development of proficiency in the use of assembled phonology.

Masterson *et al.* (1992) suggested that Seymour and Elder's findings revealed patterns of errors in the initial stage of developing reading, and continued this investigation by observing the processes involved in reading-aloud and printed-word comprehension of children in the second grade (the second stage described above) of school. It was predicted that for irregular words and infrequent homophones the children would rely more on assembled phonology in forming a pronunciation and definition. Fifty-four children participated in the study, with a mean age of 5.9 years. Task one contained a list of regular and irregular words which the children were asked to read aloud; task two consisted of regularly spelt homophones (e.g. *DAZE*), which they had to define or put into a sentence and then had to read aloud. The error rates for the regular, and irregular targets were correlated with the children's reading ability scores. The proportion of errors that were made for the irregular words (irregular word errors: total errors) was positively correlated with reading ability, suggesting the increasing use of assembled phonology with the increase in reading ability. On the occasions when the children could not pronounce the target they never were able to define it. When targets were incorrectly pronounced (i.e. read aloud as another word) the definition either corresponded to the error, or else the children said they did not know how to define it. Homophone confusions occurred 26 per cent of the time (*DAZE*, read as 'there are seven in the week'). The ten poorest readers did not make any homophonic confusions. Of the eighteen children who did make homophonic confusions, their confusions occurred significantly more frequently for the low frequency homophones. These findings strongly support the notion of phonologically mediated semantic access and that the use of assembled phonology does increase with reading ability, possibly until a stage where the vocabulary is sufficient for it only to be needed for rare and new words.

Evidence for this conversion from the use of assembled phonology, on to an orthographic stage, whereby assembled phonology is only used for rare and new words comes from Doctor and Coltheart (1980). They presented children aged 6–10 years with a visual sentence judgement task. The sentences either contained a homophone that sounded correct, or one that did not. For example:

He ran threw the street.
He ran sew the street.

The phonologically correct sentence received more false acceptances that the latter sentences. This error rate difference decreased with age, with the older children relying less on the phonological mediation and more on visual processing for meaning.

The role of memory in reading development

We have so far described the case for the association between reading development and the development of phonological awareness. These discussions have concerned the questions of what units are children aware of and when they make use of them. We have shown that phonological awareness is strongly linked with reading and vocabulary development. It is more than phonological awareness that is associated with reading performance, of course, and phonological short-term memory is also extremely important in the development of the skill of reading. Furthermore, it has been proposed that phonological awareness and phonological memory measures may both tap a common phonological processing ability (Liberman, 1989; Mann and Liberman, 1984).

There is now an established role for phonological short-term memory in the development of vocabulary and reading skill. The three main components of short-term memory (also currently known as working memory) are the phonological loop, the visuo-spatial scratchpad and the central executive (Baddeley, 1986, 1990, 1992; Baddeley and Hitch, 1974). This is the model of memory that was used in Chapter 1 to account for Kleiman's results with articulatory suppression. The phonological loop, like the visuo-spatial scratchpad, is under the control of the central executive, or supervisory attentional system. The phonological loop itself has two components in this model, a phonological short-term memory store and an articulatory rehearsal mechanism. The former stores incoming words in a sound-based code that decays quite rapidly unless maintained by articulatory rehearsal.

The phonological loop uses a sound-based code to retain speech-based information for short periods of time. It has been suggested that the maintaining of a new word's pronunciation in its phonological code enables the word to construct a stable phonological specification in long-term memory during the process of vocabulary acquisition (Gathercole *et al.* 1991b). Typical tests which have been used to demonstrate that the articulatory loop exists and that it is involved in reading are the digit span measure (how many digits someone can successfully recall) and serial recall of word lists. If the phonological loop is needed for the reading process, reading should be hindered if the phonological loop is disabled in some way. The common technique for disabling the loop is to use articulatory suppression, whereby the subject has to recite a number, word or phrase over and over whilst performing a task. If performance of the task is not hindered by articulatory suppression, then it can be concluded that the articulatory loop is not required for this task.

Using this paradigm Arthur *et al.* (1994) investigated whether the phonological loop was used for rhyme judgements and lexical decisions. Their first experiment tested children's ability to make lexical decisions with and without ariiculatory suppression (repeatedly counting digits 1 to 5, at a rate of 3 digits per second). Two types of non-word were used, orthographically legal (*GICKS*) and pseudohomophones, which sound like real words if pronounced using GPC rules (*IYUN*). Without articulatory suppression pseudohomophones took longer to reject than

orthographically regular non-words, as we would expect from Rubenstein *et al.* (1971). Arthur *et al.* suggested that the words were being
decoded on the basis of their phonological representations. If the
articulatory loop is used to produce these phonological representations,
then with articulatory suppression the pseudohomophone effect should
disappear. There was no effect of articulatory suppression, however, and
so we can conclude that the phonological loop is not used in lexical
decision judgements. The second experiment observed the time it took
for children to decide whether two words rhymed or not, with and
without articulatory suppression. There was a significant increase in
error rates when the children had to perform an articulatory suppression
task in conjunction with the rhyming task, confirming that the articulatory loop is involved in rhyme judgements. This result is consistent with
other reported findings that children do not use the phonological loop in
word recognition but that it is necessary for rhyming judgements (Barron
and Baron, 1977; Kimura and Bryant, 1983). This does not mean that
no phonological code is used in lexical access, of course. As we saw in
Chapter 1, in the discussion of Kleiman's (1975) use of an articulatory
suppression task, Besner (1987) has pointed out that there are a number
of speech-based codes available to the practised reader. These have
different purposes and different properties. Articulatory suppression may
interfere with the phonological loop necessary for the resource-demand-
ing comparison of the sounds of words in rhyme judgement tasks, but
not with other tasks involving judgements about words. A second
phonological code is said to be generated automatically in response to
the printed form of a word, and is part of the process of recognition.
Evidence in favour of the automatic creation of phonological codes
during lexical access was presented in Chapter 1 (Humphreys *et al.*,
1982; Pollatsek *et al.*, 1992; Underwood and Thwaites, 1982). This
second type of phonological code is unaffected by articulatory suppression, as confirmed by Arthur *et al.* (1994).

Gathercole *et al.* (1991a) have extended the investigation of phonological memory in reading by using several tests, the digit span test and a
more recently developed non-word repetition test. The non-word repetition task has the advantage over digit span and word recall measures
because these also contain lexical and semantic features which may be
used to support memory recall. With tasks using real words, therefore,
it may not be a pure phonological code that aids recall. Children's
abilities at repeating non-words are linked to their vocabulary development. Gathercole and Baddeley (1989) reported that non-word repetition
scores at 4 years predicted vocabulary acquisition at 5 years. Several
studies of children with developmental deficits of vocabulary development have indicated that they also have non-word repetition impair-

ments (Gathercole and Baddeley, 1990; Taylor *et al.* 1989). If a child's vocabulary development is below normal owing to deficits with working memory, he or she will inevitably experience problems with reading development.

These preliminary ideas led Gathercole *et al.* (1991a) to conduct a study of 108 schoolchildren (of 4 and 5 years old) to determine whether phonological memory and rhyme awareness skills contribute to reading and vocabulary development and whether a common phonological component underlies both phonological awareness and phonological memory. Tests of reading, vocabulary and non-verbal intelligence were given to each child in the two age groups. Two tests of phonological memory – non-word repetition and digit span – were obtained along with a rhyme oddity detection test. A factor analysis conducted on these measures indicated that there was a common phonological processing component that was shared by the rhyme oddity and phonological measures. However, these two types of phonological processing were differentially linked with reading and vocabulary development. Performance on the single word reading and multiple choice tasks were not related to any of the phonological processing measures for the 4-year-old age group, but were so related for children just one year older. Reading scores were also linked with the phonological memory measures, but again only for the 5-year-olds. Finally, for both age groups, vocabulary knowledge was linked with the digit span and non-word repetition measures but not the rhyme oddity measure. The association of digit span and non-word repetition with vocabulary development supports previous findings that phonological memory is linked with vocabulary development. The lack of an association with the rhyming task indicates that this memory with vocabulary link is not merely a reflection of a more general phonological factor. The absence of a relationship between digit span and non-word repetition with the reading tests (single word and multiple choice) for the 4-year-old age group again corresponds with previous findings (Gathercole and Baddeley, 1990). This is due to 4-year-olds relying on the visual reading strategy (Frith's logographic stage, 1985), whilst the 5-year-olds have moved on to the phonological moving strategy within one year of schooling. The rhyme awareness measurements were strongly related to reading performance. This demonstrates a well-established relationship (Bradley and Bryant, 1983; Bryant *et al.*, 1990) between rhyme detection and reading achievement scores.

Reading skill and the use of inferences

It is not only in phonological awareness and phonological memory that differences in reading ability can be seen. Skilled readers use context in different ways from less skilled readers, and differences can also be seen in the ways in which the ideas in sentences are used. Reading texts requires that we form inferences, a process that will be discussed in some detail in Chapter 6, and as children develop their reading skills their ability to form inferences also develops. Oakhill *et al.* (1986) were interested in the inferences that skilled and less-skilled readers formed from reading a story. Their subjects were 7- to 8-year-old children who were matched on chronological age, sight vocabulary and ability to read words aloud. They differed on their comprehension skill, however, with the two groups of children having reading ages of 7.34 and 8.97 years as measured by the Neale Analysis of Reading Ability (a standardized reading comprehension test). Each child listened to eight stories and were asked to try to understand them. After each story they were presented with a set of recognition sentences, two of which had not previously appeared in the story. One of these new sentences contained a valid inference and the other contained an invalid inference, according to the information presented in the original story. The children had to decide which sentences they had heard before. For example, for the passage:

The car crashed into the bus.
The bus was near the crossroads.
The car skidded on the ice.

The two new sentences would be *The car was near the crossroads* (valid inference), and *The bus skidded on the ice* (invalid inference). The results showed that skilled readers made more inferences than the less skilled readers. The good comprehenders had apparently retained more of the meaning of the story than the poor comprehenders. The poor comprehenders tended to recall the story word for word or not at all, whilst the good comprehenders appeared to make a greater attempt at understanding the sentences. In doing so the more skilled readers were more likely to accept erroneously a new sentence that agreed with the meaning of the short story.

This finding led Yuill and Oakhill (1988) to design an inference training programme for both good and poor comprehenders in an attempt to encourage them to make more inferences and improve their reading comprehension. There were three types of treatment: inference skills training, comprehension exercises and rapid decoding practice. Fifty-two children participated in total, and they were matched on the same criteria as in their previous study. After training all children were tested on a comprehension test (Neale), and their decoding speed and reading accuracy were measured. Less skilled readers benefited more from inference training than skilled readers, and they also benefited more from inference training than from decoding practice. Skilled readers obtained equal benefit from inference and comprehension training. The less skilled readers actually were slightly faster than the skilled readers on the decoding task. These findings suggest that the comprehension deficits of less skilled readers are not directly caused by a decoding insufficiency. Training of decoding skills alone is therefore unlikely to result in an improvement in reading comprehension. The absence of a significant difference between inference training and comprehension exercises suggest that both contain an element that is normally lacking in less skilled readers, and that can be taught to these readers in order to improve their comprehension ability. Although this story suggests that skill can be improved when children are taught how to use context more effectively it does not entirely support the notion of proficient reading as a result of the increasing use of context, since the skilled readers did not show much improvement with training.

Individual differences in reading development

This chapter started by suggesting that teaching reading through phonics was likely to have limited success, at least with orthographically inconsistent languages such as English. We have 26 letters to represent up to 47 phonemes – the number of phonemes varies in different parts of the English-speaking world and varies according to which phonetician is being consulted – but this is only part of the problem. We do not have a one-to-one correspondence between the units of spoken language and their representation in a written form (e.g. the identical vowel sounds in *EYE* and *STY* and *PIE* and *HIGH* have different written representations), and the converse problem is that some words with similar spellings have very different pronunciations (e.g. *LOVE/MOVE, PINT/ MINT* and *SAVE/HAVE*). These inconsistencies mean that a beginning reader of English does not have 26 decoding rules to learn, but several hundred. Some of the rules are specific to individual words, and some of them apply to large families of words.

Children's problems with the phonological decoding of English, together with observations of good readers making use of the sentence context in which words appeared, led Kenneth Goodman and Frank

Smith to suggest that we should teach reading not by phonics but by psycholinguistics. Children, they advocated, should make use of whatever information is available about a word – visual, syntactic or semantic. The experimental evidence does not entirely support the idea that better readers make more use of context than younger or poorer readers. Indeed some of the evidence suggests the exact opposite, that it is the poorer readers who are making more use of the sentence context. What appears to be happening with the beginning readers is that their word recognition is so slow that context has enough time to generate some suggestions as to what the word might be. As their reading skills develop context has less opportunity to have an influence. Word recognition becomes automatic with increased practice, and context becomes less and less necessary. Initially, however, they have little to help them. Contexts do not always define a word, and in these cases readers must make some use of orthographic information. Similarly, when attempting to make sense of words seen in their written form for the first time we need some way of gaining a representation in a familiar form. These are the times when phonological encoding will be helpful, and they are more likely to occur for beginning readers than for skilled readers. Indeed, there is evidence that even young readers do not need to recode words into a speech-based code when they read familiar words.

The intervention studies give clear evidence of the importance of phonological awareness for beginning readers however, and this is where phonics methods are most likely to be beneficial. As word recognition skills become more practised and written words become more familiar, the reader's mind will be released from the painstaking task of decoding words by a letter-by-letter or phoneme-by-phoneme process. Only at this stage of development can attention be dedicated fully to the higher level activities involved in understanding the meanings of sentences.

4

Neuropsychological Studies of Reading

The aim of this book is to discuss the question of how we read, and to outline the theories that have modelled the process of how we extract meaning from printed and written marks. The majority of the research that has been presented in the previous three chapters has concentrated on laboratory studies of normal skilled readers, frequently university students. An alternative technique which is occasionally used to develop such theories is with investigations of abnormalities of reading.

It is assumed that those people who have difficulty with the reading and the understanding of text experience such problems because of a breakdown in some aspect of the word recognition process. Thus we are able to test the word recognition models further by drawing parallels between the way in which a particular word recognition model would read if the functioning of one of its pathways or routes were impaired or abolished, and by observing the performance of impaired readers on different word recognition tasks.

It is not all poor readers who are used in neurological studies, since such people may have other cognitive difficulties in addition to their reading deficit. The readers who are of particular interest to researchers of visual processing are those who are reported to have once had normal reading skills but have suffered a loss because of some type of brain injury. These individual readers are known as the *acquired dyslexics*.

The acquired dyslexias

Acquired dyslexia involves a dysfunction in lexical access mechanisms arising from lesions within a previously normal adult brain as a result of a stroke or an accident. Dyslexia indicates 'faulty reading' in comparison to 'alexia' which denotes 'without reading'. The term 'acquired' implies that the reading disorders were caused by brain damage *after* the people had already learnt to read. In contrast, the term *developmental dyslexia* refers to reading difficulties that become apparent when children are learning to read, and such cases are discussed later in this chapter and also in Chapter 5.

Acquired dyslexia has been commonly split into four categories: surface, deep, letter-by-letter and phonological, although these do not constitute the full set of acquired disorders. Predominantly the study of acquired dyslexics has been based on their performance of reading aloud individual words rather than silent reading of text. This obviously restricts the contribution that such case-studies can make to the evaluation of word recognition models, but nonetheless their contribution is considered worthwhile.

What follows is a definition of the above four subgroups of acquired dyslexia, along with a description of some case-studies and the typical reading errors that these patients make. We will then go on to show how such patterns of errors in reading can contribute to several of the models of reading that were described in Chapter 2: the dual-route models (i.e. Coltheart, 1978) and the connectionist networks (i.e. Seidenberg and McClelland, 1989). Do the findings from the acquired dyslexics support or challenge these models? Certain acquired dyslexics show affix errors when reading aloud, e.g. *RUNNER* as 'running'. Do such errors support the notion of a morphemically organized lexicon, again proposed in Chapter 2 (Batt, 1993; Taft, 1981; Taft and Forster, 1975)? Finally, there is an ongoing debate as to whether the performance of acquired deep and acquired surface dyslexics is parallel to that of developmental dyslexics, and whether they show similar difficulties in reading. All viewpoints will be described so that readers may draw their own conclusions, drawing upon the available neurological evidence.

Types of acquired dyslexia

What follows is an attempt at defining four of the most common types of acquired dyslexia. We say 'attempt' because these definitions are not fixed and concrete in that not all patients show all of the possible symptoms suggested; there is much individual variation. Furthermore, these symptoms are not permanent, and many patients show improvement one day and yet appear to have developed a different symptom the next. Thus a deep dyslexic described by one researcher is unlikely to have identical symptoms to those of a deep dyslexic described by another group of researchers.

Letter-by-letter dyslexia

Letter-by-letter acquired dyslexia is also known as spelling dyslexia (Kinsbourne and Warrington, 1962), and word form dyslexia (Warrington and Shallice, 1980). For skilled readers the normal process of reading is not merely a matter of successive identification of each component letter in the word (see Chapter 1); however, for letter-by-letter dyslexics it is, thus reading latency is a direct function of word length (Warrington and Shallice, 1980). Such dyslexics therefore have to read every letter of a word before they can attempt to locate the word in their internal lexicon and read it as a whole unit. This slow left-to-right letter-by-letter identification procedure usually takes the form of naming each letter aloud, thus enabling clear recording of the dyslexic's errors. Furthermore, this problem is enhanced in some patients as they may also have a deficit in identification of individual letters. The severity of this deficit differs, for example, the patient RAV (Warrington and Shallice, 1980), shows no letter deficit, whilst CH (Patterson and Kay, 1982), misreads many words owing to a severe letter identification deficit. (NB: Patients are typically referred to by their initials.) Typical errors by CH are reading the word *MEN* as 'h, e, n, hen', clearly showing that the *M* has been misread as an *H*.

This is the only form of acquired dyslexia where writing and spelling can be unimpaired, and many letter-by-letter readers can write fluently and accurately, but then cannot read what they have just written, which suggests that the impairment is in letter identification not letter production. Contradictory evidence has recently been found which suggests that these patients *can* identify the letters accurately but only implicitly. When briefly exposed words are presented to these patients (too briefly for the letter-by-letter strategy to be used), they are unable to name or identify them, but on a subsequent categorical decision task they perform well above chance, selecting those previously presented words (Coslett and Saffran, 1989; Shallice and Saffran, 1986). There have been various explanations for the above finding (e.g. Humphreys *et al.*, 1988; Rapp and Caramazza, 1989), but none have as yet been accepted generally. The phenomenon of patients being able only to process stimuli implicitly is discussed again later in this chapter.

Some researchers would suggest that letter-by-letter acquired dyslexics should not be investigated in the attempt to test normal word recognition models since they believe that it is not a normal form of reading but a compensatory stage. There are many disagreements over the contribution of the evidence from acquired dyslexics, and these need to be taken into account before deciding on the fate of a model of normal reading on the basis of evidence of disabled reading.

Phonological dyslexia

There are few reports of this variety of dyslexia. These patients are able to read aloud real words but have difficulty pronouncing non-words (Beauvois and Derouesné, 1979; Coslett, 1991; Derouesne and Beauvois, 1979), typical errors are *SOOF* as 'soot', *SERSO* as 'servo' or responding 'don't know' on the presentation of a non-word. As the deficit occurs mainly for non-words it is not too disabling. Visual and affix errors occasionally occur, such as reading *BIBLIOGRAPHY* as 'biography' or *RECENT* as 'recently'. For many patients bound morphemes (e.g. -ed, -tion) cause slight difficulty, but the root form does not. Thus a patient may read *WALKED* as 'walking' or 'walks'; this suggests that free morphemes (e.g. *walk*) and bound morphemes (e.g. inflections and derivations) may be represented separately in the internal lexicon because there is no problem with accessing the stem of the word; it is the affix that causes the difficulty. However, there is not consistent reportage of affix errors across all phonological dyslexics (Funnell, 1983). There are further word type effects reported, with some patients mispronouncing function words (as for patients RG by Beauvois and Derouesné, 1979; and AM by Patterson, 1982) although again this is not observed for all patients (Funnell, 1983; Shallice and Warrington, 1980).

Surface dyslexia

This is the least understood of the acquired dyslexias and is also known as 'semantic dyslexia' (Patterson, 1981). These patients tend to assign meanings based on the pronunciation of the words, which are often themselves unsuccessful attempts at pronunciation. A consistent finding is a regularization effect, where regularly spelt words (those that conform to phonological rules) are read more accurately than irregular words (Bub *et al.*, 1985; McCarthy and Warrington, 1986). For example, a patient reported by Shallice and Warrington (1980) read correctly 36 out of 39 regular words, but only 25 out of 39 irregular words. Irregular words are often assigned the most regular pronunciation, for example, *PINT* is pronounced as 'pinnt' (to rhyme with 'mint'), and *YACHT* as 'yatchet' (to rhyme with 'hatchet'). Pronunciations can influence the semantic interpretation when the target word is a homophone, for example, the word I creates confusion as to whether it means 'eye' or 'myself', and *MOWN* could be defined as 'cry', as in *MOAN* (Marshall and Newcombe, 1973). Other errors are *BEAR* defined as a drink (beer), although there would be difficulty in knowing whether to categorize this error as a regularisation or a visual error.

There is scant evidence for an effect of word length, with Sasanuma (1980) reporting her patient KK to be better at reading aloud short non-words than long non-words. Shallice and Warrington's (1980) patient ROG also showed a clear effect of syllabic length, with an increase in reading latency with syllabic length. Again, word length effects are not reported for all patients. Some researchers (e.g. Marshall and Newcombe, 1973) have reported an abstract versus concrete word distinction with concrete words (e.g. *BABY*) being read more accurately than abstract words (e.g. *TRUTH*), although Sasanuma reports no such effects for her patients. Visual errors have been reported (Marshall and Newcombe, 1973), although they are very rare (Shallice *et al.*, 1983).

Coltheart (1981) suggests that this disorder closely resembles that of developmental dyslexia although others would disagree and suggest that it is deep dyslexia that is more similar to the errors reported for the developmental dyslexics. This argument is addressed later in this chapter.

Deep dyslexia

This is also known sometimes as 'phonemic dyslexia' (Shallice and Warrington, 1975) and is the most extensively studied of all the acquired dyslexias, and is the most disabling. Deep dyslexia is caused by massive damage to the left hemisphere and most patients have Broca's aphasia (damage to the Broca region resulting in equally poor reading and speech comprehension) as well as this deficit. Generally these patients are exceedingly poor readers: GR (Barry and Richardson, 1990) read only 21 per cent of individually presented words correctly, and errors tend to be semantically related to the word being looked at; for example *APE* read as 'monkey' (Coltheart *et al.*, 1987). Patients fail almost entirely to read non-words aloud (Barry and Richardson, 1990; Shallice and Warrington, 1980) but can repeat them. Typical responses to a non-word are 'no', or 'don't know', or responding with a visually similar word, for example *FRUTE* read as 'flute', or responding with a word semantically related, not to the non-word itself, but to a real word that looks like it, for example *RUD* read as 'naughty' (Shallice and Coughlan, 1980).

Performance on reading function words is exceedingly poor (Morton and Patterson, 1980) in comparison to content words (10 per cent v. 80 per cent). Thus, patients can read *BEE* but not *BE* (Gardner and Zurif, 1975). Abstract and low imageability words (e.g. *BELIEF*) are less likely to be correctly read aloud than concrete, high imageability (e.g. *CHURCH*) words (Katz and Lanzoni, 1992), although this is not the case for all patients. When these dyslexics attempt to read a concrete word they often make a semantically related substitution, e.g. *DREAM* is read as 'sleep', *ESKIMO* as 'iceman' (Coltheart *et al.*, 1980).

Visual and affix errors are frequently made, for example reading *SOUL* as 'soup' or *LOVELY* as 'loving'. There is equal performance on the reading of regular and irregular targets and no disruption by word length (Shallice and Warrington, 1975). Thus they are able to read *AMBULANCE* but not *AM*.

A display of the main symptoms of the described subgroups is shown in Table 4.1 as a simplified reference. It is important to bear in mind that these symptomatologies are not fixed, and that there is variation between patients within the subgroups. The four main types of acquired dyslexia and their typical errors have now been described, but what do they indicate about reading, in particular the routes from print to sound and to meaning?

Lexical and nonlexical routes to pronunciation

A popular concept is that there are two main possible ways of reading a letter-string aloud. One can be termed the lexical route, whereby a lexical entry in the internal lexicon is accessed and its correct pronunciation is produced. The other is the nonlexical route, where accessing a lexical entry is not necessary for pronunciation. Several researchers have challenged this dual-route approach altogether (Glushko, 1979; Marcel, 1980), although they have not been particularly successful, until recently, owing to incomplete formulations of the opposing models. The challengers suggest that dual routes to pronunciation are unnecessary, and that one route is sufficient to access both word meanings and pronunciations. The early one-route models proposed that the single route made use of an analogy process in order to compute pronunciations for nonlexical items (non-words). A non-word would access similarly spelt words in the lexicon and use their pronunciations to form the non-word pronunciation. These models were never particularly successful since the dual-route models were explicitly formulated and the single-route models were usually incomplete. This situation has now changed, with the development of several explicit models of reading having the concept of a single route: the connectionist parallel-distributed processing (PDP)

Table 4.1 Core symptoms of the four main acquired dyslexic subgroups

Symptom	Deep dyslexia	Surface dyslexia	Phonological dyslexia	Letter-by-letter dyslexia
Difficulty with reading non-words compared to content words	+ FOL – 'follow' PILT – 'pild'	–	+ SOOF – 'soot' SERSO – 'servo'	–
Difficulty with reading low compared to high imageability words	*	–	–	–
Irregular words more difficult to pronounce than regular words	–	+	–	–
Difficulty in reading function compared to content words	* HOW – 'where'	–	* THAT – 'which'	–
Semantic errors	+ TULIP – 'crocus' ROBIN – 'bird'	–	–	–
Visual errors	+ DAKE – 'drake' FRUTE – 'flute' WEALE – 'weasel'	*	* BIBLIOGRAPHY – 'biography'	+ MEN – 'hen'
Morphemic errors	+ EDITION – 'editor' AGAIN – 'against'	–	* INANIMATE – 'animated'	–

Key:
+   This symptom is displayed by virtually all the reported dyslexics in this subgroup.
–   never displayed by the dyslexics in this subgroup (or never reported)
*   rarely reported or inconsistent reportage of this symptom
lower case examples of the errors made
  words

model of Seidenberg and McClelland (1989), and the analogy model of Sullivan (1991; Sullivan and Damper, 1992). What follows is an in-depth comparison of dual-route and single-route models of reading based on six critical questions about reading, as asked by Coltheart *et al.* (1993): any model of reading should be able to answer them:

How do skilled readers read exception words aloud?
How do skilled readers read non-words aloud?
How is the visual lexical-decision task performed?
How does surface dyslexia arise?
How does phonological dyslexia arise?
How does developmental dyslexia arise?

Dual routes to meaning and pronunciation

With the dual-route models there are two main ways of reading a letter-string aloud. One is termed the lexical route, the other the nonlexical route. There are several dual-route models and they basically differ in the orthographic units that are used on the nonlexical route. For instance, orthographic–phoneme correspondence (OPC) theory (Shallice, 1981; Shallice *et al.*, 1983) obtains a pronunciation for its non-words by using its knowledge of correspondences between orthographic segments of various sizes and their phonological forms. Thus the pronunciation of *WINT* is produced by knowledge of individual letter pronunciations: 'w', 'i', 'n', 't', and by large segments; 'wi' 'nt', and so on. This route is nonlexical since no access to the internal lexicon is necessary, it being irrelevant whether or not the orthographic segments which used for pronunciation are words or not. The more popular grapheme–phoneme correspondence (GPC) theory (Coltheart, 1981), described in Chapter 2, breaks down the non-word letter-string into its orthographic segments, which are termed graphemes and refer to any letter or letter clusters that correspond to a single phoneme. Non-words are thus pronounced by application of grapheme–phoneme correspondence (GPC) rules, without any need to access the internal lexicon. For example, the word *CHEAT* can be subdivided into its graphemes [ch], [ea], [t], and each grapheme triggers an appropriate phonemic unit, /ch/, /ee/, /t/, which combine to create the correct pronunciation of 'cheat'. This results in the correct pronunciation of 'cheat' without the internal lexicon being consulted. The GPC theory was described in depth in Chapter 2 and will be evaluated further here, using the evidence from the acquired dyslexics, and by contrasting this account with that of a PDP connectionist network.

Grapheme–phoneme correspondence theory

Many theories have incorporated a GPC route; for example, see Figure 2.4, which shows a recent version of the logogen system containing such a route (Morton and Patterson, 1980). The best-known GPC model is that developed by Coltheart (1981), which is displayed in Figure 4.1, and it can be seen to have similarities with the right-hand pathway in Morton and Patterson's development of the logogen model (Figure 2.4). When a target is initially displayed both the lexical and nonlexical routes attempt to identify it. The lexical route (the left-hand pathway in Figure 4.1) passes through from visual feature extraction (i.e. deciding the information is verbal rather than pictorial), abstract letter identification (recognizing that 'a' and 'A' are the same letter), orthographic word recognition (does the word exist in the lexicon?) through to the semantic system (which gives the word's meaning) and finally word production. We can pronounce words without accessing their meaning, and so the left-hand pathway allows semantics to be bypassed. In contrast, when travelling along the nonlexical route within Coltheart's model, the grapheme parser decides how the letter-string is to be divided into its individual graphemes. Once the graphemes have been identified the assignment of appropriate phonemes to the graphemes (according to GPC rules) is conducted. The final stage is the blending of the individual phonemes into a single coherent whole for pronunciation. It should be noted that although this model is developed with the production of speech in mind it is able to explain other outputs, such as deciding whether a letter-string is a legal word or not (lexical decision), or producing a definition of the target.

The lexical route

The lexical route here is equivalent to the lexical route in Morton's first logogen model (Figure 2.3) and is described in detail in Chapter 2. For normal skilled readers all known real words travel via the lexical route, and once a familiar letter-string is processed and accesses an entry in the internal lexicon (within Coltheart's model this involves accessing an entry in the orthographic word recognition system, which triggers the correct entry in the semantic system) then its correct pronunciation is provided automatically. This would suggest that if the nonlexical route could not be used (e.g. if it were damaged as a result of brain injury), patients who could pronounce a familiar word would still also know its meaning, since the entry would have been located in the internal lexicon (the semantic system). However, case-studies of acquired dyslexics have shown that this is not always the finding.

An acquired dyslexic described by Funnell (1983) could not read non-

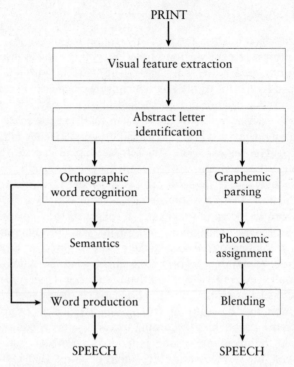

Figure 4.1   The dual-route model of reading
Source: Coltheart, 1981

words (suggesting that the nonlexical route was impaired), and was also poor at comprehending printed words (could not access the semantics), but was 90 per cent correct at reading aloud words. This suggests that there is an indirect route from orthography to phonology which bypasses the semantics. Thus there must be two lexical routes, one via semantics, and one which bypasses the semantics (See Figure 4.1, and also Figure 2.4, Morton and Patterson, 1980). The existence of this second route is further supported by neuropsychological evidence from Schwartz *et al.* (1980) and Coltheart *et al.* (1983). It can be seen that evidence from the acquired dyslexics is valuable in the interpretation and modification of the lexical route to meaning and to sound. How about the nonlexical route to sound?

The nonlexical route

It has been suggested in the sections on the four main types of acquired dyslexics that they differ in their symptomatology. For example, some dyslexics show difficulties in reading non-words and irregular words. Using Coltheart's (1981) theory, non-words are easily pronounced using GPC rules via the nonlexical route. Irregular words are not correctly pronounced by this route as the most commonly assigned phoneme associated with the particular grapheme will be allocated. For example, *PINT* will be divided into *P* and *INT*, and the common pronunciation assigned to *INT* is 'innt' (to rhyme with 'mint') thus *PINT* will be pronounced as 'pinnt'. Consequently the correct pronunciation of *PINT* would not be accessed by using the GPC route but it would be by travelling along the lexical route. It follows that any patient who can read irregular words correctly must have an intact lexical route. However, non-words cannot be processed by the lexical route as there is no corresponding lexical entry for them; therefore being able to produce a pronunciation for non-words requires an intact GPC route.

The first two major questions posed by Coltheart *et al.* (1993) for models of reading have now been answered. First, how do skilled readers read exception words aloud? We have just seen that they do this by using an intact lexical route. Second, how do skilled readers read non-words aloud? This task is easily done by a normal reader who would use GPC rules stored in the nonlexical route in order to produce an accurate pronunciation. Coltheart *et al.* go on to state four further major questions that have to be addressed. These concern explanations of how the visual lexical decision task is performed, how surface dyslexia arises, how phonological dyslexia arises, and how developmental dyslexia arises. The third of the Coltheart *et al.* questions, regarding lexical decision tasks, is again responded to with ease by the Coltheart model. The letter-string is searched for in the internal lexicon; if it is not accessed, a 'no' response is formed. Chapter 2 describes how a similar logogen model was modified also to explain non-word legality effects, and non-word neighbourhood effects. It also claims to be able to explain the behavioural patterns found in the acquired and developmental dyslexics.

How does surface dyslexia arise? The typical errors found from studies of surface dyslexics are regularization errors (irregular words being pronounced as regular forms). It results in regular words being read more accurately than irregular words, which suggests that these surface dyslexics are using the GPC route rather than the lexical route normally used for the processing of real words. Spelling errors are usually phonemically correct; for example, *SEARCH* spelt as *SURCH*, again supporting the notion that the patient can read aloud using the GPC route rather than the orthographic section of the lexical route. It is therefore suggested that the surface dyslexics tend to use an intact nonlexical route, demonstrated by the regularization errors, but on occasions may use an impaired or damaged lexical route which results in visual errors (very rarely reported).

However, if these subjects are asked to give meanings to a stimulus word they give a meaning related to the visual error. For example, Marshall and Newcombe (1973) report a classic example from AB who read *LISTEN* as 'liston ... that's that famous boxer'. This error is problematic for a dual-route model which uses GPC rules, as the nonlexical route should show no lexical influences because it has no contact with the lexicon. If *LISTEN* → 'liston' is regarded more as a GPC error than a visual error then the pronunciation of 'liston' and subsequent interpretation of the spoken word as a surname is less of a problem. Recognition of meaning, by this alternative interpretation, follows the generation of an incorrect pronunciation with aid of inappropriate GPC rules, and is a result of spoken word recognition. The reportage of uncertainty over reading homophones, with the wrong meanings being selected, e.g. *I* read to mean 'eye' rather than 'myself' also is problematic for the GPC explanation. If the word *I* is processed by the GPC route then the two alternative meanings for the pronunciation would not be known, since the lexicon is said not to be accessed. However, it is again possible that these interpretations of mispronounced words result from the lexical access of spoken words.

There is a dilemma if it can be maintained that lexical effects are occurring through what appears to be a nonlexical route. Either our view of surface dyslexia needs to be altered so that it reflects a more complicated combination of the two routes, such as targets obtaining a pronunciation via the GPC route and then achieving lexical access through a spoken word, or else our GPC nonlexical route may have to be changed to include a direct lexical influence. Some would suggest that an analogy model (i.e. Glushko, 1979; Sullivan, 1991) is already equipped for explaining these data, as the pronunciation route does involve making use of information from the lexical route.

Is the GPC theory any more able to answer the fifth question as stated by Coltheart *et al.* (1993): how does phonological dyslexia arise? The *phonological acquired dyslexics* cannot read non-words (or performance is very poor), suggesting a severed or damaged GPC route. This is further supported by the fact that the reading of real words is not impaired, showing that the lexical route is certainly intact. Function words can cause difficulty and visual and affix errors do occur, but these symptoms do not occur for all patients. These errors are therefore not a necessary feature of phonological dyslexia (Funnell, 1983). However, Morton and Patterson (1980) have taken into account the inconsistent reportage of problems with function words and bound morphemes when developing a more detailed version of the logogen model. Their model further subdivides the cognitive system into separate subsystems which deal with the semantic and syntactic processing involved in reading single lexical items, and a more comprehensive explanation of the semantic and affix errors and difficulties with reading function words is presented in Morton and Patterson.

Although we have not as yet described developmental dyslexia we can state how Coltheart *et al.* consider the dual-route model is able to explain how developmental dyslexia arises. Basically Coltheart suggests that there are several subgroups of developmental dyslexia that correspond to the acquired dyslexias. Thus we would expect to find developmental phonological dyslexics and developmental surface dyslexics. If it is damage to the GPC route that results in acquired phonological dyslexia, then the developmental phonological dyslexic probably has had difficulty acquiring the specific modules that correspond to the GPC route, resulting in a similar pattern of behavioural responses. Developmental surface dyslexia is then explained by stating that the modules specific to the lexical process of reading are somehow impaired. This explanation rests on the case that there exist subgroups of developmental dyslexics who are systematically similar to the acquired dyslexics, and this is discussed later in this chapter and is taken up again in Chapter 5. Let us now move on to to a seventh, and an eighth question that Coltheart *et al.* (1993) did not specify: how do deep dyslexia and letter-by-letter dyslexia arise?

Deep dyslexics show a failure to read non-words and frequently make semantic, visual and affix errors (e.g. 'tulip' for *CROCUS*, 'flute' for *FRUTE*, 'running' for *RUNNER*). It is arguable as to whether this type of patient can contribute to the evaluation of the dual-route model (Coltheart, 1980) as the left cerebral hemisphere is usually substantially damaged and consequently deep dyslexia may be a product of a right hemisphere reading system (for a full discussion of this view see Coltheart, 1983; Patterson and Kay, 1982). Marshall and Newcombe (1980) do attempt to review their findings in terms of the dual-route model and suggest that the almost complete inability to read non-words indicates that the GPC route is damaged. They suggest that the patients therefore use the lexical route and this results in semantic errors, since unlike the normal reader, they do not have the output from the GPC route to confirm their decision. For example, deep dyslexics may read *FOREST* as 'trees', because they do not know that the correct pronunciation must begin with an *f* (information that the GPC route would have provided had it been intact). It would then be appropriate to ask why it is that phonological dyslexics also cannot read non-words (obviously damaged GPC route) but can read real words well (few semantic errors). This pattern of disability would suggest that Marshall and Newcombe's interpretation is incorrect, and that maybe the problem lies in an impairment of the lexical route.

Furthermore, a similar criticism is raised against the interpretation of *letter-by-letter acquired dyslexia*. It may well be that this type of disorder is a strategy rather than a reflection of a normal reading process and thus should not be evaluated as evidence of damage within a previously intact reading system. However, Warrington and Shallice (1980) have attempted to review the errors made by letter-by-letter acquired dyslexics in terms of normal word recognition models and have located the deficit at the visual input logogen system (the abstract letter identification system in Coltheart's model). However Patterson and Kay (1980) suggest that the deficit is due to an impairment in the access from the visual analysis to input logogens (abstract letter identification to orthographic word recognition unit in Coltheart's model). Yet another proposal is that the visual input logogens are unimpaired but are forced to accept an abnormal source of input (i.e. a series rather than a parallel presentation of letters).

The GPC route has received mixed support from the acquired dyslexias and despite accounting for the six major questions that Coltheart *et al.* thought that dual-route models were able to answer, it would appear that the replies were not totally convincing. Would the connectionist single route models fair any better?

A single route to meaning and pronunciation

The early one-route models (Glushko, 1979; Marcel, 1980) proposed that the single route made use of an analogy process in order to compute pronunciations for nonlexical items (non-words). A non-word would access similarly spelt words in the lexicon and use their pronunciations to form the non-word pronunciation. These models were never explicitly formulated and therefore were never viable competitors against the dual-route approach. This situation has now changed with the development of several explicit models of single-route reading: the connectionist or parallel-distributed processing (PDP) model of Seidenberg and McClelland (1989), and the analogy model of Sullivan (1991; Sullivan and Damper, 1992). In the words of Seidenberg and McClelland, the claim is that 'our model, and others like it, offers an alternative that dispenses with the two-route view in favor of a single system that also seems to do a better job of accounting for the behavioral data' (p. 564). What we are concerned with is whether such claims are true. What follows is a description of one of the single-route theories, the PDP model of Seidenberg and McClelland (1989), and its ability to account for the six major questions of reading, put by Coltheart *et al.* (1993).

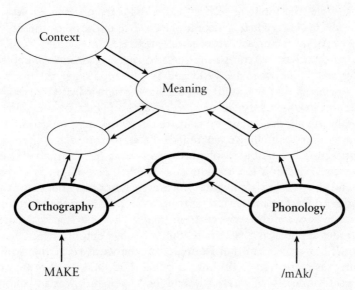

Figure 4.2   Parallel distributed processing model of reading
The larger framework for the PDP model of reading. The implemented model is indicated
by bold outline and type.
Source: Seidenberg and McClelland, 1989

This PDP network is strongly influenced by the distributed representation models of McClelland and Rumelhart (1981), and Rumelhart and
McClelland (1986), Hinton *et al.* (1986) along with Coltheart (1978),
Glushko (1979) and Morton (1969). It attempts to use a minimum
architecture and although the larger framework contains semantic and
contextual levels, and feedback from the phonological to hidden units,
this is not implemented in their simulation model. The implemented
model is illustrated in Figure 4.2.

Each word processing trial begins with the presence of a letter-string
that is encoded into a pattern of activation over the orthographic units.
These orthographic units are connected to hidden units and the degree
of activation at the hidden units is computed and fed into the phonological units. As processing in this model is interactive, the hidden unit
computations are also fed back to the orthographic units. Seidenberg
and McClelland stress that it is not necessary to activate an orthographic/
phonological unit for every letter/phoneme in a word, or to have to
specify that letter/phoneme's position (as was implemented in the rather
strict positional encoding scheme of McClelland and Rumelhart, 1981).
Rather, the representations they chose for their orthographic and phonological units are a variant of Wickelgren's (1969) triples scheme. Thus,

for example, the input *MAKE* is treated as a set of letter triples _MA, MAK, AKE, KE_ (where _ denotes a word boundary), or the phoneme string /mAk/ is treated as a set of phoneme triples _mA, mAk, Ak_.

Learning occurs by comparing the two output patterns (phonological and orthographic) that are produced by the model against the correct target patterns that the model should have produced. If there is a large difference, that is, a large error score, the learning procedure adjusts the strengths of all the connections in the network in proportion to the extent to which this change will reduce the total error score.

It therefore is possible to obtain a error score for the model's output. However, a decision has to be made whether this output is correct or not, and this is quite a complex process. As described above, the output string is compared to the input string to obtain an error score for the difference between the two representations. The next step is to compare the target input string with all other possible output strings that the network has considered. For example, for the word *HOT* the computed output was compared to the correct code, /hot/, and to all of the strings in the set formed by /X ot/, 'hX t/, and /ho$X$/, where X was any phoneme. A response was coded as correct if the error term computed for the networks output was smaller than the error term for the other output patterns, and incorrect if a correct target was beaten by any incorrect alternatives. This is known as the BEATENBY criterion.

This BEATENBY criterion was used in evaluating the model's success in reading the 2,897 words in its training set. The model proved to be very effective. Only 77 (2.7 per cent) of the words were incorrectly read and most of these errors were with low frequency exception words. This complies with behavioural data obtained from skilled readers and thus the model is able to show how skilled readers read exception words, the first of Coltheart's six questions.

How do skilled readers read non-words? Although Seidenberg and McClelland are confident that their model is able to explain the behavioural data concerned with non-word reading, they do not report how accurate the PDP model is at reading such letter-strings. A simulation of the PDP model was carried out by Besner *et al.* (1990) to test its effectiveness in non-word reading. Using Glushko's (1979) word set, the model was correct 65 per cent of the time, and using two other word sets it was correct only 59 per cent and 51 per cent of the time, compared to 94 per cent and 89 per cent accuracy for human subjects. It would appear that the network is very poor at modelling the behavioural data for non-word reading. Seidenberg and McClelland (1990) replied to this finding by suggesting that the low accuracy scores were a product of the relatively small vocabulary size of the network (2,897 words) compared to human subjects (at least 30,000 words). This would appear a plausible explanation except that Coltheart *et al.* (1993) have built a network that performs as accurately as humans with as limited a vocabulary set as the Seidenberg and McClelland network.

Is the PDP model able to mimic the high performance of humans on lexical decision tasks? The PDP model, once fully trained, performs lexical decisions by submitting a letter-string to the input unit as usual, and activation of the hidden units is computed and fed back to orthographic units (via the hidden units), which in turn recreate a representation that is compared with the input representation. An orthographic error score is then computed which is a measure of the difference between the original and the recreated input pattern. This error score is a kind of measure of the familiarity of the input pattern. Readers have to assign a criterion to this error score; if below a certain value they can respond 'yes' and if above they respond 'no'. Besner *et al.* (1990) calculated that the criterion (using stimuli from an experiment by Waters and Seidenberg, 1985) that would be needed to produce a low error rate for real word stimuli (6.1 per cent, the error rate for words observed by Waters and Seidenberg) would produce an error rate of over 80 per cent for non-words. Therefore the model would be extremely poor at correctly rejecting non-words. Seidenberg and McClelland (1989) anticipated this criticism and suggested that their model conducts the task purely on orthographic information, whilst humans may be performing the task phonologically:

> when the words and non-words are orthographically similar . . . we assume that subjects also assess the familiarity of the stimuli in terms of the computed phonological output.

They consider the possibility of training the network with the sounds of the words by connecting the phonological representation computed by the network to the hidden units (this was part of their larger framework). Even if these phonological representations were used then there would still be many instances where this modification of the PDP network may not be very productive. For example, what would the model do if presented with real words that were orthograpnically unusual, or with non-words that were wordlike and pseudohomophonic (sounded like real words)? It could not use phonology as the basis for the lexical decision as all targets would sound like words, and using a strategy of accepting those targets that looked orthographically correct, it could end up rejecting all real words and accepting the non-words. It must be noted that humans would perform very well on this task.

The PDP model has not shown a particularly high success rate so far, so how does it cope with modelling the data from the acquired dyslexics?

Patterson *et al.* (1989) and Patterson (1990) 'lesioned' Seidenberg and McClelland's (1989) word-reading network with the aim of producing symptoms of at least one form of surface dyslexia. They were partially successful in this preliminary simulation. The lesioned model was tested on four types of words and performance was very similar to that of one surface dyslexic, MP (Bub *et al.*, 1985), but not as dramatic as the performance of a second patient, KT (McCarthy and Warrington, 1986). Coltheart *et al.* (1993) query whether the lesioning studies are fruitful in the case of the PDP model, as surface dyslexics generally are very good at reading non-words, whilst the network, even when not lesioned, is extremely poor. Patterson *et al.* note that the neuropsychological implications of the PDP model are at an embryonic stage and consequently there has been no attempt to model phonological, letter-by-letter or deep dyslexia with this network at the current time: 'Much more work is needed before a comprehensive story can be told' (Patterson *et al.*, 1989).

Dyslexia provides a challenging test of the Seidenberg and McClelland model and although the model was partially successful in its simulation of surface dyslexia, on the whole it has not been tested extensively on the other three main forms of acquired dyslexia. At present they are only using impairment data rather than developmental data to test the limits of their one-network model and thus no modelling of developmental dyslexic behavioural patterns has been attempted. They do report that when they reduce the number of hidden units from 200 to 100 the performance of the network appears to simulate that of developmental dyslexics, with larger regularity effects than good readers, poor performance in reading high frequency irregular targets, yet reasonable pronunciations of non-words. This is not a full attempt at a simulation of developmental dyslexia, but no doubt this should be attempted since preliminary findings look promising.

It appears that the dual-route model provides a better account of the evidence than the one-route connectionist network. There are two main appeals of connectionist networks: first, they are computationally formal, and therefore the effective computations conducted by these networks are highly likely to resemble the computations performed in the brain; and second, they are able to learn. For these reasons Coltheart *et al.* (1993) combined the advantages of the dual-route model and that of a connectionist network and developed the dual-route cascaded (DRC) model of reading. With this model the input stage on both the lexical and nonlexical routes consists of letter units, which feed into the visual word recognition stage for the lexical route and into the grapheme–phoneme conversion stage for the nonlexical route (see Figure 4.3). The network learns the GPC rules from exposure to the 2,897 words used in the Seidenberg and McClelland (1989) training set.

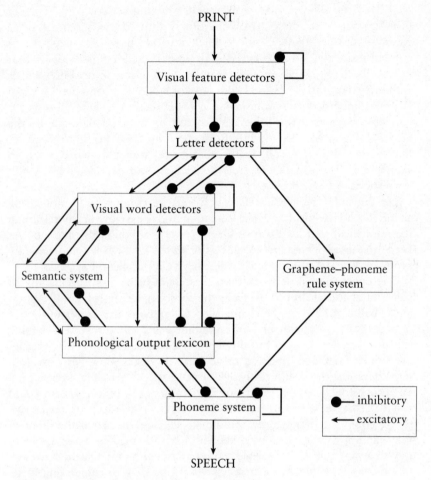

Figure 4.3   The dual-route cascaded model of reading
Source: Coltheart, Curtis, Atkins and Haller, 1993

Coltheart *et al.* provide a detailed description of how the algorithm learns these GPC rules and how it is applied to produce a string of phonemes.

How good is the DRC network in modelling human behaviour? The ability of the nonlexical route in modelling exception word reading and non-word reading is outlined below. There has been no attempt to describe reading by the lexical route as this stage of the model has not yet been implemented. The nonlexical route uses GPC rules to read inputted letter-strings, so it should make 100 per cent errors on all exception words (i.e. reading *PINT* to rhyme with 'mint'). However, it read 5 of the 47 irregular words in its training set correctly. Further investigations into these irregular stimuli showed that four of these words conformed to GPC rules and thus would have been expected to be read correctly. What is exceedingly important for this model is that using only the 2,897 words in its training set it is able to read non-words extremely accurately. Using the non-word stimuli from the Glushko (1979) experiment it pronounced 98 per cent of these non-words correctly, compared to 68 per cent correct pronunciations made by the Seidenberg and McClelland (1989) model. This confirms that the size of the training set used is sufficient to successfully train a network to a high standard of performance, despite Seidenberg and McClelland's (1990) suggestions to the contrary.

Theoretically the DRC network would be competent in simulating acquired phonological and surface acquired dyslexia by merely disabling the nonlexical and lexical routes respectively, although this has not yet been attempted. There are no suggestions as to whether it could simulate acquired deep or letter-by-letter dyslexia or developmental dyslexia.

One connectionist network that does claim to be able successfully to simulate acquired deep dyslexia is the most appealing model of Hinton and Shallice (1991). Their aim was to explore the behaviour of a network that maps from orthographic representations to semantic features when it is subject to different forms of damage. If its properties are similar to those observed in acquired dyslexia, this will provide a hypothesis for the origin of these characteristics in patients. Hinton and Shallice start by asking what possible problems within a system could result in the semantic errors that are found in the deep dyslexics (i.e. where could the damage possibly lie)? They suggest that if the input to the semantic system is noisy, then the network may be more likely to move toward one of its learned representations. Normally, the representation that it would move towards would be that corresponding to its input, but if the system is damaged, it can easily move towards a nearby attractor, which will presumably correspond to the meaning of the related word. This provides a simple explanation of the semantic substitution phenomenon. Yet some of the errors observed in the deep dyslexics are visual, and some are mixed (e.g. *CAT* read as 'rat'). Would damage to the later part of the system result in such errors? Hinton and Shallice's (1991) simulations showed that by damaging the latter part of their system they were able to produce a similar pattern of error response to that of the deep dyslexics. Furthermore, no extra mechanism or tuning was required to produce this effect.

Their network maps from the visual form of a word to its meaning. The initial components are position specific letters, which correspond to McClelland and Rumelhart's (1981) letter input units. The network consists of three- and four-letter words that use only the letters b, c, d, g, h, l, m, n, p, r, t in the first position, vowels in the second position; b, c, d, g, k, m, p, r, t, w in the third position; and e, k in the fourth position. There are therefore 28 grapheme input units. To restrict the load, just 40 words were used. These words fell into five concrete categories; indoor objects, animals, parts of the body, food and outdoor objects. The meaning of each of the 40 words used was represented by dedicating a single 'sememe unit' (e.g. green, sweet, does fly) to each of the semantic features of the words. There were 68 sememe units used in the network, with the meaning of each word being represented by a pattern of activity across these units. It was necessary to introduce one layer of hidden units (called intermediate units) between the graphemes and sememes. 'Clean up' units were also employed, which were connected to the sememe units; the effect of these units was to make actual word meanings more powerful 'attractors' than other combinations of sememes. In total the network contained about 3,300 connectors.

Hinton and Shallice (1991) then lesioned each part of the network in turn, by removing a proportion of connections (or units) or by adding noise to the connections. After each lesion they tested the network on the 40 words, and interpreted the resulting sememe patterns in terms of the best-fitting word responses. Almost every lesion condition yielded the three characteristic types of error: semantic, visual and mixed, in varying proportion. Hinton and Shallice point out that the results are rather tentative because they limited their training set to 40 words.

In general it can be seen that the evidence from the acquired dyslexics can be useful when attempting to evaluate models of word recognition and recognizing their limitations. A further question, described in Chapter 2, which benefits from the observation of the lexical and nonlexical errors made by the acquired dyslexics, is concerned with the structure of the mental lexicon.

Is the lexicon morphemically organized?

Chapter 2 discussed the substantial amount of evidence from investigations with normal readers that suggests the lexicon may be arranged in terms of morphemic units. Does the evidence from the acquired dyslexias support or challenge this notion?

Of the four subgroups described here only deep and phonological dyslexics make affix errors (this is more of a problem for the deep dyslexics). Patterson (1980) divides the affix errors made by deep dyslexics into those in which a previously suffixed word has the suffix deleted (*SOLOIST*, becomes 'solo'), substituted (*PROJECTION*, becomes 'projector') or changed (*PARTING*, read as 'apart'), and those where an unsuffixed word has a suffix added (*CONTAIN*, read as 'container'), or the tense changed (*BUY*, becomes 'bought'), or part of speech altered (*APPLAUD*, goes to 'applause'). Typically errors consist of manipulations of regular suffixes such as -ed, -ing, -er. It should be noted that although Patterson classifies suffixes such as -ing as derivational suffixes, they are more commonly found performing an inflectional function, and certain suffixes such as -er may be equally found in derivational or inflectional roles. It is important to note the function of an affix. Research on normals has suggested that inflected forms may be separated into stem and suffix prior to lexical identification, and the suffix may be stored separately in the lexicon from its stem, whereas derived forms may be stored as whole word units (Taft, 1985). Therefore, in order to avoid confusion with linguistic terminology when we refer to morphological errors we include all possible functions that an affix may play, both inflected and derived.

The morphemic decomposition hypothesis

Before we delve into the evidence from the acquired dyslexics we will briefly summarize the concept of a morphemically organized lexicon (see also Chapter 2). One search model designed explicitly with the morphemic structure of the lexicon in mind is the prelexical affix stripping model (Taft, 1979a, 1985; Taft and Forster, 1975, 1976). In this model a morphological analysis is conducted prelexically by an intelligent morpheme parser, resulting in fewer lexical entries than would be required by a whole word lexicon. The actual process that an entry such as *MIDGET* goes through prior to accessing the lexicon is seen in the step by step guide in Table 2.1. The main problem with Taft's model is that its core is centred on the processing of non-words created from the stems of truly prefixed forms (*juvenate* from *rejuvenate*) versus pseudo-prefixed forms (*pertoire* from *repertoire*). This restricts the ecological validity of the model and the generalizations that can be made concerning real reading conditions. Any evidence from the acquired dyslexics on the processing of both real and non-words would contribute immensely to the evaluation of this morphemic model.

A typical technique used in the study of normal readers is the lexical decision task. In her investigations of the errors made by deep dyslexics Karalyn Patterson (1980) adapted this technique so that the patients were each asked to go through a list of letter-strings and say aloud whether or not they thought the letter-string spelt a word. Error rates rather than response times were recorded. Although the performances of the two patients under investigation (DE and PW) were not error free, accuracy was high. This was in marked contrast to their performance when asked to read the words aloud (and respond 'no' to the non-words). Patients were generally poor at reading the affixed words although they could recognize them as real words. On the occasions when the patients attempted to read non-words (they were created by attaching a legal word stem with an illegal suffix, e.g. *HIGH + ING*), they made a large number of suffix substitutions so that the non-words were reported to be real words with the same underlying stem (*HIGHING* read as 'higher'; *LENGTHER* as 'longer').

These findings suggest that the patients can look up a target word in their lexicon with no difficulty (can say correctly whether it is a word or not); the difficulty arises in the pronunciation of the words, where the wrong affix is selected prior to spoken output. This in turn suggests that stems and affixes are decomposed prior to output, but it provides little additional information as to whether they are correctly decomposed prior to searching the lexicon, or whether the lexical entries correspond to whole word units and the problems arise at the output stage. For example, the data could be interpreted as indicating that as the patients read suffixed non-words (*HIGHING*) as real words with the same stem (*HIGHER*) they are decomposing the letter-string into stem + suffix (as Taft and Forster would maintain). After this decomposition the patients would look up the decomposed stem (*HIGH*) in their lexicon, find an entry (*HIGH*), and thus respond with a legally acceptable formation of that stem (*HIGH* + suffix), with the problem arising in the selection of the appropriate suffix to match the stem.

A second study conducted by Patterson presented her patients with incomplete sentences in which they had to select one of two possible words to complete a sentence. The two words were selected in such a way that one correctly fitted the sentence and one was morphemically similar (*RULE/RULER*). Thus the patient was presented with:

Prince Charles will one day (ruler/rule) the country.
The policeman was (directing/directions) the traffic.

In each sentence the incorrect alternative was a response which had been made earlier in response to the correct target word (e.g. the patient had previously been asked to read aloud *DIRECTING* and had responded 'directions'). Each patient was asked to read the sentences silently and cross out the wrong word so that the sentence would read correctly. One month later the test was conducted again with the patient listening to the sentences being read aloud. Patients found the task extremely difficult when they had to read the sentences silently (and performed below chance), whilst performance was very good with the auditory presentation. The initial finding that subjects' performances are very poor on the visual task would suggest that the lexicon is morphemically organized because the correct entry cannot be accessed in the lexicon. However, the discovery that performance is reasonably accurate on the auditory presentation of sentences may suggest that the difficulties experienced by these patients are due to the visual aspects of the words. Thus what appear to be affix errors may in fact be visual errors. This visual interpretation would not explain how tense errors occur (*BUY* pronounced as 'bought') or how the deep dyslexics performed so well on the variation of the LDT in Patterson's (1980) first experiment.

The question of how the internal lexicon is organized clearly needs more research to be conducted before any firm conclusions may be drawn. A further problem that arises when examining morphemic errors made by acquired dyslexics is knowing how to define an error as morphemic (it may be a visual or even a semantic error). Although the acquired dyslexics can contribute to the clarification of well-established models this area of study needs further developing before their errors can provide deeper insight into the structure of the mental lexicon.

One final area that is receiving a great deal of attention is the comparison of acquired dyslexia with developmental dyslexia. This is based on the proposal that there are striking similarities between the reading abilities of certain acquired dyslexics and those reported for the developmental dyslexics.

The developmental dyslexics

Although the subtyping of acquired dyslexia can cause debate, the acquired dyslexics as a whole are not difficult to classify. They are people who once had normal reading capacities and after brain injury have lost some of their reading capabilities. The definition of a developmental dyslexic is not so clear-cut. The descriptions that researchers have used to distinguish the developmental dyslexics from poor readers do differ slightly but usually involve a diagnosis by exclusion. Thus one definition provided by the World Federation of Neurology (see Critchley, 1970) refers to developmental dyslexia as:

> a disorder manifested by difficulty in learning to read despite conventional instruction, adequate intelligence and sociocultural opportunity

Such criteria have been referred to by some as a 'counsel of despair' (Rutter, 1978). This is because such a diagnosis makes it extremely difficult to classify children from a 'disadvantaged background' as dyslexic, as their socioeconomic circumstances cannot be ruled out as a possible cause of their poor reading. The alternative therefore is a diagnosis by symptomatology (the technique used to subdivide the acquired dyslexics into their many proposed subgroups). This again is problematic as it is not clear what symptoms we should use. Some researchers have produced symptoms that appear to have little linkage with the reading process. For example, Levinson (1980) regards dyslexia as a cerebellar-vestibular dysfunction, and therefore suggests diagnosis on the basis of whether subjects can ride a bicycle, or how good they are at balancing on a beam. As dyslexia is often referred to as a 'specific reading disability' we might safely disregard this evidence.

Despite the difficulty with the definition of developmental dyslexia we shall accept the classifications (usually by exclusion) made by the researchers, and move quickly to accounts of the disorder. Our starting point is Anthony Jorm's (1979a, 1979b) contention that a theory of developmental dyslexia should account for the disorder at a variety of levels: the nature of the reading deficit the cognitive deficit, and the neurological basis of the deficit.

Jorm's approach: similarities with the deep dyslexics

In addressing the first level, the nature of the reading deficit, Jorm draws attention to the unpublished work by Firth (1972) on developmental dyslexics which suggests that they are capable of accessing the meaning directly from the visual form of a word but have difficulty with the phonological recoding of the written word. If we were to evaluate such findings using Coltheart's dual-route model we would conclude that the direct visual route was intact, but the phonological route was impaired. Relying on such an interpretation of the actual reading deficit Jorm went on to evaluate which of the basic cognitive abilities were necessary for effective phonological recoding and thus were likely to be deficient in developmental dyslexics. A variety of studies was reviewed and the general conclusion was that dyslexics are able to perform normally on tasks that reflect normal perceptual registration and iconic memory, but that tasks requiring large memory loads were performed poorly, indicating a memory deficit. Jorm then proceeded to suggest that a similar deficit is observed in brain-damaged patients (Warrington, 1971; Warrington and Weiskrantz, 1973) who have had lesions to particular areas of the brain resulting in impairment of memory performance. More specifically, the area of the brain which resulted in these short-term memory function deficiencies was the inferior parietal lobe (Warrington *et al.* 1971).

Jorm concluded that developmental dyslexics are capable of accessing the meanings of words directly from their visual forms, but that they have difficulties with phonological recoding. As the phonological recoding of words requires the use of short-term memory the difficulty that the developmental dyslexics have with such tasks may indicate memory deficiencies. Previous memory research has implicated the inferior parietal lobe as a core area in short-term memory function. Patients with lesions in this area (e.g. deep dyslexics) produce similar findings on tests of reading (difficulty reading non-words, visual and semantic errors, etc.) to the developmental dyslexics. It therefore seemed reasonable to conclude that the developmental dyslexics are likely to have underdeveloped inferior parietal lobes (similar views have been proposed since the nineteenth century) and that there are functional similarities between acquired deep dyslexia and developmental dyslexia.

Until this link between the research on acquired deep dyslexia and developmental dyslexia was made by Jorm few attempts had been made to connect the research conducted in the two areas. Ellis (1979) congratulated Jorm on his attempt to bring together the developmental dyslexic and acquired dyslexic fields and noted that it is regrettable that few psychologists had attempted this. However, Ellis went on to criticize Jorm's views and to present a contrary view, initially presented by Holmes (1978), as being more valid. Holmes argued that the misreadings made by the developmental dyslexics are comparable to those made by the acquired surface dyslexics. Thus Holmes's view (direct visual route dysfunctional) is almost directly opposed to Jorm's view (GPC route inadequately functioning).

Ellis's approach: similarities with the surface dyslexics

Ellis (1979) criticized Jorm's (1979a) paper on several points, two of which will be described here. Firstly, it was claimed in Jorm's paper that developmental dyslexics were poor at reading non-words. Ellis stated that this information was inadequate. Were the developmental dyslexics unable to read the non-words or did they attempt to pronounce them but were incorrect? This is an important issue, as the acquired deep dyslexics tend to produce real word responses to non-word targets, for example, *FOL* pronounced as 'follow', or else they do not attempt a pronunciation at all. Jorm (1979b) replied that the developmental dyslexics reported by Firth often attempted pronunciations of the non-words. Jorm had reported that the developmental dyslexics, like acquired deep dyslexics, made visual errors, but Ellis notes that so do the surface dyslexics. This leads to the suggestion that visual errors should not be used as a defining feature of deep dyslexia. However, visual errors do occur in surface dyslexics but *very* rarely. Only 2 per cent of errors of the surface dyslexic patients of Marshall and Newcombe (1973) were visual errors, and usually visual errors are not reported at all, suggesting they do not occur (Shallice *et al.*, 1983). It certainly is not a core symptom of surface dyslexia and we do not include it as such in our Table 4.1 of defining symptoms. A more challenging criticism made by Ellis was that semantic errors are common in acquired deep dyslexics but none were reported by Jorm with the developmental dyslexics. In reply, Jorm notes that developmental dyslexics did sometimes make semantic errors (*SHEEP* read as 'shepherd'), although it is debatable whether this should be regarded as a visual or a derivational error.

It therefore appears that Jorm defended his position reasonably well, but how about Ellis's proposition that Holmes's (1978) linkage of developmental dyslexia with acquired surface dyslexia is a more valid suggestion? Holmes reported that many of the errors made by her developmental dyslexics indicated partial failure of GPC rules. However, many of the errors cited by Holmes as demonstrations of the use of failed GPC rules could be equally plausibly classified as visual errors, for example, *CERTAIN* pronounced 'carton', *MUSCLE* as 'musical', *REIGN* as 'region'. Furthermore, Jorm criticized Holmes for presenting selected examples of errors to illustrate her conclusions, declaring that a quantitative analysis of all the data would have been more informative. Even if Holmes's personal analysis of errors were to be accepted as indicating usage of faulty GPC rules, it is difficult to see the primary deficit as being in the direct visual route. It seems more plausible that there is a deficit in the phonological route.

Ellis supported Holmes with evidence from Seymour and Porpodas (1980). They studied four dyslexic boys and concluded that there was impairment of both routes (visual and phonological). However, this may not be incompatible with Jorm's approach. Seymour and Porpodas assessed the functioning of the direct route with tasks that compared performance on high frequency versus low frequency words, irregular versus regular words, and word versus non-word. Jorm notes that these tasks measured *achievement* of the direct route rather than the *ability* of the direct route. As Seymour and Porpodas themselves point out, the development of an extensive word sight vocabulary may depend partly on having an adequate phonological route. Children with good phonic skills have an inbuilt teacher which they can use to add words to their sight word vocabulary, whereas children with poor phonic skills have to rely on an external teacher to build or increase their sight word vocabulary. Poor achievement of the direct route is thus predicted if the child has poor phonic skills (not because the direct route is disabled or dysfunctioning – since it is perfectly able to function – but because it is the insufficient sight word vocabulary that results in the poor achievement). Thus Seymour and Porpodas's evidence is inconclusive on this point. Their findings could be used to support either Jorm or Holmes.

The use of the phonological route was also emphasized by Baron (1977) and Brooks (1977). They taught subjects to associate strings of printed symbols from an artificial alphabet with spoken responses. In one condition the symbols could be related to the responses using GPC rules (the orthographic condition) but in the other there was only an arbitrary relationship between symbols and responses. After several hundred practice trials the words in the orthographic condition were read faster than the words in the arbitrary condition. This clearly demonstrates how a deficit in the phonological route in dyslexic children would produce not only a limited sight word vocabulary, but also slow performance with highly familiar words. This gives support to Jorm's suggestion of the potential importance of an impaired phonological route in developmental dyslexia.

The weight of evidence so far appears to lie more in the direction of developmental dyslexics being functionally similar to the deep dyslexics. However, a thorough study by Baddeley *et al.* (1982) gives cause for doubting Jorm's theory. Three groups were selected: 15 dyslexic boys, 15 boys matched for chronological age (normal reading age), and 15 boys matched for reading age (younger chronological age). The boys were presented with four lists of 17 words and 17 non-words in a pencil-and-paper version of the lexical decision task. For two of the lists the non-words were homophonic with real words (pseudohomophones). The boys' task was to underline the letter-strings they recognized as being real words. Overall, the dyslexic boys were slower and less accurate than the controls (boys of comparable chronological age). Both groups showed slower and less accurate responses to the homophonic non-words. If the dyslexic boys had an impairment in the phonological encoding of written words then their decision should not have been affected by the phonological characteristics of the word, and so they should have been no slower or no more inaccurate at rejecting homophonic non-words. The results found 27 per cent pseudohomophones falsely accepted by the dyslexics, and 5 per cent falsely accepted by the controls, and of the nonhomophonic non-words 15 per cent were falsely accepted by the dyslexics and 2 per cent by the controls. This pseudohomophone effect suggests that both the dyslexics and the controls were using phonological encoding, and thus the results are difficult to interpret from Jorm's position.

In the second experiment the boys had to work through two lists of words and non-words reading each letter-string aloud. The dyslexics were again slower at reading aloud the targets than either of the control groups, although their error rate (42 per cent for non-words) was similar to that of the reading age controls (32 per cent for non-words). These results are used against Jorm's suggestion of a functional similarity between deep dyslexics and developmental dyslexics because one of the key striking features of deep dyslexics is their severe inability to read out non-words correctly.

An additional feature of deep dyslexics is the difficulty they have in reading words of low rated imageability (although this is not the case for all patients). Accordingly, the boys in the Baddeley *et al.* (1983) study were also asked to read aloud words varying in degree of imageability. Certainly the dyslexics had more errors when reading the low imageability words (37 per cent for low imageability, 13 per cent for high imageability), but so did both the matched reading age control (29 per cent low imageability, 8 per cent high imageability) and the matched chronological age control groups (7 per cent low imageability, 0 per cent high imageability). One of the features of deep dyslexia turns out to be a more general phenomenon, and so it is questionable whether it should be used as a crucial feature of dyslexia. Indeed, in our Table 4.1 of symptomatology it is not proposed as a key feature, as not all patients show such errors. In any case, Jorm's argument that developmental and deep dyslexia are similar because they both are sensitive to imageability is drastically weakened.

A misinterpretation?

While the evidence used to evaluate Jorm's position is not consistently supportive, Baddeley *et al.* (1982) and Ellis (1979) may have misinterpreted the argument, which is that deep dyslexics and developmental dyslexics are functionally *similar*, not *identical*. Thus if the GPC route is not operating efficiently in the developmental dyslexic then performance on reading non-words would be reduced, but this does not mean that it would be eliminated. Baddeley *et al.* agree with Jorm in suggesting that developmental dyslexics may suffer from an impairment of verbal short-term memory. They suggest, however, that it may be more profitable to explore the relationship between developmental dyslexia and surface dyslexia, as proposed by Holmes. This surely is also not supported by their findings because surface dyslexics characteristically do not have problems reading non-words, whilst the developmental dyslexics observed by Baddeley *et al.* showed a clear disadvantage at reading non-words in comparison to real words. Ellis (1993) has argued convincingly that developmental dyslexics show marked differences, posing the question of whether we should be thinking of developmental dyslexia as a unitary disorder. We must also wonder whether we are gaining any extra insight by comparing it to another disorder, acquired dyslexia. As Ellis notes in his more recent analyses, some developmental dyslexics resemble acquired surface dyslexics, and others resemble acquired phonological dyslexics. However, we do not have total agreement as to the subgroups that exist within acquired dyslexia or within developmental dyslexia, and there may be a limited amount to gain by attempting to understand one poorly defined problem by comparison with another.

The division into subgroups

Although Jorm does not dismiss the notion of subgroups he considers there to be no satisfactory evidence to support the notion and suggests that we should adopt the more parsimonious view that developmental dyslexia is a unitary disorder. Ellis (1979) also asks why genetic neuropsychological syndromes should be less varied than those resulting from brain injury. The evidence in favour of subtypes of developmental dyslexia is the subject of a long-standing controversy, however, with little agreement over the question of how many subtypes exist, let alone whether there is a unitary or a multifactor disorder (see Snowling, 1987; Vellutino, 1979; Wright and Groner, 1993). The principal candidates for subtypes are an auditory-linguistic deficit and a visual-perceptual deficit (which is discussed in more detail in Chapter 5). The auditory-linguistic deficit has also been seen as being composed of separate subtypes that emphasize the similarities with surface dyslexia and similarities with deep dyslexia.

Although there may be grounds for classifying the developmental dyslexics into subgroups their division into the same categories as acquired dyslexia should only be attempted with extreme caution. Concerning the acquired dyslexics it would be entirely wrong to think that there is an established and agreed number of acquired dyslexias. We have outlined what are the four most agreed upon subgroups with acquired disorders but not all researchers' views and not all patients' symptoms are consistent, as we have stated. Cognitive neuropsychologists have had considerable success in discriminating between individual patients but the attempt to identify acquired dyslexic syndromes has proved to be fraught with difficulties. For example, the borderline between some of the categories is extremely blurred. Sartori, Barry and Job (1984) reported a patient who made 5 per cent semantic errors immediately after his cerebral injury, but one month later made no semantic errors at all. On both test occasions he was poor at reading non-words. Using the criteria of symptomology described in Table 4.1 it can be seen that immediately after injury he was defined as a deep dyslexic, but at what point did he then become a phonological dyslexic (as would be deduced from the pattern of errors at test two)? How many semantic errors make a deep dyslexic (Ellis, 1985)? Furthermore, what constitutes a semantic error as opposed to a morphemic or visual error? For instance Funnell (1983) classified the error in reading *LIGHT* as 'night' by her patient WB as a semantic error, but other researchers would disagree with such a classification.

This problem of subgrouping within the acquired dyslexics can be demonstrated further by the recent suggestion that there are two types of deep dyslexia, input and output. This arises from the finding that in some patients the damage appears to occur at the output stage, when they are attempting to produce a phonological output from a semantic representation. Such a patient is JA (Katz and Lanzoni, 1992). As with most deep dyslexics his reading errors varied according to the imageability, concreteness, legality and frequency of the words. Comprehension of printed words outstripped his oral reading ability, suggesting that the printed words could activate their semantic representations more easily than they could activate their correct phonological outputs. As the tasks ordinarily used to test deep dyslexics involve explicit, controlled processing, a lexical decision task was used as an alternative technique to see if printed words could be activated on an automatic basis. It has been shown that letter-by-letter dyslexics are able to process briefly presented words implicitly, and the lexical decision task has the advantage of not requiring a transcription of a visual sequence of letters into a compiled phonological sequence. If JA's responses on the lexical decision task were influenced by the phonology of a word in the same manner as normal readers, it would suggest that his problem lies with the conscious compilation of the phonological output.

Katz and Lanzoni (1992) used a task that had previously demonstrated that the phonology of a word influences its processing (Meyer *et al.*, 1974). Subjects had to decide whether two words presented on a screen were both legal words or not, and these words were either phonologically and orthographically similar (*BRIBE/TRIBE*), or phonologically dissimilar but orthographically similar (*TOUCH/COUCH*). Faster responses were recorded for both normal readers and JA on the first set of words (phonologically similar) than for the second set (phonologically dissimilar). This suggests that JA was able to access the phonological representation of the word. A second experiment was conducted using pairs with dissimilar spelling and sounds that included function words (which deep dyslexics, including JA, are poor at reading). No influence of phonology was found for JA, but it was for normals. For the normal readers, *BUT/CUT* was easier than *HAD/WAD*, but JA found these pairs equally difficult. This suggests that JA was unable to access the phonological representation for function words, and that the semantic route was working and was able to produce accurate phonological representations. Why in that case are the 'output' deep dyslexics only able to identify words implicitly? Katz and Lanzoni (1992) suggest that this is because to produce the correct pronunciation takes time (and the deep dyslexics often suffer from aphasia), and whilst the articulatory response is being prepared a competing lexical entry may become dominant. This also may explain why many dyslexics try to correct themselves after making an error, knowing their response was incorrect. For example, JA read *SHORT* as 'long, short, long, tall, no, long'. The next logical question is to ask, if output deep dyslexics such as JA can automatically activate phonological entries, can 'input' deep dyslexics do likewise?

This may be difficult to test since input deep dyslexics may well have difficulty with the LDT. This subgroup's problem appears to arise not at the accessing of the word's pronunciation but at an earlier stage of the reading process. The input deep dyslexics not only have difficulty producing an oral response to written words, they also have problems with matching pictures to written words (Coslett *et al.*, 1985). Additionally, some of this subgroup have greater difficulty accessing semantic representations for visual rather than auditory stimuli (Sartori, Bruno, Serena and Bandin, 1984), suggesting that it is a difficulty within the orthographic input lexicon, not at the output stages. The evidence supporting the existence of input and output deep dyslexics appears quite convincing. The logical question is, when do we stop subdividing into these different groups? If we only have one patient demonstrating the behavioural patterns of output deep dyslexia are we justified in creating this subgroup or are we in danger of giving each case-study a defining title of its own?

Contributions from the neuropsychology of reading

The GPC dual route, connectionist single- and dual-route models and the plausibility of a morphemic lexicon have been examined here using evidence from the acquired dyslexics, but is this evidence useful in evaluating the models? It is possible to argue that single case-studies of individuals with unique disorders do not constitute sufficient evidence for an evaluation of normal reading. It is plausible that having suffered brain damage, mechanisms that have already been established are further developed in unique and unrepresentative ways. These routes to a word's meaning and pronunciation would usually be considered inefficient in normal readers and would not usually be utilized. Impairments may therefore not reveal the components of a fractionated system so much as the strategies used under unique circumstances. These strategies might not be used at all by the unimpaired skilled reader. For example, if the direct route to a word's pronunciation is blocked, then its meaning may be determined and the phonology determined after an indirect route to the lexicon. However, some suggest that after damage to the left cerebral hemisphere structures and processes in the right hemisphere are used, and thus an entirely new set of procedures take over the task of reading. If this happens the analysis of errors from acquired dyslexics will tell us little about the processes normally used in reading. Furthermore, the comparison of acquired dyslexics with developmental dyslexics should only proceed with caution. There is little agreement among investigators of the acquired dyslexias about what the subgroups are and what symptoms they should demonstrate. To try and impose this poor set of criteria on the developmental dyslexics may be more limiting than enlightening.

These warnings having been made, a model that is able to predict or simulate impaired as well as intact performance is a more powerful model of human behaviour than one that can only simulate intact performance. Additionally, the models developed from this neuropsychological research have important applications. If we have a precise understanding of the reading mechanism, and of how specific damage to a system translates into symptoms, we can help guide the design of rehabilitation and teaching programmes to aid the acquired and developmental dyslexics. For example, from the findings from Hinton and Shallice's model we could conclude that it might be advantageous to retrain the reading system using distinctive orthographic styles for words that tend to be confused semantically. While we must be cautious in using the behaviour of dyslexics when investigating the intact reader, the research described throughout this chapter, and the models that have attempted to explain and simulate the dyslexic performance, are looking promising in the building of an efficient and accurate model of the reading process, both intact and impaired.

5

The Role of Eye Movements in Reading

For over a century eye movements have been considered as a sensitive indicator of the reading process (Huey, 1908; Javal, 1879; Tinker, 1958). When readers process a page of text their eyes do not move in a continuous sweep across the page, but instead the movement (a saccade) tends to be quite jerky, occasionally stopping to inspect a word (a fixation). Not every word is fixated, however, and not for a consistent duration of time. Further, the movement is not consistently from left to right along a line of text. Occasionally readers may move back to a part of the sentence that they may have previously fixated (a regression). The purpose of an eye movement is to bring a piece of text under the scrutiny of the fovea of the eye, where vision is sharpest. Visual images fall on different parts of the retina, and these can be divided crudely into three areas: the fovea, the parafovea and the periphery. When we fixate an object in the world we bring an image of that object on to the fovea centralis, where there is the greatest concentration of retinal cone cells. The foveal area provides the greatest amount of visual acuity and subtends outwards 1 to 2 degrees from fixation. As distance from fixation increases, visual acuity decreases quite rapidly, and the region of reduced acuity up to 5 degrees to each side of fixation is known as the parafovea. Any visual image projected on to the retina further than 5 degrees from the fovea is counted as being in the periphery. Eye movements deliver new areas of text for foveal inspection, and the main question to be considered in this chapter concerns the sensitivity of the mechanism that controls this inspection process to the cognitive processes that act upon the inspected text. This question asks the extent to which we can observe the processing of words in sentences as they are being read by observing variations in fixation durations and fixation locations, as the difficulty of the text is varied. We shall also plot changes in fixation patterns as children acquire their reading skills, and consider the hypothesis that developmental dyslexia is a product of an impaired eye guidance mechanism.

The technique of monitoring eye movements is considered by many to be more ecologically valid than the other traditional methods (i.e. LDT, tachistoscopic identification) used to tap into the reading process. Subjects can read 'normally' in preparation for some questions about the meaning of the text, rather than having to press response buttons or name words under time pressure. Unfortunately the technique is not without its critics, and we will address them later. Its popularity is based on the assumption that the direction of our eyes can tell us something about the processing that is being conducted by our mind. Variations in eye fixations reflect variations in the difficulty of the word being inspected, and so eye movement and fixation measures can be considered as providing a direct indication of the current difficulty of processing.

During reading the movement of our eyes is ballistic. This means that once the direction and distance of the movement has been programmed and triggered it cannot be altered *en route*. This rapid eye movement is known as a *saccade* and can cover a distance of 1–18 degrees although usually it spans 8–9 characters in length (approximately 2 degrees visual angle, depending on the distance between the reader and the print). The duration of the saccade is dependent on the distance to be covered and on average takes 25–30 msec. to be accomplished (for a 2 degree saccade). The total proportion of reading time taken up by saccadic movement is usually 10 per cent. During the saccade virtually no visual information can be collected. We say 'virtually', since laboratory studies have shown that in a darkened room a pattern which is presented during a saccade is perceived as a blurred image, as long as no other visual stimulus is presented prior to or following the saccade; another stimulus would mask the saccadic image (Campbell and Wurtz, 1978). However, it can be safely assumed that under normal reading conditions no useful visual information is detected during a saccade. After the saccade has been completed the eyes come to rest at a predetermined location in the text; this resting time is known as a *fixation*. Typically, readers fixate for 200–400 msec., and there is a considerable amount of variation within this range. Although readers of alphabetic scripts such as English read in a left-to-right fashion, they occasionally do go back to a point in the text

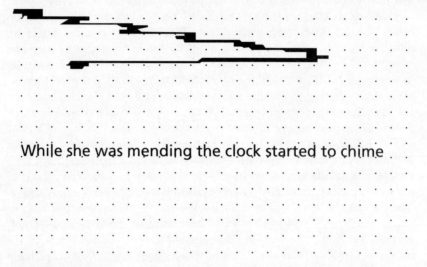

While she was mending the clock started to chime

Figure 5.1   Eye movement pattern of a normal reader reading a sentence
Source: Underwood and Everatt, 1992

that may have been previously fixated, or to text that may have been passed over during a saccade. This return fixation is known as a *regression*; and these regressions occur on average 10–15 per cent of the time for a normal adult reader.

Regressive fixations usually are launched to areas of the text that have caused linguistic confusion, or contain particularly complicated words. For example, Figure 5.1 shows a reader's fixation pattern on a 'garden path' sentence. These are sentences that are characteristically misinterpreted on their first reading, either as a result of the syntactic structure or as a result of a lexical ambiguity. In the example here the noun *clock* is attached to the verb *mending*. This parsing, or calculation of the syntactic structure, is quite legal until the words at the end of sentence are encountered. They cannot be integrated with the rest of the sentence, and at this point the syntactic structure of the sentence must be recalculated.

Fixations are indicated in Figure 5.1 by the short vertical 'stacks' and saccadic eye movements are indicated by the horizontal lines that connect the stacks. Time can be thought of as flowing downwards from the top of this print-out. The first fixation within the sentence occurred on the word *while* (duration 370 msec.), followed by *she* (240 msec.), *mending* (280 msec.), *the* (350 msec.), *clock* (270 msec.), and *started* (370 msec.). A regressive saccade then resulted in a second fixation on the word *she* (210 msec.). There was no fixation on the words *chime*, *was* or *to*. Six out of the nine words were fixated, and there was one regressive saccade. A fixation on the space immediately before the first letter of a word is counted as a fixation on the word, for our purposes. The total reading time for this sentence was 2.29 sec. Indicators of the difficulty that the reader had with this sentence are the long fixation on *started* that was followed by a regressive movement. The fixation on *started* was 90 msec. longer than the fixation on the other seven-letter word, *mending*, even though it is a more frequently encountered word. Usually high frequency words attract shorter fixations, but in this case a parsing difficulty has resulted in a longer fixation. We can conclude that it was when the reader reached *started* that it was realized that the syntactic structure that was being used was inappropriate, as this verb cannot be attached to a noun in the sentence if *the clock* is first interpreted as the object of the phrase *while she was mending*. When the reader realizes that an incorrect syntactic interpretation has been made, a recovery is necessary, and this is indicated by the long fixation and a regressive movement.

The appeal of measuring eye movements is that they give an indication of what processes are going on in the reader's mind. This linkage between the direction of the reader's eyes and the cognitive processes stimulated by what is being inspected is formalized as the *eye–mind assumption*:

the eye remains fixated on a word as long as the word is being processed ... [and] ... the eye-mind assumption posits that there is no appreciable lag between what is fixated and what is being processed. (Just and Carpenter, 1980)

With no linkage at all, of course, there would be no point in recording a reader's eye movements. They would provide no information about the cognitive processes prompted by fixation. The assumption is validated by reports that the number of regressions and forward fixations increase with text difficulty, and that these fixations tend to be of a longer duration than those associated with less complex text. Simple words receive less visual attention than low frequency and otherwise difficult words, and there are individual differences that also lend support to the assumption. For example, poor readers make more regressive fixations, and longer fixations, on a piece of text than good readers. There is an accumulating body of evidence that, in general terms, the eye–mind assumption is valid and that we can learn a great deal about reading processes by watching reader's eyes as sentences are understood. There are limiting cases, however, and we have suggested that the assumption can be challenged by (i) demonstrations of people fixating one point in space while amending or thinking about something elsewhere in the field of view; (ii) demonstrations of the recognition of words that are not being fixated; and (iii) demonstrations of speed reading and skimming associated with good comprehension. In these special cases knowing where the readers' eyes are pointing will tell us little about what is going through their minds, but these are not a part of normal reading and the assumption holds well enough for us to use eye fixation behaviour as a reliable and direct guide to changing cognitions. By changing the words in a sentence, or by changing the structure of a sentence, we can induce difference patterns of fixation, and these changing patterns tell us about differences in cognitive processes. When readers make longer fixations upon certain kinds of words, as they do with low frequency words for example, we can infer that these words require more processing than high frequency words.

Eye movement measurements

The recording of eye movements can be accomplished in a number of ways. One of the more popular methods is to direct an infra-red beam of light on to the outer surface of the eye – the cornea – which is then reflected back on to a photo-electric detector mounted on a spectacle frame or head frame. When the eye moves the reflection changes, and it is this change that can be used to indicate the location of fixation. As such equipment cannot distinguish head movements from eye move-ments the head needs to be restrained. This is done by placing the head in a clamp-like device or by using a bite bar which is moulded to the shape of the subject's mouth. More advanced equipment is also available which can subtract head movement from eye movement without any need for restraining devices, and this gives an accurate measure of eye fixations while eliminating the need for head restraint. Other methods of eliminating head restraint use detectors mounted on the subject's head in conjunction with video images of the scene being inspected (taken from a lightweight video camera that is mounted on the subject's head), and observation of the eye with a video camera. These methods often provide less accurate estimates of fixation locations than methods dependent on corneal reflections.

There are several measures used in eye movement investigations. The main ones are duration of the first fixation on a word, first fixation location, total number of fixations, and gaze duration. 'First fixation duration' is self-explanatory: the amount of time spent on the first fixation in a word. Location of the first fixation is usually measured in terms of character spaces within the word, with the first letter being counted as the first character. If the word is long it may receive more than one fixation, some researchers measure the duration of the second and even third fixations and analysis them as separate independent measures, others merely sum all the forward fixations together to obtain the gaze duration. If a regressive fixation is made to a word this is summed with the forward fixations to obtain the total inspection time for that word. Obviously, for short words which only obtain one fixation, gaze duration and total inspection time would be identical.

The eye movement problem that a researcher is investigating will influence the measurements that would be selected. For example, if investigating the direct, on-line processing of particular words in sentences, then gaze duration may be considered to be a suitable measure of the difficulty of processing of a word. Location of the first fixation would be unimportant in this study. On the other hand if an investigator wants to know about the extent of parafoveal processing then gaze duration might be still considered to be a good measure of the processing of the fixated target, but the experiment would also take account of possible influences from words other than that being fixated. Thus, the location of the first fixation on the next word would also be considered to be a useful measure. If eye guidance is influenced by the word ahead of the current fixation, this can only be checked by looking at measures that are sensitive to pre-processing. Processing of the target might be influenced by the context in which it appears. The words prior to the target will generate expectancies, both semantic and syntactic, and pre-processing of the next word may even influence the amount of time that we decide to spend fixating the current word. There are therefore a number of possible influences upon fixation duration and gaze duration. These multiple influences can be taken into account not only by taking different measures of eye movements, but also by taking control of the words and sentences that are to be displayed. One way to overcome the possible contamination of a foveal measure such as first fixation duration from pre-processing of the word ahead of fixation, is to keep all the other words in the sentence constant.

In the following discussions we shall describe research on eye movements in two central areas of interest: that which tries to determine what fixations can tell us about the processes which are occurring in the mind, and that which concentrates on how the reader knows where to look next, that is, what influences the extent of the next saccadic movement.

Processing during fixations

To what extent is the duration of an individual fixation under the control of the cognitive processes that are extracting information during that fixation? Our fixations may be autonomous, and may give little indication of the difficulty of the cognitive processing taking place. In this case all processing of the information extracted during a fixation would have to occur *after* that fixation has been completed (post-fixation theory). Such a view contrasts strongly with the on-line (eye–mind) and parafoveal processing theories, which both agree that some cognitive control is exerted by the reader in determining the duration of eye fixations. The more difficult the processes involved in comprehending the sentence, the longer should be the fixation, so as to allow more time for extraction of information from the word being inspected, and more time for consideration of how the word should be integrated with the sentence.

Post-fixation processing

The notion of post-fixation processing, as the term suggests, is that processing occurs after a fixation has been terminated (Gonzalez and Kolers, 1985). According to this model the locations and durations of fixations do not provide an index of cognitive processing because the processing is deferred until after the fixation that collects the information. If this were the case it could be predicted that all fixations and saccades would be of the same duration and distance, because the eyes are pre-programmed to move a constant distance alone the line. The post-fixation hypothesis has difficulty explaining why a low frequency word receives more visual attention than a high frequency word (Rayner and Duffy, 1986). If we did not process any information until we had reached a convenient spot in the text in which to do so we could not manipulate our fixation patterns. Clearly the post-fixation processing position cannot be strongly defended.

On-line processing of individual words

There is a considerable body of evidence to suggest that processing is not postponed completely during reading, and that fixations provide an 'on-line' indication of reading difficulty (Just and Carpenter, 1980), which involves moment-to-moment control. When fixating a relatively important part of the field, our eyes will remain for a duration that indicates the amount of processing being performed. The extreme version of this theory proposes that words that are not fixated are not processed. Just and Carpenter's view of reading is in fact based on two assumptions: the *immediacy assumption,* which states that 'the reader tries to interpret each content word of a text as it is encountered', and the *eye–mind assumption*, which says, as we have already described, that the reader's eye remains on a word as long as the word is being processed. The time it takes to process a newly fixated word is directly indicated by the gaze duration. Support for this model comes from Rayner and Duffy (1986), who presented single target words on a screen. They found longer fixation durations upon low frequency words (*gondola*) than upon high frequency words (*vehicle*) of similar length, and also found longer fixations upon ambiguous nouns with equally likely meanings (*coach*) than upon ambiguous nouns with a dominant meaning (*perch*). This confirms the assumption that those words that need more visual processing do indeed receive longer fixations.

Further support for on-line processing of differences *within* words comes from studies conducted by Hyönä *et al.* (1989), O'Regan *et al.* (1984) and Underwood, Clews and Everatt (1990), whose readers showed a sensitivity to the information structure of long words, with longer fixation durations upon the informative halves of the words. This again supports the notion of moment-to-moment control. Ehrlich and Rayner (1981) also reported more fixations and longer fixations upon words containing misspellings (for example, the word *horse* appearing in a sentence where *house* was anticipated).

Just and Carpenter (1980) have provided data showing that during the reading of paragraphs taken from scientific text, the length of the inspection was directly related to the difficulty of processing. For example, one subject looked at the word *question* for 300 msec., but at the equally long but less frequent word *transfer* for 633 msec. Further support for the on-line approach comes again from Carpenter and Just (1983) who showed that gaze duration on a target was not influenced by the length or frequency of the preceding word. They concluded that cognition is locked to fixation and that there is no influence of material prior to or ahead of fixation.

Just and Carpenter state in their definition of the immediacy assumption that readers try to interpret every content word. This is supported by their data, which show that only 18 per cent of content words are skipped compared to 62 per cent of function words. This finding in itself is problematic for the on-line processing approach. If readers try to inspect only every content word, not function words, how would they know which ones to land on and which to avoid? When skipping shows a sensitivity to word type, then we have a suggestion of processing without fixation.

A major source of evidence that suggests that our eyes are under the control of the cognitive processes involved in sentence comprehension comes from studies of the sensitivity to sentence contexts and sensitivity to syntactic structure. We shall illustrate the immediacy of the effects of varying the processing load upon eye movement control, with investigations of sensitivity to the predictability of words in sentences and sensitivity to parsing difficulties.

On-line processing of words within sentences: context effects

The probability of fixating a word varies as a function of its predictability, and when it is fixated; the fixation duration also varies. Ehrlich and Rayner (1981) showed that during the reading of passages subjects fixated words that were predicted by the preceding context less often (51 per cent of the time) than words appearing in neutral contexts (fixated 62 per cent of the time). In this experiment the subjects read passages including:

> *He saw the black fin slice through the water ... He turned quickly toward the shore and swam for his life. The coast guard had warned that someone had seen a shark off the north shore of the island ...*

in which the target word *shark* is more predictable than it is in a passage such as:

> *The couple were delighted by the special attention that they were getting. The zoo keeper explained that the life span of the shark is much longer than those of the other animals they had talked about: ...*

When a predictable target word was fixated then the fixation duration was shorter than if the same target had been fixated in neutral context (221 msec. versus 254 msec.).

There are two results of interest here. The variation in fixation duration demonstrates that the current processing load has an immediate effect on the mechanism that decides whether it is time to move our eyes. The more difficult it is to relate a word to what has preceded it, the longer we will spend looking at it. This is a recurring result in studies using eye fixation data.

When target words were fixated, they had shorter fixations, and a second result of interest is the variation in probability of fixation. Predictable words were fixated less often than unpredictable words in the Ehrlich and Rayner study, begging the question of how readers with the predictable passage knew they need not fixate the target. It may be that the context alone was sufficient to tell them what the next word was, but this seems unlikely. The sentence could have continued in a number of ways, with *shark* as one of any number of candidates. For instance, the coast guard might have warned that someone had seen a great white shark, or a blue shark, or a man-eating shark, or a large shark, or any number of qualified sharks. The point is that *shark* itself could have been preceded by an adjective, and this exact word is not required by the sentence structure as the word immediately following *had seen a* . . . in this sentence. The word *shark* will appear somewhere – this much is very predictable – but not necessarily in the sentence slot that it does occupy. (There is a potential problem with Ehrlich and Rayner's experiment that makes *shark* almost inevitable. The target word appeared in a prior sentence, informing the readers that this is a passage about a shark before their eyes came to the target.) Given that the target word does not have to occupy the particular position that it does, the readers were probably skipping the word with the aid of additional information. If they could extract information about the target during the fixation immediately prior to the fixation that would take them to the target, then a decision could be made to make a longer saccadic movement and to avoid fixating it altogether.

When we read we do not fixate every word on the page, but these 'skipped' words are not unprocessed (Fisher and Shebilske, 1985). There is also some evidence of parafoveal processing during reading, and the incidence of skipping of predictable words leads to the suggestion that one of the purposes of parafoveal processing is to help us make decisions about how far to move our eyes next. With a predictable word, and with early processing of the shape of the next word that is consistent with our expectancies, we can risk making a longer saccade, bringing the possible benefit of an increase in reading speed without loss in comprehension. After all, if we make a wrong guess we can always make a regressive movement and take a look at the word we have recently skipped.

If we are anticipating an outcome in a sentence – as the Goodman–Smith psycholinguistic guessing model suggests for skilled readers – then we see different patterns of fixation and re-fixation when our interpretations are confirmed and when they are violated by the way that the sentence is actually completed. What happens if the reader is led to anticipate one interpretation of the text and then is given contradictory evidence? Carpenter and Daneman (1981) were able to subject their readers to just this with sentences containing homographs (words with one spelling but multiple meanings, e.g. *tears*). These ambiguous words appeared late in sentences that encouraged one interpretation of the target (to cry) and then concluded with another interpretation (to rip). For example, they gave the readers sentences such as:

Cinderella was sad because she couldn't go the dance that night. There were big tears in her brown dress.

Such 'garden-pathing' of the reader resulted in longer fixations on the word *dress* and more regressions back through the text. This suggests that contextual information is used to disambiguate lexical ambiguities within a text as they are encountered. It also shows that readers will interpret information in one way until subsequent information suggests an alternative interpretation. This incompatible information then leads to a slowing down in the overall processing of the text because reanalysis is required, and on occasions this will result in a regressive saccade and a rereading of the text.

Further evidence for the finding that readers only interpret one meaning of a lexically ambiguous word when initially encountering it is provided by Rayner and Duffy (1986). They presented subjects with ambiguous words within sentences whose interpretation varied in relation to how dominant one meaning was within the language. For example, *boxer* is usually interpreted as one who fights rather than a breed of dog, whilst *coach* can refer either to a vehicle or a person who teaches (American subjects were used). Gaze durations on the ambiguous words with a dominant meaning were shorter than those ambiguous words with equally dominant meanings. Furthermore, dominant meaning ambiguous words did not differ from control words in measures of gaze duration. Rayner and Duffy concluded that for the dominant meaning ambiguous words and the control words only one meaning was accessed, whilst the ambiguous words with equally dominant meanings accessed both meanings, resulting in longer gaze durations on these targets. If prior context makes one of these equally dominant meanings more plausible, then gaze durations are reduced. This suggests that context is necessary to disambiguate the various interpretations of text and thus reduce processing times.

On-line processing of words within sentences: effects of parsing difficulty

In the Cinderella example the misinterpretation is induced by a temporary lexical ambiguity, but reanalyses can also be seen with sentences containing a temporary syntactic ambiguity, as with the sentence:

Because her sister loves to teach kids learn.

The difficulty in this case is in assigning *kids* to *to teach* whereas it is only on progressing to the final word that it becomes apparent that *kids* is part of a new clause and is not to be attached to the existing one. This becomes clearer once the sentence is rewritten with a comma after *teach*. In other sentences the words to *teach kids* could easily form a complete phrase, correctly parsed and consistent with the meaning of the text. In this garden-path sentence, however, there is a temporary ambiguity that demands reanalysis of the syntax. The ambiguity in this example revolves around the tendency to continue adding new words to a phrase unless there is good reason to do otherwise. Thus a sentence such as:

Since he always jogs a mile this seems like a short distance to him.

is easier to process than:

Since he always jogs a mile seems like a short distance to him.

Frazier and Rayner (1982) suggest that the difficulty in the second sentence arises because *a mile* is interpreted as the direct object of *jogs*, owing to a hypothesized characteristic of the syntactic processor, that of 'late closure'. The principle of late closure is one of two general principles that guide the reader, according to the Frazier and Rayner model of parsing. As each word in a sentence is encountered, it is added to an existing phrase or a decision is made that it should form the start of a new phrase. In this way all of the words in a sentence are related to each other in a process that analyses the syntactic structure. The first of the parsing principles is:

The principle of late closure: Newly encountered words should be attached to the current phrase whenever grammatically permissible.

Late closure says that new words are added to current phrases until the rules of syntax say otherwise, rather than being allocated to new phrases. This strategy usually works, but does not in cases such as the second sentence above. The initial reading of this sentence can result in misparsing, with the reader failing to close the phrase after *jogs*. The second sentence deserves a comma after *jogs*, to indicate that the phrase is complete, and without it the immediately following words are incorrectly attached to the first clause. Frazier and Rayner (1982) found that this error in processing is represented by the longer reading times needed for the second sentence. Also there were longer fixations on the post-ambiguity region (*seems like*) and more regressive fixations to the ambiguous information (e.g. *jogs a mile*). The eye movement data once again show that immediately on encountering ambiguous information or inconsistent information regressive fixations occur to the area of the text that can disambiguate and clarify interpretations.

If the second of the sentences about jogging a mile (early closure sentence) is disambiguated by including a comma to indicate the separation of clauses the sentence is no longer difficult to read (Clifton,

1992; Underwood *et al.*, 1992). For example, the early closure sentence with the comma:

While Pam was washing, the baby started to cry.

became easier to process than similar sentences without the comma:

Though Ben read the book really bothered him.

Such findings support the previous interpretation of Frazier and Rayner, that the difficulty of processing early closure sentences is a result of inappropriately attaching words to a phrase under development until a parsing failure suggests otherwise. This suggests that the mind processes the meaning of text as it encounters it (support for the eye–mind assumption), because when it encounters text incompatible with the prior interpretation longer fixations and regressions are made until this conflict is resolved.

The second of Frazier and Rayner's principles, a principle of parsimony, says that readers attach new words to the existing sentence structure using the fewest syntactic nodes consistent with the syntactic rules known to the reader. The fewer the number of syntactic nodes, the simpler will be the description of the syntax of the sentence. The sentence will be interpreted as containing fewer phrases. An alternative strategy would be to avoid simplicity, but if the accessing of syntactic rules requires processing time, then minimal attachment will lead to a faster recognition route. The second of the parsing principles is:

The principle of minimal attachment: Newly encountered words should be attached to the existing syntactic structure using the smallest possible number of syntactic nodes.

These two principles assume that sentence comprehension proceeds through the recognition of individual words, to the analysis of the syntax, and then to the processing of the meaning of the sentence. The idea that sentence meaning does not influence sentence parsing is controversial, and has been challenged. The principle of minimal attachment is supported by results from Rayner *et al.* (1983), who found differences in the processing times between sentences that comply with the principle and those that violate it. For example,

The spy saw the cop with the binoculars but . . .

complies with the principle, but the sentence:

The spy saw the cop with the revolver but . . .

does not. In the first sentence the prepositional phrase *with the binocu-lars* modifies the existing verb *saw*, but in the second sentence the equivalent prepositional phrase *with a revolver* should be attached as a modifier to the noun *cop*. The first sentence complies with the principle simply because to attach a prepositional phrase to a verb requires one less syntactic node than it does to attach it as a modifier to a noun. The second sentence therefore induces an incorrect parsing if minimal attachment is followed. It must then be re-parsed using a different, non-minimal attachment strategy. Rayner *et al.* found that reading times were longer in the disambiguating region for the second type of sentence than the first, where a non-minimal attachment strategy was required. The disambiguating region in these sentences is the prepositional phrase (*with the binoculars/revolver*).

The longer reading times for sentences that violate the minimal attachment principle support the idea that as we read sentences we initially construct the simplest syntactic structure consistent with what we know at that moment. When a new item makes the interpretation implausible (that is, when we realize that the revolver would have to be an instrument to allow the spy to see with), then it is discarded, and a new interpretation attempted. Semantics are regarded, by this garden-path model of sentence comprehension, to have an influence on parsing late in the sequence, and only when a parsing based on syntactic principles has failed. The model claims that the parser is 'modular' and 'informationally encapsulated', two features of Fodor's (1983) influential description of the mind as having a 'faculty' architecture that is fixed and innately constrained. A number of psychological abilities are ordered in separate faculties in this model, with no interference in the processing by one faculty or modular unit upon the processing in another. The modules are insensitive to our central cognitive goals. Modules cannot use information being processed by another module until it is exported by the module's output system. Three such modules, we might argue, involve word recognition and the syntactic and semantic processing of sentences. The relationships between words are said to be determined by a modularized parser that resolves any ambiguities and that builds phrases using syntactic strategies. Support for the modular independence of the syntactic and semantic processors was reported in the Rayner *et al.* (1983) experiment. Readers had difficulty with sentences such as:

The actress sent the flowers was very pleased.

and

The florist sent the flowers was very pleased.

which have reduced relative clauses. In these examples the unreduced versions would be:

The actress/florist who was . . .

Rayner *et al.* argued that because difficulties were encountered with both sentences, the greater plausibility of the first sentence was irrelevant. Our knowledge of the world suggests that whereas it is plausible that an actress would be sent flowers, it is less likely that this would happen to a florist. Semantic constraints do not appear to be able to assist the correct parsing of the first sentence any more than the second.

This argument of the late involvement of semantics, separate from and after the initial syntactic structure has been analysed, is in dispute. Taraban and McClelland (1988) demonstrated *easier* processing of sentences that violated the minimal attachment principle under some circumstances. In the sentence:

The bird saw the cop with the binoculars.

there is no ambiguity and no difficulty. The prepositional phrase must now be attached to the second noun, rather than – as when *bird* is replaced by *spy* – to the verb. In this example the meaning of the sentence appears to guide the parsing process. What is crucial is the plausibility of the sentences, and Taraban and McClelland's sentences requiring the minimal attachment strategy were simply less plausible than those with non-minimal attachment. Tanenhaus *et al.* (1989) also report an experiment in which semantic information aids parsing. They compared sentences such as the following pairs:

The man recognized by the spy took off down the street.

and

The van recognized by the spy took off down the street.

In both sentences there is an ambiguity at the begining, but this is resolved more easily in the second sentence in which the verb *recognized* cannot apply to the inanimate noun *van* and so must (according to our knowledge of the world) apply to another agent later in the sentence. For at least some cases parsing is influenced by semantics, although the absence of an influence in the Rayner *et al.* (1983) experiment suggests that semantics do not always help.

Clifton *et al.* (1991) discuss a second difficulty with the data that appear to support minimal attachment. To appreciate this study we need to take a very brief diversion into syntactic structures. Consider the attachment of the prepositional phrase *in the Porsche* in the following sentence:

The driver expressed his interest in the Porsche.

The prepositional phrase may be attached to the noun *interest*, in which case the driver is declaring an interest in driving or buying a Porsche, say. This interpretation is suggested by the early appearance of a driver. With this interpretation the prepositional phrase is an argument of the noun (*interest*) in that it qualifies the noun. Alternatively, the phrase may be attached to the verb *expressed*, in which case it provides currently non-essential information about the location of the incompletely described occurrence of the driver of the Porsche expressing his interest. We are told that he expressed his interest in something or other, but not what. If it is intended by the writer as an adjunct phrase, then it could be attached elsewhere, as in:

The driver in the Porsche expressed his interest.

However, in the case of an argument phrase it follows the noun that is to be qualified, and is part of a general left-to-right accumulation of incoming words as we read through the sentence. The difficult task for the readers in the Rayner *et al.* experiment is to attach the prepositional phrase correctly. Rather than use the principle of minimal attachment, however, they may have been using another principle, a preference to analyse prepositional phases as arguments rather than adjuncts. Parsing a prepositional phrases as an argument or as an adjunct will result in differences in processing time as well as differences in sentence comprehension.

If readers prefer to read propositional phrases as arguments rather than as adjuncts, then the effects seen in the Rayner *et al.* experiment may not be a product of a minimal attachment principle at all. Clifton *et al.* (1991) pointed out that a problem with the Rayner *et al.* study is that, in a large number of the sentences requiring minimal attachment, the prepositional phrase was an argument (as in *with the binoculars*, where *with* signals the head of the phrase). In contrast, many of the sentences requiring a non-minimal attachment strategy contained prepositional phrases that were adjuncts (as in *with the revolver*, which is an additional property of the previous noun).There was therefore a confounding of these two variables in the Rayner *et al.* experiment. The easier reading of the minimal attachment sentences may have been a product of using a minimal attachment strategy or of a preference for interpreting prepositional phrases as arguments. Clifton *et al.* clarified this issue with four types of sentence. The prepositional phrase was an argument half the time in a minimal attachment sentence, and argument half the time in a non-minimal attachment sentence. Examples are:

The salesman tried to interest the man in a wallet . . .
(minimal attachment, argument prepositional phrase)

The man expressed his interest in a hurry . . .
(minimal attachment, adjunct prepositional phrase)

The man expressed his interest in a wallet . . .
(non-minimal attachment, argument prepositional phrase)

The salesman tried to interest the man in his fifties . . .
(non-minimal attachment, adjunct prepositional phrase)

In sentences starting in these ways the word *interest* potentially signals the arrival of a prepositional phrase (e.g. *in a wallet*) taking the form of an argument. The minimal attachment hypothesis was supported by the fixation patterns in the Clifton *et al.* experiment, but so was the argument preference hypothesis. The first reading of the prepositional phase was faster for minimal attachment sentences than for non-minimal attachment sentences, thereby confirming Frazier and Rayner's principle. This prepositional phase was also read faster in the two sentences in which it was an argument rather than when it was an adjunct. (Reading times were calculated per letter in this study, to get over the difficulty of different types of sentences containing prepositional phases of slightly different lengths.) The total reading times for these sentences showed that readers were having more difficulty with the adjunct phrases, especially in the regions of the sentences following the prepositional phrase. This study suggests that both of these parsing strategies are operating, and present a case for the initial operation of minimal attachment whereby the prepositional phrase is attached to a verb (as in the example of *saw* / *with the binoculars*) rather than a noun, but when this renders an implausible product (as in *saw* / *with the revolver*) reinterpretation is necessary. Reinterpretation can run quite smoothly when it is prompted by an argument phrase that is attached to a noun (*revolver* / *saw*), because there is a standing preference for arguments over adjuncts. Most difficult in the Clifton *et al.* study was a sentence in which an adjunct phrase was to be attached to a noun, as with:

The salesman tried to interest the man in his fifties during the storewide sale at Steigers.

These investigations of parsing strategies not only demonstrate that the reader's eyes are sensitive to the current demands of syntactic and contextual processing but also that observations of eye movements can help inform us of the cognitive processes that are operating from moment to moment. Increases in the amount of visual attention (more fixations, longer fixations) given to words in these studies tell us not only that a difficulty has been encountered, but also where the difficulty is located. Chapter 6 will take up this theme of using eye movements as direct indicators of the integration of information in texts, when we consider the problem of how the reader decides whether an agent in one sentence is the same agent as appeared in an earlier sentence – the problem of using inferences to identify anaphoric referents.

The results from the studies of parsing described here are consistent with Just and Carpenter's (1980) immediacy assumption. They provide evidence that readers attempt to interpret words as they come upon them; there is no postponement of interpretation. Evidence of word skipping is more problematic for the eye–mind assumption. In Ehrlich and Rayner's (1981) study of context, for example, and in the fixation of function and content words systematic differences appeared. The phenomenon of skipping begs the question of how readers knew which words they should avoid. Skipping is not random, and leads to the suggestion that there is some processing of the text ahead of fixation, or processing without fixation.

Parafoveal processing

We have distinguished between the foveal and parafoveal regions of the eye according to the visual acuity that each region possesses. When we fixate an object in the world the centre of its image is projected to the fovea. As described earlier, the parafovea starts 1 to 2 degrees from the centre of the fovea, and extends up to 5 degrees each side of the centre of fixation. The fovea has greater acuity than the parafovea, but it is doubtful that there is no processing of words projected to the parafovea. The extent of parafoveal processing has been addressed by the two questions of whether words in the parafovea of vision can have any influence either upon eye movements and skipping behaviour or upon the processing of what is being fixated. The first of these possibilities is suggested by evidence of the selective skipping of certain kinds of words and evidence of the selective fixation of certain parts of long words. The second possibility suggests that some aspect of material not yet fixated can influence our understanding of the text currently fixated. This is a very controversial hypothesis with little evidence in support except from tachistoscope (single frame displays) studies of the effects of parafoveal words upon the recognition of fixated words. Evidence in favour of either of these hypotheses is necessarily evidence against the strong form of the eye–mind assumption, because this would be evidence of an influence upon cognitive processes from text that is not fixated.

Evidence leading to the suggestion that words not being fixated can influence those that are fixated came initially from single frame tachisto-scope studies. Eye movements are not possible with these displays because they are too brief. Tachistoscopic displays mimic the presenta-tion of information that is available during a single fixation, though they underestimate the use of context while reading, and because they are considerably briefer than a fixation during reading they may underesti-mate the influence of parafoveal processing. In such an experiment subjects named line drawings of familiar objects (Underwood, 1976). They knew the locations of the drawings and had good reason to fixate them since presentations were very brief (60 msec.). The dependent variable was the time taken to name the drawing, and this was found to vary according to the presence of a word printed to the right of the drawing. For example, when the word (*TREE*) was related to the drawing (a bird), then a slower response was made than when an unrelated word, non-word or no word was presented. This finding suggests that the meaning of the parafoveally presented word was influential without fixation, providing another challenge for the eye–mind assumption. Eye fixations were not monitored in this exper-iment, but it can be inferred that the drawing was fixated because it was presented too briefly to be recognized without full attention. Response times increased in a second experiment, in which the subjects were not able to fixate the drawing. Experiments with single frame displays can only be suggestive of processes that occur during the reading of sen-tences, of course, and stronger evidence comes from the on-line monitor-ing of what readers look at and what they do not.

Systematic differences in the fixation of content words and function words pose a more direct problem for the eye–mind assumption. How do readers know that certain classes of words may be skipped unless they have processed them prior to fixation? Just and Carpenter may have replied to this criticism by suggesting that as function words are always short then maybe the reader has learnt to skip short words. Unfortu-nately their own evidence (Carpenter and Just, 1983) challenges this view in that they report that three-letter function words (*was, can, off, for*) were skipped more frequently (57 per cent skipped) than three-letter content words (*act, red, use, not,* 47 per cent skipped).

Along with the report that we are more likely to skip function words, and more likely to skip predictable words (Ehrlich and Rayner, 1981), comes a further problem for the eye–mind assumption from Fisher and Shebilske (1985). They recorded subjects' eye movements (first group of subjects) whilst reading a short essay, and noted which words had not been fixated. Words were classified as unfixated if there were no fixations on it or on the two letter spaces to either side of it. In these short essays readers in the first group of subjects skipped 21 per cent of the meaningful content words. Fisher and Shebilske then presented a second group of yoked subjects (who had not previously seen the essay) with the same essay as the first group, but with the unfixated words removed from the display. Readers in the first group were presented with sentences such as

Pets have funny names such as my favorite dog, Jingles.

and one subject may fixate only the words that are underlined here; the words *funny* and *dog* may be skipped. These two unfixated words would then be deleted when the sentence was shown to the yoked subject, as in

Pets have   names such as my favorite   , Jingles.

Blank spaces occurred where the first reader had skipped a word. Both groups of subjects had to attempt to recall the passage. Of particular interest was the recall of unfixated words by subjects in the first group, in comparison with the 'recall' of these words by their yoked partners in the second group. Skipped words were correctly recalled 59 per cent of the time by the first group, whilst only 30 per cent of the blanks were correctly guessed by the yoked controls. This study argues against the eye–mind assumption as it is evidence that the words that were not fixated by the first group had been processed to some degree since these readers could correctly fill in 29 per cent more missing words than the control group.

Content words are skipped less than function words, and content words themselves are skipped more when they are predictable than when they are not. This suggests that it may be the combination of two sources of information that determines whether a word will be skipped or fixated. As we read through a sentence we may be able to anticipate what is coming next, and if a predictable word is confirmed by parafoveal processing, then it need not be fixated. The benefit in selective skipping on the basis of this information is in an increase in our overall reading speed. The evidence does indeed suggest that readers selectively skip words, but what of the evidence that we can extract sufficient parafoveal information for the skipping to be based on an informed decision?

Evidence of changes of fixation positions supports the parafoveal processing hypothesis because it is evidence of an influence upon behaviour prior to fixation. The first fixation upon a word is further into long words than into short words, and is nearer to unusual combinations of letters than to common combinations. This evidence is described in more detail in the following section of this chapter, when we consider theories of eye guidance. A second source of evidence comes from the *parafoveal preview effect*, in which there is easier processing of a fixated word if it is first available in parafoveal vision. One of the first demonstrations of the preview effect was reported by Balota and Rayner (1983), who used a contingent display: the words on the screen changed according to where the subject was looking. In this experiment a word that was to be identified and named aloud changed immediately before it was fixated. As the reader's eyes crossed an imaginary boundary close to the location of the target word, the target changed from one word to another. This is sometimes called the *boundary technique*. If we can use parafoveal information, then the reading time should be increased when the target was very different from the original word. In the Balota and Rayner experiment the target location was originally occupied by a non-word (e.g. *snckks*) and when the reader's eyes crossed the boundary this changed to a word that was either visually similar to the preview (e.g. *snakes*) or dissimilar (e.g. *lizard*). Targets similar to the previews were named faster than those that were visually dissimilar, suggesting that information is extracted from printed words prior to direct fixation.

The parafoveal preview benefit in the Balota and Rayner (1983) study was even larger when the word fixated prior to the eye movement was semantically related to the eventual target. The two effects could be additive or interactive. Additive effects would suggest independence of the use of context and the use of parafoveal information, while interactive effects would suggest that context influences the extraction of information from the parafovea. If skipping is to be based on the use of parafoveal information in predictive contexts, then interactive effects should be observed, with a larger preview effect for semantically associated words. As with so many psychology experiments the answer was not straightforward. In an experiment in which the subjects saw the first word very briefly (250 msec.), the effects were additive, but when this context was shown for 1,250 msec. the effects were interactive. If we can argue that the longer exposure duration is more representative of the build-up of context during the reading of a sentence, then there is evidence here in support of the informed skipping hypothesis.

The boundary technique with a contingent display was also used by Henderson and Ferreira (1990) to demonstrate that the parafoveal preview benefit depended upon the difficulty of the word inspected on the prior fixation. Subjects read sentences in this experiment, and prior to fixating the target word, its location was occupied by a non-word letter-string, as in:

Mary bought a chest zqdloyv the high price.

In this example the letter-string *zqdloyv* changed to the word *despite* when the reader's eyes crossed a boundary at the end of the preceding word *chest*. The letter-string only existed as a letter-string during the period until the reader's eyes crossed the boundary; thereafter it was replaced by the target. In some sentences the letter-string was dissimilar to the eventual target (as with *zqdloyv*), sometimes it shared the first three letters of the target and retained word shape (*desqlda*), and sometimes the preview was the actual word itself (*despite*). Visually similar non-words gave a preview benefit in this experiment, in comparison with dissimilar non-words, with shorter fixation durations on the target when letters and word shape were preserved. It is important that this effect only held when processing of the prior word (*chest*) was easy. The difficulty of processing the prior word was manipulated in two ways by Henderson and Ferreira, and both manipulations were effective. In one experiment the prior word was either a high frequency word, as in the sentence above, or a low frequency word, as in:

Mary bought a trunk zqdloyv the high price.

Trunk has a much lower word frequency than *chest*, and the increased recognition difficulty resulted in a perceptual span so reduced that there was less attention available for processing of the parafoveal word. A similar effect was found when the prior word was part of an easy or a difficult syntactic structure. Difficulty was manipulated by including or excluding the complement *that* from sentences, such as:

She warned that Harry bought tipoa gifts.
She warned Harry bought tipoa gifts.

In these sentences the non-word *tipoa* changed to the target *small* as the reader's eyes crossed the boundary at the end of *bought*. In the case of the first, structurally unambiguous, sentence there was an advantage gained by a preview letter-string that shared letters and shape with the eventual target. There was no advantage for words in the second, temporarily ambiguous sentence. Parafoveal previews of words can influence the ease of processing, but only when the prior fixation is upon simple text. Only when our current processing load is light can attention capture information ahead of fixation.

Theories of eye guidance

These experiments that demonstrate an influence of parafoveal information also suggest an answer to the question of how readers know where to guide their eyes to next. The theories that are the main contenders in providing an answer to this question can be classified according to the amount of cognitive control that we have over our saccadic eye movements.

The minimal control hypothesis

The theories of fixation control did not explain how the eye is guided to its next location in the text. The first theory, in advocating post-fixation processing only, is similar to the minimal control hypothesis of eye guidance (also known as the oculomotor control hypothesis). This suggests that the reader's eyes move a constant distance along a line of text, with the distance perhaps increasing as the skill of the reader increases, or decreasing as the perceived difficulty of the text increases. The same criticisms face this hypothesis as did the post-fixation theory, in that it cannot explain why within a sentence the saccades and fixations vary in length and duration.

The strongest version of this viewpoint is the process-monitoring or gain control hypothesis, which states that as the text difficulty changes it can have an indirect effect upon eye-guidance by altering the lengths of saccades and durations of fixations. Again this view would be challenged by the evidence which indicates that eye movements can be influenced by information ahead of the fixation as well as by that which preceded it. There are two more plausible guidance hypothesis which do acknowledge the importance of parafoveal preview in guiding eye movements: the visual control hypothesis and the linguistic control hypothesis.

Visual control hypothesis

This hypothesis, which is sometimes known as peripheral search guidance, proposes that reader's eyes can be guided by non-linguistic features within the text. McConkie and Rayner (1975) collected some interesting data by using a computer system that enabled a manipulation of the display such that the subject could see a restricted amount of the text around each fixation. As with the parafoveal preview benefit experiments described earlier, a contingent display was used, so that the text on the screen changed according to where the reader was looking. This is known as the *moving window technique*. In the McConkie and Rayner experiments it was the number of letters around the point of fixation that was varied. The extreme was a display in which only one character on the screen was visible, with the other letters mutilated by the removal of some of their features, or changed to *x*s until they were themselves fixated. Or the window could be increased so that more characters around the fixation point could be clearly seen. This enabled McConkie and Rayner to determine the area of the text from which the reader could extract useful information. Whenever the subjects moved their eyes to a new part of the text this became visible and the previously fixated sections (now in the parafovea) become mutilated.

Using this moving window technique McConkie and Rayner could measure how far into the parafovea the subject could obtain useful lexical and non-lexical information. They reported that viewing up to 15 characters either side of fixation was helpful. This was indicated by increases in processing speed when the window size increased. The fact that readers can make use of adjacent information to this extent suggests that if we have a symmetric perceptual field around the point of fixation then our perceptual span is in the order of 31 characters. The effective perceptual field was, in fact, asymmetrical, with a field that was biased to the right of fixation, in the direction of the next eye movement.

Instead of subtracting some of the letters' features there are many different types of text patterns that can be used, such as the unfixated words being replaced with *x*s or all unfixated locations (including the spaces between words) being replaced with *x*s. When *x*s were used but spaces between words were preserved, then reading speed was aided up until a window size of 31 characters, and above this window size it did not matter whether spaces were maintained or not. Thus readers appear to be making use of word boundary information (the spaces between words), perhaps to help guide their eye movements so that they land on a word and not a space. This suggestion is further supported by data from a study by Abrams and Zuber (1972), who found that readers are more likely to fixate words rather than the spaces between words. There is much to be gained from knowing when a word begins and when it ends; from this basic processing the length of the word can be calculated, and this information may be important in guiding the eye to particular locations within the word.

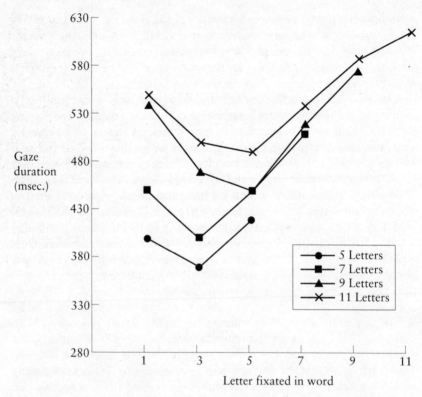

Figure 5.2   Convenient viewing location within words of varying length
Source: O'Regan, Levy-Schon, Pynte and Brugaillere, 1984

There is support for the notion that the location of the first fixation within a word influences the ease with which it is processed. This is demonstrated by O'Regan *et al.*'s (1984) experiment with single words abruptly displayed to fixation. Readers were presented with isolated words of different lengths such that their initial fixation was forced on different positions within the word. Once the subjects were fixating a specific point on the screen a word appeared and the task was to name the word aloud. Words of five, seven, nine and eleven letters in length were used. Figure 5.2 displays the targets' mean gaze durations as a function of the letter position within the word that the eye was forced to fixate at the moment the word appeared. It can clearly be seen that for five- and seven-letter words the shortest gaze durations occur when the third letter within the word is landed upon. As the length of the word increased to nine or eleven letters this 'convenient viewing location' shifted rightwards so that the shortest gaze durations were when the fifth letter within the word was fixated. It can be seen that ideally the reader would desire to land on the convenient viewing position within the word to maximize reading efficiency and that this is the centre of the word, or for long words just left of centre. If word length information were therefore available within the parafovea it could be used to the reader's advantage.

There are numerous studies which demonstrate that readers make use of information about word length available in the parafovea, to guide their initial fixations to the convenient position within a word. As can be predicted from O'Regan *et al.* (1984) the convenient viewing location for a ten-letter word would be close to centre, probably the fifth character. Underwood, Clews and Everatt (1990) conducted a study that presented ten-letter words embedded in sentences to subjects who had to inspect these sentences in preparation for comprehension questions. Those words that gained just one fixation received this fixation nearer to the word's centre than in the case of words which gained two fixations, and thus had longer gaze durations. It can be seen that if readers do land within the convenient viewing position they benefit in terms of a reduction in the duration of the processing time needed.

Knowing the length of the word ahead of fixation could be useful in guiding the eyes to the optimal viewing location, but do readers actually make use of this word length information? Rayner (1979) investigated this by asking what is the preferred landing position within a word, i.e., where do readers land when they have the choice? He measured the location of the first fixation within words of three to ten letters in length, embedded in text, and found that the majority of first fixations fell near the middle of the words, and as word length increased there was a tendency for fixations to fall slightly nearer the beginning of the word. Figure 5.3 displays the data that was collected by Rayner for the three-, five-, seven- and nine-letter words used in his study. The lighter bars indicate those occasions when only one fixation was made on the word, and the darker bars indicate the location of the initial fixation when two or more fixations were made.

The next question to be asked is why didn't the readers land on the convenient viewing position every time? One possible explanation is that the eye cannot always move to the exact location that it may wish to because of oculomotor reasons. Studies that have embedded a clearly marked target letter within a random letter-string that subjects are asked to fixate have shown that the eye is unable accurately to land on this requested location (Coeffe and O'Regan, 1987). This suggests that readers can and do make use of the word length information appearing in the parafovea in order to guide their eye movements although performance may not be as accurate as planned.

The evidence so far is very supportive of the visual control hypothesis,

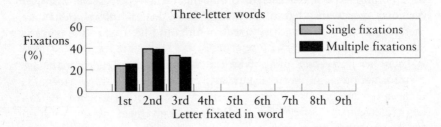

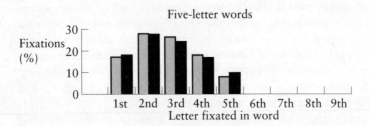

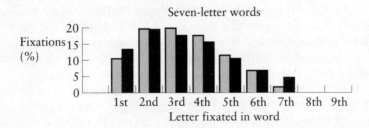

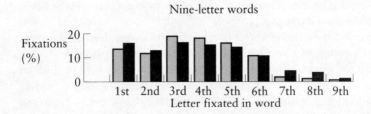

Figure 5.3 Bar charts showing the location of the initial fixation within words of differing length

The number of fixations on each letter position is shown as a percentage of all fixations on each type of word.

Source: Rayner, 1979

which can obtain information about word boundaries and word length in order to guide saccades and thus benefit text processing. If it were found that lexical or semantic variations in the text ahead of fixation influenced saccades to parafoveal words the simple visual control hypothesis would have to be rejected in favour of the linguistic control hypothesis. Some consider the linguistic control hypothesis to be the most controversial of all of the guidance models.

Linguistic control hypothesis

The evidence that was used to support the parafoveal processing theory of eye movement control can also be used here. We have also considered a large body of evidence that demonstrates that the reader's eyes indicate the difficulty of sentence interpretation. Effects of contextual predictability and syntactic complexity are observable through changes in fixation behaviour as they occur. Further evidence for this control hypothesis comes from studies such as Kennedy (1978) which lean more towards the linguistic rather than the visual control models. He asked adults to read a three-sentence passage in which the word in the final sentence was sometimes preceded by a highly associated word which had appeared in the first sentence. Reader's eyes arrived at the target word in the final sentence *faster* if it had been preceded by an associate word in the first sentence. This suggests that a primed word can attract fixations, and that semantic information is available in the parafovea (otherwise why would they be attracted to the primed target?).

Nonlexical guidance

As described earlier, McConkie and Rayner (1975) demonstrated that word boundary information is useful 15 characters either side of fixation when the mutilated text consisted of subtracting some of the letter features. If the mutilated text consisted of letters visually similar to those in the text, as opposed to dissimilar letters, this consistent letter shape information was only more useful for a window size up to 21 characters (10 either side of fixation); these displays are illustrated in Figure 5.4. Therefore beyond a window size of 21 characters it did not matter whether the mutilated text consisted of similarly or dissimilarly shaped letters, as this information was not being used to aid text processing.

Common sense would suggest that although McConkie and Rayner's findings indicate that the perceptual span is 31 characters for subjects who are familiar with alphabetic languages (15 to the left of fixation, 15 to the right), the information to the left of fixation may not be processed to the same extent as the information on the right. This is because

A Letter shape maintained

> aiukemjasvheoclaiolemfing is the new book bjavokaemxchizaboeeis
> *

B Letter shape not maintained

> yghmgqdadkjetxwqlkrstjing is the new book btaghjdszbnqgihlsoswqp
> *

Figure 5.4   Example of displays from a moving window experiment
A. Letter shape maintained
B. Letter shape not maintained

The asterix (*) denotes the location of the fixation. It can be seen that the next 10 characters either side of a fixation are clearly visible; beyond this region the letters of the word presented in the parafovea either have their shape maintained (in A) or they do not (in B). Letter shape is defined in terms of the possession of ascending and descending features.

The difference between the two boxes is entirely in the changes to letter shapes outside the 21-character window. In A, letter shape is maintained although the letter itself is changed, so 's' changes to 'a', 'p' changes to 'y', etc. In B, the same 's' now changes to 'y' and the same 'p' changes to 'k', etc. The experiment demonstrates that information about the shape of a letter is only useful within the 21 letters around the point of fixation.

alphabet readers tend to read from left to right and so incoming information is to the right of fixation. McConkie and Rayner (1976) tested this view by manipulating the window size asymmetrically. They discovered that, similarly to their previous finding, the perceptual span to the right of fixation is 14 characters, whilst to the left it is only 4 characters. Therefore if more than 4 characters of information was made available to the left of fixation it did not result in greater comprehension or faster reading speed.

The perceptual span for languages that are read from right to left also show asymmetrical effects. Pollatsek *et al.* (1981) measured the perceptual span of Hebrew readers and reported that it was greater for information appearing to the left than to the right. However the bilinguals he tested showed the opposite effect (greater perceptual span to the right than to the left) when he asked them to read text written in English. Therefore the asymmetry of the perceptual span can be altered according to which sort of text is being processed.

Lexical and semantic guidance

Inhoff and Rayner (1986) were interested to know whether anything more than letter information was available in the parafovea. They presented targets to the right visual field (right of fixation) and manipulated their frequency. When the word appearing in the parafovea was of a high frequency, the fixation on the word presented to the fovea was of a shorter duration than if a low frequency parafoveal word had been presented. This would suggest that the subjects were getting more than letter information from the parafovea: they possibly were obtaining lexical or semantic information.*

A study by Rayner (1978) suggests that lexical or semantic information can be obtained up to four letter spaces to the right or less. Thus it is possible that this information can be obtained prior to a fixation. However at the screen to subject distance usually used, and with a foveal region of 1 to 2 degrees the prediction of four character spaces (approximately 1 degree) away from the central fixation point is not as impressive as it might originally seem because the majority of the stimulus would actually be falling within the fovea region.

Other studies have manipulated the information distribution of words appearing within sentences in order to measure the type of information available in the parafovea. Underwood, Clews and Everatt (1990) and Everatt and Underwood (1992) embedded targets differing in information distribution (*YEARNINGLY, FEATHERING*) into sentences and found that the distribution of the information within the words led to changes in the fixation pattern, with the observed influence being on the location rather than the duration of the fixations. Rayner *et al.* (1986) conducted a similar study in which they failed to find support for the linguistic guidance hypothesis (preferring the visual control hypothesis). However, they used fixation duration as their dependent measure, which raises the question of whether pre-processing has a more noticeable effect on the location of fixations than on their durations.

The evidence that suggests that eye movements can be guided by the

* A note on the use of the terms lexical and semantic may be appropriate here. It is possible that lexical information is processed parafoveally; this does not necessarily mean that semantic information is also available. Consider the logogen model of word recognition (see Chapter 2). When a word is recognized as being stored in the mental lexicon the relevant logogen fires. In order to access that word's meaning (its semantic attributes) the cognitive system also has to be accessed, but this is not necessarily automatic. Thus parafoveal preview may result in lexical access but it does not always result in semantic access. However, in order to obtain semantic access, lexical access is required. Of course, if the lexicon stores not only a list of words but also other information in an associative network, then the distinction between lexical and semantic information becomes less clear-cut.

information ahead of fixation (Everatt and Underwood, 1992; Hyönä *et al.* 1989; Underwood, Clews and Everatt, 1990) does not necessarily indicate that semantic parafoveal processing is occurring. It may be the case that highly familiar orthographic patterns can be detected ahead of a fixation, which results in saccades being guided away from these redundant components. It is not clear from these experiments whether the reader's eyes are guided *towards* particularly interesting or informative groups of letters – unusual sequences of letters, perhaps – or whether their eyes are guided *away* from very frequently occurring groups of letters such as those that occur with familiar prefixes and suffixes. But it is clear that this influence of parafoveal information is not consistent. Henderson and Ferreira (1990) found that the parafoveal preview benefit was only observable when the foveal load was light, suggesting that when the reader's attention is captured by a word that is difficult to process there will be little useful information extracted from the parafovea. If little information is extracted then the landing position will be determined by preprogramming, with a saccade of predetermined length.

As the reader's eyes move over the words and sentences in a paragraph there will be considerable moment-to-moment variation in the difficulty of word recognition and integration. As this difficulty increases the reader's attention will become focused on the fixated word, and parafoveal processing will be minimal. During some fixations there will be greater opportunity for using parafoveal information than during others. This source of variation may also explain why the landing position effect appears in some experiments but not in others. Underwood *et al.* (1988) found an effect of uneven information distributions in words upon fixation durations, but not upon landing positions, and Hyönä *et al.* (1989) found an inconsistent effect. More recently, Rayner and Morris (1992) found no effect upon landing position, while Hyönä (1995) found an effect in which fixations were attracted in the direction of unusual patterns of letters at the beginnings of words but he found no effect for unusual sequences at the ends of words. It seems likely that the appearance of the effect depends upon the foveal load imposed by the difficulty of recognizing and integrating the prior word.

Morphemic guidance

Evidence from Inhoff (1987) suggests that lexical information does guide the eye, in fact it is information concerned with the morphemic structure of the parafoveal word that is used. If the reader was exposed to a parafoveal preview of the first morpheme in a compound word (the *cow* in *cowboy*) there was less foveal inspection of that word than of a pseudocompound (e.g. *carpet*, where the first three letters *car* had been parafoveally presented). This suggests that individual morphemes may be decoded in the parafovea. This finding was not supported by Lima (1987) who recorded subjects' eye movements whilst they read sentences which contained prefixed (*remind*) and pseudoprefixed (*relish*) words. Previews of the targets were such that either the whole word was present before fixation upon it, or only the prefix was present, or none of the word was present. Preview advantages (shorter fixation times on the target) were only obtained when the whole word had been parafoveally presented as opposed to the prefix or no word; there were no word type effects (both prefixed and pseudoprefixed words benefited equally from whole word parafoveal preview). Although Lima's finding does not support parafoveal morphemic decomposition it does demonstrate that whole word information is available from the parafovea, as this condition resulted in short fixation times on a target compared to prefix preview or no preview.

Underwood, Petley and Clews (1990) conducted a study in which they varied the morphemic structure of the words embedded in sentences, and primed either the first morpheme, the second morpheme or the whole word whilst measuring the location of fixations. The stimuli used were transparent (*houseboat*) or opaque compounds (*backgammon*), and a comprehension test was given after presentation of the sentences to ensure that they had been read properly. By setting compound words into sentences that primed one morpheme, they predicted that those morphemes would then contain less information and would attract shorter fixations. Fixations within these words were therefore expected to be located towards the informative (unprimed) morpheme rather than towards the primed morpheme. There were no reliable effects of priming upon fixation durations or locations within the compound. There was a significant difference on the measure of gaze duration with transparent compounds responded to 29 msec. faster than opaque compounds (surface frequency of the compounds was not reported). The main bulk of evidence appears to challenge the notion of morphemic information being detectable in the parafovea.

So far we have discussed three theories of eye movement control; the first one, post-fixation processing, has no evidence to support such an extreme view. However, neither the on-line or the parafoveal processing views are fully supported by the evidence cited here. We do appear to be able to detect some information from the parafovea; however this is limited to only 4 to 10 character spaces to the right of fixation. Perhaps a combination of the two viewpoints is more realistic. The duration that our eyes spend at a location is some indicator of the difficulty of processing that piece of text, but also can be influenced by the information that is available in the parafovea. And whether the parafoveal information used to guide eye movements is lexical or nonlexical is still a hotly debated question. The authors consider there to be an abundance of evidence demonstrating that word boundary, word length and letter shape information is available in the parafovea to guide fixations. Whether lexical or semantic information can be parafoveally detected still needs further research, with all investigators ensuring that they report all measures, including fixation durations and locations of durations. The inconsistent reportage of eye movement measures stems from which theory a researcher prefers to adopt, since this generally influences which eye movement measurements he or she choose to record.

It can be seen that the measurement of eye movements could be a useful tool in studying the processes involved in reading. One major area of usage popular since the late nineteenth century attempts to investigate differences between poor readers and good readers, with the hope of diagnosing and understanding reading difficulties.

Individual differences in reading

We have acknowledged that there is much individual variation in eye movement measures such as saccadic distance and fixation duration, why should this be so? If the word *question* is fixated for 300 msecs. by one reader, why should another reader take 270 or possibly 470 msecs. in fixating it? There are many explanations for this variation, such as that eye movement behaviour is random, thus there should not be consistencies between readers, or even within a reader. This first explanation is challenged by all the evidence cited in the previous section which shows that eye movements are not random, and that we can predict to reasonable accuracy where within a word a saccade will land depending on its length (O'Regan *et al.*, 1984), or on information distribution (Underwood *et al.*, 1989; Underwood, Clews and Everatt, 1990). Furthermore, we know that certain words will have longer fixations than others, even when we control for word length. If eye movements were random then such predictions could not be formed. A second explanation is that eye movements are heavily influenced by the reading experience of the subject.

Reading ability and experience

In a large-scale study of school and college students Buswell (1922) monitored students' eye movements whilst reading text. The findings suggest that numbers and durations of fixations and also the numbers of regressive fixations decrease with an increase in schooling age. Figure

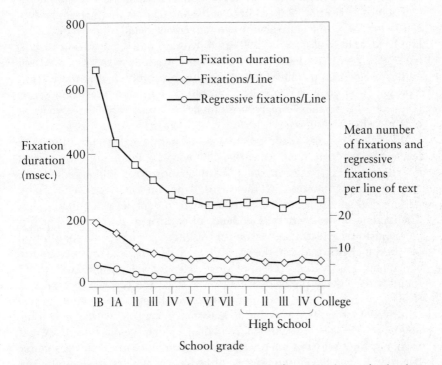

Figure 5.5 The development of eye movements from Grade 1 of schooling though to college level
Source: Buswell, 1922

5.5 shows the three dependent measures that were recorded; mean fixation duration, mean number of fixations per line and mean number of regressive fixations per line. It can be clearly seen that there is a sharp decline in all three measures until the fifth grade of school when these measures of reading have stabilized. Are these changes due to reading ability, reading experience or age of the child?

When reading experience is controlled, the fixation durations of children do not vary a great deal (Murray and Kennedy, 1988). What kind of pattern of data do we get if we monitor the eye movements of children of the same age (and therefore similar reading experience) but with different reading abilities? If eye movements are merely a function of age or experience, then the duration, and number of fixations and regressions should be similar for both groups. Olson *et al.* (1983) found that below average readers produced fixations which were 50 msec.

longer than normal readers. They also reported a relationship between reading ability and number of regressions through a text, with fewer regressions as reading ability improved. This suggests that reading ability can be strongly associated with eye movement behaviour. Underwood, Hubbard and Wilkinson (1990) and Everatt and Underwood (1994) have also reported that shorter fixation durations were observed for adult readers who produced better scores on a comprehension test. Thus fixation duration was negatively associated with comprehension score. However, the number of regressions made was not a significant predictor of comprehension score.

Do skilled readers make greater use of parafoveal information than less skilled readers? We have earlier discussed the landing position effect in which the first fixation on a word is sometimes influenced by the information distribution of the word, with informative letter combinations attracting closer fixations than redundant letter combinations. The landing position effect is evidence of parafoveal processing, but it is an inconsistent effect. One reason for this inconsistency is that parafoveal processing depends upon the attentional load imposed by recognition and integration of the preceding word. Henderson and Ferreira (1990) found a parafoveal preview benefit only when the preceding word was easily recognizable or was easily integrated into the syntax of the sentence. A second reason for inconsistency may be with the reading ability of the subjects, with more skilled readers being able to extract more information from the parafovea. While this seems like a reasonable hypothesis, we have two pieces of evidence against it. Everatt and Underwood (1994) correlated reading ability and vocabulary knowledge of adults with their eye movements in a sentence-reading experiment. One of the measures was the size of the landing position effect, but this was not predicted by their performance on the pencil-and-paper language tests. Using a related approach, Kennison and Clifton (1995) looked at the relationship between the size of the parafoveal preview benefit and the individual's reading span. Reading span is a measure of the capacity of working memory that has been related to reading comprehension (Daneman and Carpenter, 1980), and is described in Chapter 1. Efficient readers have been found to have larger reading spans than poorer readers, who are less able to keep a number of words in temporary storage in preparation for word integration. If reading span is a good measure of reading ability then it, too, might be expected to vary with the use of parafoveal information. Kennison and Clifton found that the parafoveal preview effect varied according to whether the prior word had a low frequency or a high frequency, thereby confirming Henderson and Ferreira's result, but reading ability was again unrelated to the use of parafoveal information.

Taylor (1957) reported that as reading experience increased so did the perceptual span, a measure that might be thought to be related to the use of parafoveal information. We have already discussed how the reader can make use of word boundary, word length and letter shape (and possibly lexical) information that appears in the parafovea and periphery. If a reader has only a small perceptual span then he or she would be unable to make use of the information available within it, thus disabling reading. Taylor reported that the range of recognition (the number of words processed per fixation) increased from about half a word (assuming an average word length of 10 characters) when beginning to read to about one and a third words in adult life. Rayner (1986) on the other hand found that this was a massive overestimation of the increase and that beginning readers had a perceptual span about 25 per cent smaller than that of an adult reader (11 characters as opposed to 15).

One problem emerging is that we are trying to determine the relationship between not two but three variables: reading experience, reading ability and age. Although the perceptual span is reported above to increase with reading experience and age, it is not necessarily true that this is correlated in any way with reading ability. Indeed Underwood and Zola (1986) found no difference in the perceptual span of children who differed in reading ability. What if we were to increase our perceptual spans? Our reading experience would not have been increased, but would our reading ability improve? It is highly plausible that an increased span would result in improved reading ability, because we would have a larger source of information to make use of in our reading task.

Speed readers and the perceptual span

Increasing the reading span size is actually a technique taught on speed reading courses. A speed reader can pass through a passage of text very quickly, supposedly with no loss in comprehension compared to a normal reader. Observers of speed readers have reported that they move their eyes down the left hand side, or middle of a page, fixating each line only once if at all (see Gibson and Levin, 1975). These rare fixations are often longer than the average ones made by normal readers, suggesting that more parafoveal, and possibly peripheral information is being detected by the speed readers than would be by a normal reader.

Some would suggest that the claims made by speed reading course organizers that comprehension is equivalent to that of normal readers is a bit far-fetched. Masson (1985) and Just and Carpenter (1987) found their speed readers were disadvantaged in answering both high level questions about the text they had read and also low level questions

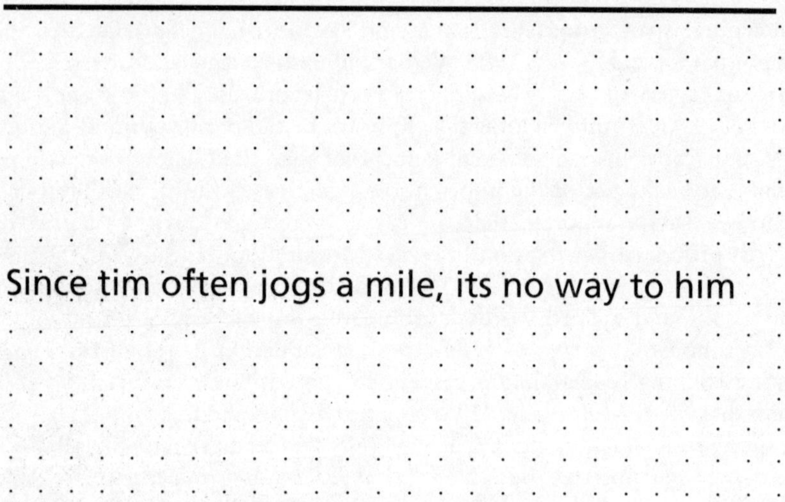

Since tim often jogs a mile, its no way to him

Figure 5.6   Eye movements of a speed reader
Source: Underwood and Everatt, 1992

about specific details. On one particular passage taken from the *Reader's Digest* accuracy on high level questions was 65 per cent, compared to 80 per cent for normal readers and on low level questions was 30 per cent, compared to 50 per cent for normal readers.

Underwood and Everatt (1992) described the eye movements of a speed reader accidentally discovered in a text reading study. This reader, identified here as HA, made far fewer fixations than the normal readers in the study and these were slightly faster than the average fixation duration. The small number of fixations made is consistent with reports of other speed readers. The report of shorter fixation durations is not consistent, showing that there is no single pattern of eye movements for speed readers. The eye fixation pattern for HA is displayed in Figure 5.6, and this should be compared to the pattern from a 'normal' adult skilled reader shown in Figure 5.1. The almost completely horizontal line in this plot represents a series of a few saccadic movements with very brief fixations between them. The pattern can be characterized as a fast sweep of the eyes across the line of text, broken by a small number of brief fixations. With such a cursory inspection of the text we might expect HA's understanding to be minimal. However, HA's performance on the comprehension questions that followed the reading task was actually superior to most of the other subjects in the study. It is possible that HA was merely guessing the answers to the comprehension questions, but considering the complexity of those questions we consider this to be highly unlikely, although we are unable to ignore this explanation. In general however, speed reading is achieved at the expense of comprehension.

Poor readers and developmental dyslexics

As we have discussed, perceptual span is inconsistently linked with reading ability and therefore can not be considered at this stage as a valid explanation of the performance of poor readers and dyslexics. It was previously mentioned that poor readers make more forward and regressive fixations than normal readers when reading text. A pattern of eye movements of even greater irregularity has been reported with dyslexics. Figure 5.7 shows three fixation patterns taken from a normal, a poor and a dyslexic reader (Pavlidis, 1978, 1981b) whilst they were reading text. The horizontal lines represent fixations whilst the vertical lines represent eye movements (saccades). A downward vertical line indicates a forward saccade, and an upward vertical line a regressive saccade. It can be seen that although the poor reader makes more fixations and regressions than the normal reader, there is the same staircase-like pattern, and the length of the regressive saccade is also smaller than the preceding forward saccade. On the other hand the eye movements of the dyslexic child displayed here is extremely erratic; there are a high number of regressive saccades (an upward vertical line) which often are greater (showing a longer saccade) than the previous saccadic movement. Furthermore, regressive saccades appear to occur in clusters of two or more.

There are a few other studies that have compared dyslexics with matched controls (students with equally poor reading ability and matched for chronological age) which have also reported that their dyslexics' eye movements during reading were more erratic and idiosyncratic than their controls (Gilbert, 1953; Pavlidis, 1981a, 1981b, 1985) although this is finding is not consistently replicated (Brown et al., 1983; Olson et al.,1983; Stanley et al. 1983)

Eye movements: cause, effect or a parallel phenomenon of dyslexia?

What exactly is the relationship between eye movements and dyslexia? It was once thought possible to improve reading ability by changing eye movement behaviour, this assumption being based on the early observations that poor readers' eye movements differ from those of normal readers. Although there are some physiological disabilities such as congenital-jerk nystagmus which will result in reading difficulties as a

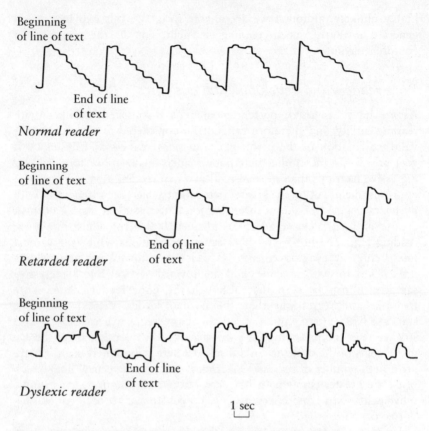

Figure 5.7   Eye movements of normal, retarded and dyslexic readers
Source: Pavlidis, 1986

result of this oculomotor disturbance, generally the hypothesis that eye movements cause or lead to reading difficulties (Gilbert, 1953; Goldrich and Sedgwick, 1982) is no longer supported. Tinker (1958) reviewed studies that attempted to train readers to make more efficient eye movements and concluded that the relationship between eye movements and reading ability is only correlational and not causal.

A second hypothesis is that the eye movements are a result of the reading problem (Goldberg and Arnott, 1970; Tinker, 1958). If this hypothesis were true then controls matched on reading ability would show the same pattern of eye movements as the dyslexics. Figure 5.8 suggests that they do not. We will return to this hypothesis later.

Pavlidis (1986) asked why researchers appear so keen to impose a cause and effect relationship with eye movements and dyslexia. He proposed a third hypothesis that they are both a result of the same, or parallel but independent, brain malfunctions. Thus dyslexics would experience many problems other than their reading difficulties as a result of this brain malfunction. This idea is certainly supported by the evidence: there are reports of their having language deficits (Liberman, 1983), their performance is significantly worse than matched normal readers in sequential tasks (Bakker, 1972), they are poorer at scanning digits than normal or retarded readers (Gilbert, 1953), as well as having many other difficulties. We shall return to this hypothesis when we consider the work of Lovegrove and his colleagues on a specific deficit in the visual subsystems of dyslexic children.

When children were asked to fixate at lights that moved sequentially from left to right, or right to left, the dyslexics made more forward and regressive eye movements than the matched advanced, normal and retarded readers (Pavlidis, 1981a). The proportion of regressive to forward eye movement did not differ significantly among the advanced, normal and retarded readers, but regression did increase proportionally as well as numerically in the dyslexics.

It would appear that erratic eye movements characterize many dyslexics but not their matched controls. Thus the use of eye movement monitoring in the diagnosis of dyslexia appears very worthwhile, particularly as it may lead to diagnosis before the child attempts to learn to read. It would thus spare such children the secondary emotional problems that tend to emerge with their unexpected failure in reading and spelling.

Pavlidis's work looks very promising but it does have its critics. We have already acknowledged that there are problems in defining a reader as dyslexic. Furthermore, it is questionable as to whether dyslexics form a single homogeneous group (Pirozzolo, 1979). Although their defining criteria differ, those researchers who propose dyslexics should be divided into heterogeneous subgroups tend to agree that there are at least two broad types of dyslexic. The most common subtype is the dysphonetic dyslexic (Boder, 1973) alternatively known as the language disorder dyslexics (Mattis *et al.*, 1975). The second, less common, subgroup is referred to as dyseidetic (Boder, 1973) or visual-perceptual dyslexics (Mattis *et al.*, 1975). It has been suggested (Rayner, 1986) that the language disorder dyslexics outnumber the visual-perceptual dyslexics by a factor of 10:1.

The reason that we draw attention to the possible heterogeneous subgroups of dyslexia is a suggestion by Rayner (1986) that the dyslexics studied by Pavlidis may have been from the less common visual-perceptual subgroup. This is because Pavlidis is well known for specializing in visual problems, and it therefore is plausible that more of this type of dyslexic would be referred to him for treatment. This may well explain why Pavlidis's finding of erratic eye movement patterns on non-reading tasks for dyslexics compared to poor and normal readers is not consistently reported (Brown *et al.*, 1983; Olson *et al.*, 1983; Stanley *et al.* 1983).

A further criticism raised in particular over Pavlidis's earlier work (1981a) is concerned with his definition of dyslexia. We mentioned in Chapter 4 the difficulty of comparing dyslexic children with poor readers, since how a child is defined depends on the criteria used for the diagnosis. It is possible that a child may be categorized as dyslexic by one researcher but as a poor reader by another. Pavlidis's (1981a) definition of dyslexia has frequently been criticized for being particularly vague (although it must be stated that his later studies were more explicit about the definitions used).

Rayner (1986) therefore draws attention to the work of Brown *et al.* (1983), Olson *et al.* (1983) and Stanley *et al.* (1983), who reported no difference between the eye movements of dyslexics and normal readers on a tracking task. All three researchers have produced similar findings using similar procedures to that of Pavlidis, that is, of no difference between normal and dyslexic readers using a non-reading task. It appears that the problems arise when the dyslexics are asked to read text (Stanley *et al.*, 1983). Pirozzolo (1979) characterized dyslexics into the two subgroups previously described and compared their performance on a saccadic latency task to that of normal readers. She found that both language-deficit dyslexics and normals were faster at moving their eyes from left to right to reach a target (three ### symbols or a three-letter word) than from right to left to reach a target. However, the visual-perceptual dyslexics were faster at moving their eyes from right to left than from left to right. These findings are displayed in Figure 5.8 and it should be noted that all three groups have similar movement times for the right-to-left movement (to the target in the left visual field), yet the visual-perceptual dyslexics are particularly slow at making the left-to-right movement necessary to reach the targets appearing in the right visual field. The delay in starting to make a saccadic eye movement (saccadic latency) is shown in Figure 5.8 for the three groups of readers moving their eyes in each direction.

Using the findings from such studies Rayner (1986) proposes that the erratic eye movements displayed by language-deficit dyslexics in reading tasks is due to the difficulty the reader is having processing the language (hypothesis 2 above: eye movements are a result of the reading problem). On the other hand, the problems experienced by visual-perceptual dyslexics are a reflection of an underlying spatial processing disorder. Rayner does not go into detail describing the spatial processing disorder,

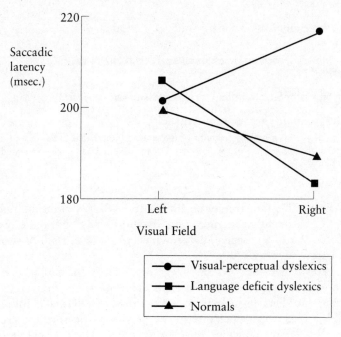

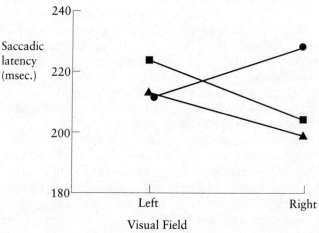

Figure 5.8

    A. Saccadic latencies for eye movements to symbols (###) displayed in the right and left visual fields

    B. Saccadic latencies for eye movements to words displayed in the right and left visual fields

Source: Pirozzolo, 1979

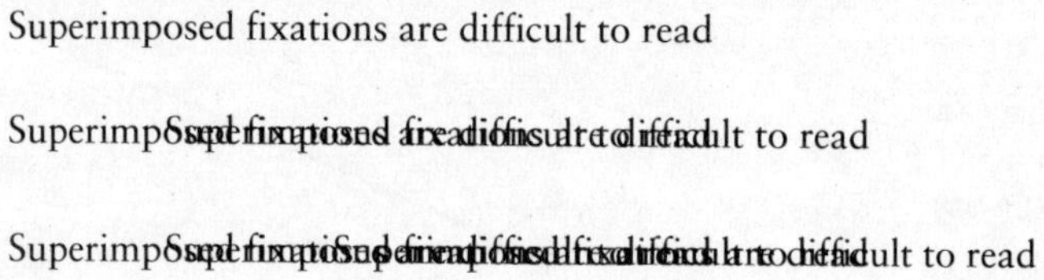

Superimposed fixations are difficult to read

Superimp6septifirapiosas ñreadiōfisudteoliffaldt to read

Superimp6septifinptoSupdtinapiōfasdlfixolifōnda kroctefidult to read

Figure 5.9   Carrying images between fixations

Overlaying images as a sensory memory of the sentence are carried to the second fixation (simulated in the second line of text here) and then to the third fixation (simulated in the third line).

and it is plausible that it may be similar to Pavlidis's brain malfunction theory. Consequently Rayner and Pavlidis may both be correct (hypotheses 2 and 3), depending on which particular group of dyslexics are being considered.

Further evidence supports the suggestion that both reading disability and unusual patterns of eye movements can result from the same underlying problem. In moving our eyes rapidly from one location on a page to another we must eliminate any persisting traces of the previous fixation. If we carry an iconic image of one fixation as our eyes move to the next fixation, then two images would be superimposed: the iconic image from the first fixation would be seen as an overlay on the text newly fixated. This overlaying of images would mean that reading speed would be impeded, with a saccadic movement only possible after a slowly decaying iconic image had faded to a state where it no longer interfered with perception. Reading with slowly decaying iconic images is simulated in Figure 5.9, in which the top line represents the appearance of the sentence with just one fixation.

With a long-lived iconic image the top line will be perceived without difficulty provided that only one fixation is made. Multiple fixations would result in a percept something like the bottom line. Suppose that with each new fixation saccadic movement takes the eyes eight character spaces to the right. The whole image of the sentence in the top line of Figure 5.9, collected from the first fixation and now stored in the form of an iconic memory, is then moved eight spaces to the right. The effect of two superimposed images is simulated in the second line of text. This is what the sentence would look like if we retained an iconic image that could not be separated from newly arriving visual information. If the image has still not decayed by the time we move our eyes a second time, then the problem will get even worse. In the third line of Figure 5.9 another saccade and another fixation have been added. There are now two 'iconic images' superimposed on the sentence.

According to Breitmeyer (1980, 1993) most of us do not see the world with superimposed images like those in Figure 5.9 because the saccadic image is suppressed whenever we move our eyes. The suppression is triggered by activation of the transient visual subsystem. This subsystem, sensitive to contrast and displays containing low spatial frequencies, responds at stimulus onset and offset, and, most importantly for the present discussion, can inhibit the second visual subsystem, the sustained system. Activity from the sustained channel occurs during fixations of the eyes, and lasts for several hundred milliseconds. This activity is curtailed when an output from the transient channel is initiated by an eye movement. Both of these visual subsystems are necessary for reading, otherwise processing of visual information from one fixation will continue when the eyes are collecting information from the next. The transient response effectively limits what we see to whatever we are looking at. Saccadic movements allow the sustained channel to collect visual information from a new location and at the same time they activate the transient channel that inhibits the sustained activity from the previous fixation.

Normal reading entails alternating activity from the sustained and transient visual subsystems, and the hypothesis being investigated by Bill Lovegrove and his colleagues is that developmental dyslexics have a deficit in the operation of the transient channel (Lovegrove and Williams, 1983; Lovegrove *et al.*, 1980; Lovegrove *et al.*, 1986). Their research has compared normal readers and dyslexics on a number of tasks sensitive to differences between the sustained and transient systems, and have found that the dyslexics consistently show reduced activity in the transient system. For example, dyslexics have been found to be less sensitive than other children on a task requiring detection of patterns with low spatial frequencies but not with high spatial frequencies. Secondly, dyslexics are less sensitive in a task determining their flicker thresholds. In both of these tasks, the dyslexics show impaired performance in the operation of their transient subsystems, supporting the hypothesis that their reading difficulties stem from reduced inhibition of the sustained system as they move from one fixation to another. Finally, when dyslexics read sentences shown one word at a time, a task in which eye movements are not required and in which transient activity is at a minimum, their reading performance improved to the level of other children (Hill and Lovegrove, 1993). These results suggest that the reading difficulties of children diagnosed as dyslexics or specific reading disabled may be attributed to a deficit in their transient visual subsystem. Such a deficit would also influence their pattern of eye movements, supporting the hypothesis of a common cause underlying both dyslexia and the control of eye movements.

On-line processes in reading

The main theme of this chapter has been to compare the on-line processing approach as an explanation of eye movement behaviour to the parafoveal processing approach. As has been seen, neither stand up well to the evidence provided. Certainly the location and the duration of a reader's eye movements are strong indicators of the processes being conducted by the mind, but they also are influenced by certain nonlexical information ahead of fixation and possibly by some lexical and semantic information. As the research stands at present, the eye–mind assumption does account for a high proportion of the variance in fixation durations, but it is unable to account for saccadic length and location of fixations within words.

The usefulness of eye movement recording as a tool for further developing our knowledge is apparent in such questions as: how we process syntactic and semantic information, why dyslexics appear to show erratic eye movements when reading text, whether speed reading is a trade off between speed and depth of comprehension. Our eyes selectively fixate the words on the page, and as the reading task gets more difficult, longer fixations occur, providing researchers with a means of directly observing processing difficulties as they occur.

6

Reading Comprehension
from Words to Propositions and Inferences

> Some Nottingham Forest fans are psychologists, and as all of their fans are misguided, it follows that some psychologists must be misguided.

The doyen of cognitive psychology, Ulrich Neisser, has described reading as externally guided thinking (1967, p. 136). In order to understand the sentence about Nottingham Forest fans the reader needs to do more than recognize each word and determine which words refer to each other. What is required here is that we follow an argument in order to judge the validity of the conclusion that some psychologists must be misguided. Reading in this sense is equivalent to reasoning, and Neisser's definition helps us to go beyond word meaning to the understanding of sentences and texts. Reasoning about statements such as these is not restricted to reading, of course, and much of the research that is to be discussed in this chapter could be repeated with spoken statements. When we read anything more complex than the label on a cornflakes packet or anything more novel than a political cliché, we need to think about the words and the relationships between them. Our discussions so far have dwelt upon the processes necessary for the identification of words, and in the present chapter we present the second and third levels of representation that are necessary for reading and understanding. These are representations of the propositional structure of the sentence, and of the reader's personal model of the ideas being presented.

The agents and events in a text can usually be described as forming propositions that must be recognized and then linked in a mental model of the text based upon the relationships between the ideas. The meaning of the text may be contained in this propositional model alone, but we often need to reason about the propositions. This is not a chapter about reasoning, although the point it makes is that in order to understand we often need to make inferences about the relationships of the agents and events. These inferences often require the use of our existing knowledge, and are often calculated as we read them; they are processed 'on-line'.

Thinking while reading

When we read we are usually attempting to recover the meaning of a passage, and in order to do this we need to think about the ideas represented by the words on the page. The basic processes of word identification and syntactic parsing are rarely part of reading in this sense. Only when our eyes come upon an unfamiliar word (or a misspelled word), or when the writer has used a difficult sentence construction that perhaps has resulted in our being 'garden-pathed', do we need to think about these processes.* For the most part reading is equivalent to thinking about the ideas that the writer has attempted to represent in print, and beyond a mundane level of prose or tabloid journalism reading involves the understanding of inference and the development of argument. This might be a circular statement, of course, for what we regard as mundane might be exactly the kind of text that does not require us to think. If a sentence is purely descriptive of an object, then perhaps we would consider it less interesting than when we need to go beyond the actual words appearing in print. Consider a couple of simple examples involving a necessary inference:

> *The carnation won a prize.*
> *It was the best flower in the show.*

and

---

* These sentences are discussed in more detail in Chapter 5, and depend upon lexical or syntactic ambiguities that are not resolved until late in the sentence, for example:
  When George punched the boxer he found that its bite was worse than its bark, and: *Because her sister loves to teach kids learn.*

A motorcycle came around the corner.
The vehicle nearly hit a pedestrian.

No word in these sentences should present a difficulty to any reader who has managed to get this far through this book, and indeed the relationship between the sentences themselves is transparent. In each case the first sentence is descriptive and can be presented as a simple proposition; reasoning is not called upon, and all the information we need to understand them is contained in the words as presented. However, if the two sentences in each example are to make sense, then an inference must be calculated. In the first example the pronoun *it* clearly refers to the *carnation*, but deriving this relationship requires inference. This is generally described as an example of an anaphor, and in this particular case the sentences contain a pronominal anaphor. The second sentence poses no difficulty because the first sentence contains a matching antecedent. In the second example the referent *vehicle* unambiguously points to *motorcycle*, and again there is a simple inference: the two words refer to the same object.

Resolving anaphoric references

The process of inferential reading can run into difficulty if the anaphor is not a typical exemplar of the antecedent. From sentence verification tasks we know that it takes longer to judge that

A penguin is a bird.

than it does to respond to

A robin is a bird.

and this typicality effect (Smith *et al.*, 1974) can also be seen to work in the processing of pairs of sentences. The anaphor is sometimes an instance of the set of items suggested by the antecedent. Garrod and Sanford (1977) had their readers answer simple questions after seeing pairs of sentences containing typical and atypical antecedent/anaphor pairs of the kind:

A bird would sometimes wander into the house.
The robin was attracted by the larder.   (typical instance)

and

A bird would sometimes wander into the house.
The goose was attracted by the larder. (atypical instance)

When the anaphor was an atypical instance, then it took longer to read the second sentence. This effect was also found when the order of referents was reversed, with the specific instance presented in the first sentence and the category item used as the anaphor in the second sentence.

Anaphoric referents such as these serve a number of purposes, in that they avoid tedious repetition and can provide enriching information about the antecedent, but more interestingly they can also inform the reader about a topic change. The following short texts, taken from Vonk *et al.* (1992), illustrate how anaphoric pronouns can be used first to avoid repetition and then, in passage 2, how the thematic structure can be signalled by the reappearance of the original referent.

Passage 1:

1 Sally Jones got up early this morning.
2 She wanted to clean the house.
3 Her parents were coming to visit her.
4 She was looking forward to seeing them.
5 She weighs 80 kilograms.
6 She had to lose weight on her doctor's advice.
7 So she planned to cook a nice but sober meal.

Passage 2:

1 Sally Jones got up early this morning.
2 She wanted to clean the house.
3 Her parents were coming to visit her.
4 She was looking forward to seeing them.
5 Sally weighs 80 kilograms.
6 She had to lose weight on her doctor's advice.
7 So she planned to cook a nice but sober meal.

The first passage is awkward because sentence 5 introduces a new topic without a signal, and only in sentence 7 does the appearance of the new topic start to make sense. By marking the thematic shift with the specific referent *Sally*, it becomes clear that sentence 5 is telling us something new, and that this sentence does not need to be integrated with what has preceded it. Replacing the pronoun with *Sally* in other sentences is quite legal, but does not have the same effect.

In a series of experiments Vonk *et al.* (1992) showed that the reappearance of a specific referent is used both in sentence production and in sentence comprehension. In a production experiment subjects read two sentences, the first of which introduced a character by name or role. The second sentence referred to this character with a pronoun. At this point the subject continued the story, and after a few sentences had to include a target word in the next sentence. Sometimes this target was the original name or role and sometimes it was a pronoun. The sentences written by the subjects were scored according to whether there was a topic shift in the sentence containing the target. If a pronoun was the target there was a topic shift on 17 per cent of occasions, but when the original specific name or role was reintroduced then 88 per cent of the sentences used a topic shift.

Vonk *et al.* found a similar result in the comprehension experiments, involving recognition of a probe word that required the readers to judge whether or not a single word had appeared in the preceding story. The probe word was always contained in the sentence prior to a critical sentence that sometimes introduced a topic shift. When a topic shift was introduced it was sometimes signalled by the reappearance of the specific referent and sometimes the referent was the appropriate pronoun. The recognition times indicted that the probe was more difficult to retrieve when followed by a sentence containing a specific referent: the probe recognition time increased from 930 msec. to 1,007 msec. This result suggests that when we read a specific referent we anticipate a topic shift, and that this makes the words in the previous sentence more difficult to retrieve because they form part of a different topic. These experiments together suggest that pronouns are interpreted by readers to indicate a continuous theme in a text and that this is understood by writers, implicitly at least.

Anaphors and mental models

The anaphoric expressions that we have used in the examples so far have all been quite straightforward in that the antecedent (a category name, or a specific name) and the anaphor (a specific member of the category, or a pronoun) are easily identified. Before progressing beyond this introductory tour of the domain we should mention some varieties of anaphoric expressions that make reading more problematic.

When *the flower* follows the *carnation* it is clear that the two nouns refer to the same object, but computing the inference becomes more difficult when the anaphor can refer to more than one antecedent. The following pair of sentences illustrate this problem:

When the aardvark saw the anthill, it trembled with delight.

compared with

When the aardvark saw the anthill, it trembled with fear.

In each these cases *it* might refer to either the *aardvark* or the *anthill*, though pragmatically there will be a different probability generated by the knowledge that aardvarks eat ants.

Oakhill and Garnham (1992) have catalogued some published instances of anaphors according to their linguistic acceptability, and have recorded skilled readers' judgements of examples of each type. They categorized the examples into a number of linguistic types. One of the more interesting forms is the 'anaphoric island', in which the antecedent is isolated from its anaphor, as in:

They had a feature on violent youngsters, attributing it to drink.

Although this may be acceptable in a psycholinguistic sense, the anaphoric *it* does not agree with the exact form of the antecedent *violent*. Readers in this experiment were able to comprehend sentences containing such anaphoric islands, presumably by extending the meaning of the antecedent. In rewriting the sentences the subjects usually focused their attention on the two referents, by changing either the antecedent or the anaphor, but usually the anaphor. In the present example, almost all subjects replaced *it* with *violence, the violent behaviour,* or an equivalent. Garnham and Oakhill (1987) established that readers not only judge such implicit constructions to be less acceptable than their explicit forms, but that forming judgements about anaphoric islands also takes longer than their explicit equivalents.

A second type of difficult anaphor that Oakhill and Garnham investigated is 'ellipses' or surface anaphors. They can be regarded as giving the impression that writers have used incorrect phrasing. They are characterized by the omission of a referent when that referent has appeared recently. So, rather than writing:

There's nothing magic about sailing a ship. Columbus sailed a ship.

an elliptical form might be preferred for stylistic reasons:

There's nothing magic about sailing a ship. Columbus did.

In this case the surface anaphor does not have an antecedent that provides a perfect syntactic match. The tense of *sailing* has to be changed to correspond to something that *Columbus* did in the past. If the anaphor is used to avoid a direct copying of the exact surface form of the antecedent then there should really be no tense change. When rewriting the texts subjects again tended to change the anaphors rather than the antecedents.

Deep anaphors are also known as 'model-interpretative anaphors' in that they require the use of knowledge that is not presented in the sentence. They are interpreted through a mental representation of the situation described, and the linguistic antecedent in a surface anaphor is not necessary in a deep anaphor:

> *A vast amount of ill-health is self-inflicted, but there are things you can do to promote it.*

In this case the anaphoric pronoun *it* appears to refer to *ill-health*, but that is pragmatically wrong and the second clause must mean that there are things that you can do to promote better health. Subjects judged sentences of this form difficult and poorly written, and rewrote a variety of sections.

A central distinction between surface and deep anaphors rests upon whether a mental model is needed for interpretation, and Garnham and Oakhill (1987) have found evidence that suggests that the distinction is not psychologically valid. Although surface anaphors require only the reinstatement of superficial features of the preceding text, readers do tend to interpret them through a mental model in the same way that they interpret deep anaphors. Subjects were given short passages to read of the form:

> *The new houses had been left in an untidy state.*
> *The plumbers had been blamed by the contractors.*
> *The electricians had too.*

The anaphor in the last sentence has a surface form because a clause from the second sentence appears to have been replaced directly by an elliptical clause. After reading this passage subjects answered questions such as:

> *Did the contractors blame the electricians?*
> *Did the electricians blame the plumbers?*

For some subjects the *electricians* was replaced in the text (and in the questions, of course) with the *estate agents*. By this simple replacement the whole meaning is changed because our knowledge of the world of house building specifies the roles taken by electricians, plumbers and estate agents. Whatever we may know about the difficulties caused by estate agents, our knowledge of this domain suggests a simple reply to the question:

Did the contractors blame the estate agents?

In the original form the surface anaphor leads to the interpretation that the *electricians* were at fault, but pragmatically the *estate agents* will not be blamed for the mess by the *contractors*. Knowledge of a domain is represented by a mental model, and the presence of the elliptical clause calls for an interpretation inconsistent with our mental model. Readers in the experiment responded to the comprehension questions incorrectly more often when the mental model was violated. In addition, reading times for the third sentence of the passage were longer when pragmatics suggested an interpretation that was violated by the linguistic prescription. From this study it appears that we cannot distinguish between the reading of surface and deep anaphors and that mental models are used when we attempt to understand both forms. Garnham and Oakley conclude, on the basis of this comprehension study and on the basis of similar responses in the rewriting experiment, that we read anaphors in similar ways, regardless of their linguistic descriptions.

From words to propositions

The suggestion that readers use mental models when understanding prose – represented very strongly in the work of Alan Garnham and Jane Oakhill described above – is supported by a classic experiment on sentence memory reported by Bransford and Franks (1971). The essential feature of a mental model here is that it is the reader's own reconstruction of the ideas presented in the text, and such models can be seen to have close similarities with Bartlett's (1932) notion of the schema. A schema is used to integrate the incoming information into a meaningful, organized framework, and is constructed by the perceiver using existing knowledge. When readers recall prose they use a generalized schema into which the original is assimilated. Distortions of the original text may occur in order that it can be integrated with familiar concepts, and the most common distortions reported by Bartlett were *flattening*, whereby an individual writing style is lost, *sharpening*, whereby some details are exaggerated, and rationalization, whereby prose is made more coherent and consistent. When readers encounter unusual prose such as Bartlett's 'War of the Ghosts', many of these distortions occur, resulting in recollections very different from the original folk-tale. As sets of ideas are encountered readers are said to abstract the meaning and to reconstruct or assimilate the material.

Sentences and ideas

These processes of abstraction and reconstruction can also be seen in the Bransford and Franks (1971) experiment in which subjects listened to groups of sentences, answering questions about each one, and then performing a recognition memory task. The experiment suggests that when understanding language we integrate the ideas contained in sentences, forming them into a mental model, or schema. Ideas are not retained in isolation, but are combined into an abstracted form that is consistent with the general meaning. The actual surface form of the original presentation is lost in favour of this abstracted form, which itself is a mental representation of the meaning of the story as extracted by the listener or reader. The Bransford and Franks experiment has been well described in a number of textbooks, but it is sufficiently important to justify another summary here.

A number of sentences presented ideas from stories, with each sentence containing up to three ideas. Sentences from four stories were jumbled in each list. After each sentence a simple question was answered, with the following as an example from one of the lists of sentences.

The girl broke the window on the porch.	(Broke what?)
The tree in the front yard shaded the man who was smoking his pipe.	(Where?)
The hill was steep.	(What was?)
The cat, running from the barking dog, jumped on the table.	(From what?)
The tree was tall.	(What was?)
The old car climbed the hill.	(What did?)

The sentences were formed from simple ideas that we can regard as propositions, with a variable number of ideas in each, for example

One idea:	The cat was scared.
Two ideas:	The scared cat jumped on the table.
Three ideas:	The scared cat was running from the barking dog.
Four ideas:	The scared cat, running from the barking dog, jumped on the table.

It is important to note that the complete sentence of four ideas was not actually presented in this phase of the experiment; only sentences containing one, two or three ideas were heard by the subjects.

After working through the list of sentences and questions, the subjects were given a recognition test in which they had to say whether further sentences were 'old' or 'new' according to whether they had appeared in the first part of the experiment. As part of the recognition test they also stated the confidence with which they declared a sentence as having been presented previously or not, giving each sentence a rating between +5 and −5. Positive values were for familiar sentences and negatives were for newly presented sentences. The 'new' sentences were created by putting together ideas from different sentences, for example, *The scared cat climbed the tree* and *The barking dog jumped on the old car in the front yard*. It was in the recognition stage of the experiment that the complete set of four ideas came together for the first time in one sentence, with the correct recognition response being 'new' of course, because the exact sentence was not presented in the first part of the experiment even though all of the composite ideas had been.

The dramatic finding from the experiment was the confidence of the subjects that they had seen sentences that legitimately combined all four ideas of each story. The confidence rating for having heard the four-idea sentences was very high – a value of +4.26 out of a maximum of 5 – suggesting that subjects were certain that the complete form had been present. As each test sentence became shorter, the confidence rating also reduced, but provided that the combination of ideas was legitimate there was little to choose between the ratings given for 'old' and 'new' sentences. The subjects had remembered the meanings of the sentences and had integrated the ideas into an abstract meaning, and had not remembered their specific surface forms.

When the sentences are read rather than heard subjects can remember some of the surface, visual structure (Katz and Gruenewald, 1974), but even with this cautionary note it is safe to conclude that readers do acquire an abstract representation of the meaning rather than a sequence of words in sentence format. That readers remember the meanings of sentences rather than their surface forms was well illustrated by Keenan and Kintsch (1974). Subjects read one of two short paragraphs, with either an explicit or an implicit relationship between the two sentences:

A carelessly discarded burning cigarette started a fire.
The fire destroyed many acres of virgin forest.   (explicit relationship)

or

A burning cigarette was carelessly discarded.
The fire destroyed many acres of virgin forest.   (implicit relationship)

The subjects then verified as true or false a sentence requiring the integration of information:

The discarded cigarette started the fire.

The verification times indicated a large difference between immediate and delayed testing, suggesting that the surface form of the explicit paragraph had been available to help an immediate decision, but was unavailable after 20 minutes. With the implicit paragraph, readers must use the meaning derived from an inference, because the surface form of the test sentence is not present in the paragraph itself. Verification times did not change very much between immediate and delayed testing, confirming the conclusion that surface forms of sentences are remembered for only a short time after their presentation. After the delay there was no difference in the verification times between the explicit and implicit paragraphs, which suggests that the inference was made during reading. If the inference had been derived during verification then the extra time required for the inferential processing would increase the time required for the judgement, resulting in slower decisions in the implicit condition.

The propositional analysis of text

The ideas that were remembered in the Bransford and Franks (1971) experiment are related to the propositions in Walter Kintsch's (1974) model of the representation of meaning. Propositions are the basic units of meaning in text comprehension. They take the reader beyond the level of morphemes and words which are dealt with in the lexicon, and are created by the reader as words are related to each other. As a noun collects a verb or an adjective, then a proposition is formed. In the Bransford and Franks experiment the four 'ideas'

The ants were in the kitchen.
The jelly was on the table.
The jelly was sweet.
The ants ate the jelly.

can be considered as the basic units of meaning or propositions that form the story-sentence:

The ants in the kitchen ate the sweet jelly which was on the table.

While we retain an accurate representation of these units of meaning we are less clear of the vehicle that was used to deliver them to us. We remember the propositions at the expense of their surface appearance. Kintsch's descriptions of propositional structures analyses the units of meaning and their relationships within a text, and for simple texts this is sufficient to capture the way that a reader extracts text meanings from lists of words in sentences. There are occasions when this level of processing is sufficient for understanding, but there are often times when the reader must supplement the propositional textbase with prior knowledge, and in so doing a mental model or 'situation model' is constructed. The essential difference between the level of processing derived from an analysis of the propositional structure and the deeper situation model is in the necessity of inference. We shall turn to the formation of the situation model and the use of different types of inference after first outlining Kintsch's propositional model of the representation of meaning and describing some evidence from studies of reading that offer support to the model.

The propositional richness and complexity of a text help determine not only the time taken to read it, but also the parts of the text that will be recalled. By way of introducing the propositional model, it is worth considering just one experiment that justifies this approach. Kintsch (1974, ch. 6; see also Kintsch and Keenan, 1973) presented subjects with sentences containing 16 or 17 words, but which varied in their number of propositions. Each sentence had between 4 and 9 propositions. The task was to read a set of sentences and recall each of them, and the reading time for each sentence was recorded along with the recall protocol. The accuracy of recall was scored according to inclusion or omission of each proposition in the sentence. Accuracy of word order was not important to this study.

The results indicated two linear functions: one plotted reading time as a function of the total number of propositions presented in each sentence, and the other plotted reading time as a function of the number of propositions recalled. It might be considered more appropriate to use the measure of number of propositions recalled because not all of the available propositions are necessarily processed by a less than careful reader. Both functions were linear however, indicating that as the number of propositions increased, so reading time increased by a constant amount for each additional proposition. For each additional proposition presented in a sentence, reading time increased by 0.94 sec., and for each additional proposition recalled, reading time increased by 1.48 sec. It is important to note that the sentences contained the same number of words and varied only in their number of propositions. It is arguable which is the better measure – propositions presented or propositions recalled – but the linear functions in each case indicate the significance of this measure of the content of sentences.

Kintsch (1974) proposes that our representations of texts are formed of a textbase that lists the propositions and their relationships. The propositions themselves are the basic units of meaning, and to maintain the meaning of the whole text we need a representation of the importance or level of each proposition together with the connections between each of them. This is perhaps best explained with the help of a couple of examples. A simple sentence such as:

Romulus, the legendary founder of Rome, took the Sabine women by force.

contains the four propositions:

Romulus: took women by force
Romulus: founded Rome
Romulus: was legendary
Women: Sabine

that together form a textbase written in the following format:

1   (TOOK, ROMULUS, WOMEN, BY FORCE)
2   (FOUND, ROMULUS, ROME)
3   (LEGENDARY, ROMULUS)
4   (SABINE, WOMEN)

The syntax of the propositions reflects the significance of the verb in Kintsch's model. These verb frames are constructed of a predicate followed by an argument, and so if the proposition contains a main verb, then this is primary. Other propositions can describe characteristics of various kinds (as with propositions 3 and 4). The indentations indicate something of the structure of the textbase, and propositions can be related to each other explicitly in a tree:

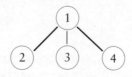

The diagram simply represents the structure of the textbase, as with the indentations, by presenting proposition 1 as superordinate to each of the other three, which themselves have direct connections only to proposition 1. The hierarchical organization has implications for how the text is recalled, but before looking at this performance evidence we shall present a second, more detailed, example. Consider the following, taken from Kintsch (1975):

Turbulence forms at the edge of a wing and grows in strength over its surface, contributing to the lift of a supersonic aircraft.

This is clearly more complex than the *Romulus* sentence, and Kintsch's model captures the difference in complexity, not only with an increase in the number of propositions, but also in their inter-connectedness. The formal textbase can be written as follows:

1	(FORM, TURBULENCE)
2	(LOC: AT, 1, EDGE)
3	(PART OF, WING, EDGE)
4	(GROW, TURBULENCE, STRENGTH)
5	(LOC: OVER, 4, SURFACE)
6	(PART OF, WING, SURFACE)
7	(CONTRIBUTE, TURBULENCE, LIFT, AIRCRAFT)
8	(SUPERSONIC, AIRCRAFT)

The numbers in propositions 2 and 5 refer to earlier propositions, with proposition 2 representing, in longhand, 'The location of the turbulence mentioned in proposition 1 is at an edge'. The hierarchical tree to describe the relationships is shown in the diagram:

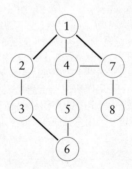

The hierarchical tree is a representation of the textbase that allows us to identify additional connections between propositions. The advantage of the textbase over the tree is that the meaning of the propositions is apparent, and by use of indentation some of the structure of the text is preserved. In both forms it is clear that proposition 1 ('turbulence forms') is at the head in that all other propositions are supplementary, or subordinate. Three immediately subordinate or second-level propositions (2, 4, 7) each describe some property of the formation of turbulence (location, growth, contribution to lift). In turn these properties are each qualified (by 3, 5, 8) by sub-subordinate or third-level propositions. Proposition 6 is a fourth-level proposition that qualifies proposition 5 (the growth in turbulence specified in proposition 4 is located over a surface). The presence of the possessive pronoun indicates that the surface is part of a wing that was also mentioned in proposition 3.

The redescription of texts in terms of their propositional structures gives us a way of capturing the units of meaning and the relationships between them. The reading and recall experiment reported by Kintsch and Keenan (1973) presented sentences of constant length but of varying propositional density. Both the reading time and the recall of propositions increased as the number of propositions increased. We can conclude that the unit of meaning that readers deal with is the proposition. Recall is dependent upon the hierarchical structure, with high level propositions being more likely to be recalled than lower level propositions. This makes good intuitive sense if we consider an attempt to recall the 'turbulence' sentence. It is difficult to imagine someone being able to recall something about, say, the surface of the wing (level 3 or 4 proposition) without knowing that the sentence was about the formation of turbulence (level 1 proposition).

Kintsch *et al.* (1975) confirmed the importance of hierarchical level in a recall experiment in which subjects were presented with paragraphs of about 70 words. Level 1 propositions were twice as likely to be recalled as level 3, 4 or 5 propositions, and recall of a high level proposition also had consequences for its subordinates. When the superordinate is recalled then recall of the subordinate increases from around 15 per cent to 50 per cent. Again, this makes good sense if we look at the turbulence sentence as an example: having recalled that the formation of turbulence is located at an edge (propositions 1 and 2) it seems more likely that a subject would be able to recall that the edge is part of a wing (level 3 proposition).

Individual differences in the use of propositions

Knowing the propositional structure of a text allows us to predict how long it will take a subject to read it and also gives an indication of what parts of the text will be recalled and what will happen if one proposition is either recalled or not. Kintsch's model provides a valuable tool for our understanding of how readers process the relationships between ideas in texts. The model has also been used to illustrate differences between readers of varying ability (Graesser *et al.*, 1980) in an investigation of the best textual predictors of reading speed.

Graesser *et al.* had 12 passages read by 24 university students, and on the basis of their average reading time per sentence, they were classified as fast readers or slow readers. Half the readers were allocated to each group. The fast readers were able to read the sentences in an average time of 3.55 sec., while the slow readers took 5.02 sec. per sentence.

The purpose of the study was to identify the features of the text that best accounted for differences in reading speed between the two groups as they read passages sentence by sentence. As each sentence appeared on a screen the subjects read it and pressed a response button to indicate that they had finished reading. The reading time per sentence was the interval between first appearance of the sentence and the subject's action on the response button. Each subject read a total of 275 sentences. Subjects were instructed to read for meaning, and a comprehension test was used to ensure this. The textual features that Graesser *et al.* considered were:

Narrativity: Each subject rated each passage on the basis of how near it was to a story in which events unfolded. A passage entitled 'Snow White' would be expected to be rated highly here, while a passage called 'Armadillos' would have low narrativity. The rating for the whole passage was entered as the narrativity value for each sentence within the passage.

Familiarity: Each subject also rated each passage according to how familiar he or she was with the topic being discussed.

New nouns: The number of nouns in each sentence that had not been used previously in the passage.

Serial position: The position of each sentence in the passage was entered into the analysis, with the expectation that sentences presented early in a passage would be read more slowly than those presented later.

Number of words: The total number of words in each sentence.

Propositions: The number of propositions, defined according to Kintsch's criteria, in each sentence.

Syntactic predictability: This is a measure of syntactic complexity, based on 'augmented transition network' (ATN) grammar, in which the syntactic class of each word is predicted. The proportion of words correctly predicted by the ATN grammar was entered as the value for the sentence.

The seven variables can be classified as providing either macrostructure or microstructure measures. Narrativity, familiarity, serial position and the number of nouns not encountered in earlier sentences each relate to the relationships between sentences, and are referred to as macrostructure variables. In comparison, the number of words per sentence, the number of propositions per sentence, and the predictability of the syntactic class of each word each vary from sentence to sentence independently of their values in other sentences and these are the microstructure variables. The seven variables were used to predict reading time per sentence. Four good predictors were identified, and these can be described by their simple correlations with reading time: narrativity ($r = -0.57$), new nouns ($r = +0.25$), number of words ($r = +0.29$) and number of propositions ($r = +0.44$). These correlations come from the undivided group of subjects, and to identify individual differences in reading speed separate comparisons were made for the 12 fast readers and the 12 slow readers. The measure used here was the difference in reading time caused by an increment in the value of each of the seven measures. This is the slope of the graph of the reading time against the number of units on a measure, and separate slopes were calculated for the two groups of readers. Serial position is omitted as it is a very weak predictor of reading time. The slope values (in seconds) are shown in Table 6.1.

So, as the 'narrativity rating' of a story increases by one point in the estimation of the judges, then the reading time for each sentence in that story would decrease by 0.272 sec. for the fast readers and by 310 msec. for the slow readers. Similarly, the sentence reading time for the fast readers increases by 0.114 sec. each time a single word is added to a sentence. With this measure we can also compare the fast and the slow readers, and the right-hand column shows the ratio of slow to fast readers for each of six text variables. The ratio is simply the slope value for slow readers divided by the value for fast readers, and indicates the relative difficulty that slow readers are having as each text variable adds difficulty.

Only the microstructure variables showed statistically reliable differences between the two groups of readers. Although the differences look quite small, and although the overall slope values for the microstructures look smaller than those for macrostructures, the critical factor is in the amount of time processing each unit of microstructure. There were on average 11.92 words in each sentence, and so the difference between a

Table 6.1 Comparisons of how fast and slow readers process macrostructures and microstructures

	Fast readers	Slow readers	Slow to fast ratio
Macrostructures			
Narrativity	−0.272	−0.310	1.14
Familiarity	−0.207	−0.170	0.82
New nouns	+0.149	+0.156	1.04
Microstructures			
Number of Words	+0.114	+0.198	1.74
Propositions	+0.075	+0.191	2.55
Syntax	−0.106	−1.607	15.16

Source: Graesser, Hoffman and Clark, 1980

fast reader and a slow reader must be multiplied by 11.92 in order to see the true extent of the difference here. Similarly, there was an average of 4.93 propositions per sentence, and so the difference between slow and fast readers must be multiplied by this figure to see the total difference during the reading of a sentence. The slow to fast ratio gives some indication of the difference between the two groups. This shows that slow readers take 1.74 times as long as fast readers to recognize individual words, for instance. They process propositions even more slowly, but there are fewer propositions in each sentence, and so the overall disadvantage is not as large. The disadvantage in processing syntactically unpredictable words is also large, but the overall effect is reduced because there are not as many of these words as there are words per sentence, of course. All three microstructure variables are potent relative to the macrostructure variables, suggesting that it is the processing of these features of text that should receive attention when attempting to develop the skills of slower readers. Processing of the propositional structure of the text is one of the three microstructure variables that helps differentiate between fast and slow readers.

From propositions to inferences

The model of reading presented in this chapter describes three levels of activity. As the reader collects visual information and combines it with knowledge in the lexicon, and makes use of syntactic rules, a surface level representation is formed. Understanding of the sentence follows a semantic analysis in which a propositional textbase is formed, and this is the second level of activity. For some sentences this may be all that is necessary, but readers are often called to go beyond the specific words appearing in the sentence, and to construct what van Dijk and Kintsch (1983) called a 'reader's situation model', in which a sentence is interpreted. To go from a purely propositional level of understanding to an interpretative level, inferences will be made.

We have already seen how inference is necessary when anaphoric references are to be interpreted, and many of the inferences that we make are as simple as this. There are roles for inferences in addition to the solution of anaphoric problems, however, and the principal roles involve the formation of causal connections and in the construction of elaborative relations. These two main forms can be illustrated with the following examples. Singer (1979) provides a clear example of an elaborative inference:

The boy cleared the snow from the stairs. The shovel was heavy.

The first sentence implies that a tool will be used for clearing the snow, but the tool is not specified at this point. By inferring that the shovel mentioned in the second sentence is the tool used by the boy, a mental model has been developed by the reader. The model is based on inference because the identity of the non-specified tool requires the reader to use information in the second sentence. The shovel is not necessarily the tool, of course, and may have been something that the boy kicked while clearing snow with his boots. It is reasonable to suppose that it is the nonspecified instrument, but this requires an act of construction on the part of the reader. In a similar way information in the second of Singer and Ferreira's (1983) sentences specifies or elaborates an earlier noun phrase until we read the second sentence:

Bob threw the report into the fire. The report burned.

At the time of reading the first sentence there are uncertainties, and we cannot be sure whether the report put the fire out, or whether the report was after all combustible. The second sentence eliminates these uncertainties and specifies the event. Inferences of this kind are sometimes called forward inferences, in that the first statement calls for information that is yet to be presented (but may not actually appear, of course).

Causal inferences (sometimes called 'causal bridging' or backward inferences) do more than give identity to previously unspecified agents such as the specification of the snow-clearing tool as a shovel or the specification of what happened to the report when it was thrown into the fire. Whereas elaborative inferences provide more information about something that is already known to exist, causal inferences are made when we conclude that there is a relationship between two separate events. The following example is taken from Trabasso and Suh (1993):

> *One day Betty found that her mother's birthday was coming soon. Betty really wanted to give her mother a present.*

Betty's new knowledge, described in the first sentence, has clearly caused the intention described in the second sentence. The inference that the newly discovered upcoming birthday resulted in Betty wanting to take some action can be seen to form a causal bridge between the two sentences. A similar example, from Noordman *et al.* (1992) requires a causal inference between two clauses within a sentence:

> *Chlorine compounds make good propellants, because they react with almost no other substances.*

The assertion that chlorine compounds are both good propellants and generally unreactive, together with the word *because* signalling a causal relationship, leads to the inference that good propellants should react with few substances.

One of the main questions to be asked of these inferences is whether they are formed during reading, as a routine part of the comprehension process, or whether they occur some time later, perhaps when we are asked about them. Evidence has come from studies of reading time and verification time and also from observations of eye movements during the initial reading of the sentences. The conclusion is not straight-forward, but with some qualifications we can say that the generation of inferences does occur during comprehension. There is good evidence to suggest that causal inferences are made on-line and form part of the reader's situation model, but there is some dispute over the formation of elaborative inferences. Elaborative inferences are not essential for comprehension to proceed, and so the question becomes one of when readers do or do not make them.

Elaborative inferences

The evidence of the on-line formation of inferences comes from the comparison of reading or verification times of the implicit and explicit forms of texts. When they are similar we can conclude that the information provided in the explicit form is also available in the implicit form, and that an inference has been made. Singer (1979) found a difference between these two forms in connection with elaborative inferences, comparing texts such as:

The boy cleared the snow with a shovel. The shovel was heavy.

against

The boy cleared the snow from the stairs. The shovel was heavy.

In the first case no elaborative inference is necessary when reading *The shovel was heavy*, and this is the explicit form. This same sentence requires an elaborative inference in the second case, the implicit form. Singer found that reading times on the identical sentence were longer when an elaborative inference was required, suggesting that it is at this point that the connection is made. The readers had not inferred the presence of a shovel in the implicit form until the second sentence called for that elaboration. The important point concerns the point at which the elaborative inference is formed. If it is formed during the reading of the sentence about the clearing of the snow, then there should be no difference in reading the second sentence. The extra reading time required in the implicit form of Singer's texts suggests that extra thinking was required in order to develop the connection between the two sentences.

The conclusion that elaborative inferences are not formed on initial reading is supported by a number of studies using a number of different methods. The method used to test the formation of the inference is at least as important in studies of inference formation as it is in other areas of psycholinguistics, and some seemingly contradictory findings are summarized by Keenan *et al.* (1990). One of studies that suggests that elaborative inferences are made on-line, in some circumstances at least, observed readers' eye movements. O'Brien *et al.* (1988) found evidence of inferences being formed early, but only when good context had been presented prior to the point where the inference could be made. O'Brien *et al.* presented their readers with short paragraphs such as:

Sally's diet called for her to eat lots of fresh vegetables. Her favourite vegetable was corn that she could eat right off the cob. This was a diet she didn't mind one bit. She always had plenty of corn with every meal.

Of particular interest was the inspection of the target word *corn* in the final sentence. This is the high-context version of the paragraph, with an explicit antecedent in the form of *corn* in the second sentence. To form an implicit version of the same paragraph, *corn* in the second sentence was replaced by the word *one*. To form a low-context version the second sentence was replaced with:

> *Her favourite vegetable was corn that she could get fresh only in the summer.*

Again, *corn* was replaced with *one* in this sentence in order to produce an implicit form. The study therefore used four forms of each paragraph, to compare fixation durations on the target word in the final sentence under conditions of strong or weak preceding context and with an implicit or explicit antecedent. The results indicated that with strong context the elaborative inference was formed on-line, because there was no difference in gaze durations between the implicit (211 msec.) and explicit forms (209 msec.). These are durations of the first fixations on the target word in the final sentence. When the text was changed so that the context was weaker the pattern of inspection also changed, with the implicit form resulting in longer fixations (234 msec.) than the explicit form (215 msec.). With poor context the result is consistent with Singer's (1979) conclusion that elaborative inferences are not made at the point when they could be formed but only when it is necessary to make them. The effect of the context was to encourage readers to form the elaborative inference, so that the difference between the implicit and explicit forms was eliminated. With another of the paragraphs, the implicit but contextually constraining *long-legged animal with a hump on its back* induced the readers to draw the conclusion that a *camel* was implicated, and reduced fixation durations were observed.

Garrod *et al.* (1990) were not entirely convinced by this conclusion, however, and reanalysed the results according to whether the prior context took the form of a sentence that strongly constrained the target, or a sentence that invited the reader to make a prediction. Both types of context were included in the O'Brien *et al.* study, and in the example above (the passage about *Sally's diet*) the elaborative inference is encouraged by the presence of strong biasing context. In other passages the inference is encouraged by a demand sentence, as in the following:

> *Joan was delighted when Jim gave her a ring with a large stone in it. He had asked her to marry him, and now they were officially engaged. She went to show her father. He asked what kind of gem it was. She excitedly told him that it was a diamond from her boyfriend.*

Prior to the sentence containing the anaphoric target word *diamond* there is a sentence that forces the reader's attention to the question of what kind of large stone is in the ring and suggests that the final sentence will provide an answer. Garrod *et al.* suggested that different passages used in the original experiment produced either a passive form of elaborative inference in which a context of interpretation was created, when there were strong contextual constraints, or the prediction of a subsequent referent when a demand sentence was present. These are two situations in which elaborative inferences may be observed. Garrod *et al.* also demonstrated that they are only observed with unambiguous anaphoric referents. In their experiment passages contained sentences that introduced antecedent/anaphor pairs such as *bird/robin* and in which the anaphor was accompanied by a definite or indefinite article. So, a sentence about a *bird* was followed either by *the robin* or by *a robin*. In the first case it was clear that the two words refer to the same object and so there is an unambiguous anaphor, while in the second it is ambiguous. In another pair of passages the antecedent was explicit, by having the same word appear in separate sentences. With the unambiguous anaphoric target there was no difference in gaze durations whether the antecedent was explicit (234 msec.) or implicit (237 msec.) – the elaborative inference had been made in the implicit condition – but there was a difference with the ambiguous forms, with explicit antecedents requiring less visual attention upon the target (236 msec.) than the implicit antecedents (269 msec.). Elaborative inferences may be made during reading, but only under specific conditions. They are made when an antecedent is made very predictive by a strongly constraining context or by the presence of a demand sentence that invites a prediction; but in any case an unambiguous anaphor is necessary for the effects of the inference to be visible.

Causal inferences

Successful comprehension depends not only upon identification of the individual words and propositions, but also upon the reconstruction of the relationships between them. As the reader identifies these relationships the causal dependencies are mapped in a mental representation or network of the ideas. The relationships provide the text with coherence. To illustrate the network of causal relationships consider the following text, taken from van den Broek and Lorch (1993):

Label		Statement
SETTING	(S)	*There once was a boy named Bob.*
INITIATING EVENT	(E)	*One day, Bob saw his friend's new 10-speed bike.*
GOAL	(G)	*Bob wanted to get a 10-speed.*

ACTION	(A1)	*He looked through the yellow pages.*
ACTION	(A2)	*He called several stores.*
ACTION	(A3)	*He asked them about the prices of bikes.*
ACTION	(A4)	*He found the store with the lowest prices on bikes.*
ACTION	(A5)	*He went to the bike store.*
ACTION	(A6)	*He asked the salesperson about several models.*
ACTION	(A7)	*The salesperson recommended a touring bike.*
ACTION	(A8)	*Bob looked at the selection of touring bikes.*
ACTION	(A9)	*He located some that were his size.*
ACTION	(A10)	*He found a bike that was metallic blue.*
OUTCOME	(O)	*Bob bought the beautiful bike.*

The network representation of this story has causal links between the goal (*Bob wanted to get a 10-speed*) and several statements (A2, A3, A5, A6, A10, O). Without these links the story would have no coherence, and so the reader is left to infer the relationships. For instance, the link between *Bob wanted to get a 10-speed* (G) and *He called several stores* (A2) is implicit, with A2 being caused by Bob's intentions as specified in G. Without the inference being made, A2 has no meaning as part of the story. The statement is understood only if a bridging inference allows the causal relationship to be appreciated. The question asked by van den Broek and Lorch, in a series of experiments, was whether these relationships are formed only between adjacent statements or whether distant causal connections are also formed. These are alternative ideas of the reader's mental model of the events in the text, and are related to two extreme hypotheses concerning the on-line recognition of relationships by the reader.

The conservative hypothesis of the formation of causal connections suggests that links are formed for purposes of local cohesion. Each statement will be connected only to the immediately preceding text event, according to this hypothesis, so forming a linear chain as the reader progresses through a paragraph. This hypothesis is close to the minimal inference model suggested by McKoon and Ratcliff (1986), in which any connections that are formed are predominantly local or are invited by a constraining context. In this model inferences are formed only if they are necessary to preserve local coherence or if they are supported by readily available knowledge. The linear chain version of this model sees readers as linking each statement only to the preceding statement, and connections are not made between non-adjacent units of text.

An alternative hypothesis suggests that multiple connections are made as a text is understood, including distant causal connections, even when the text is locally coherent. This is the global hypothesis of inference formation, and is related to causal network models that suggest that all relevant connections will be formed (e.g. Trabasso and van den Broek, 1985; and see Singer, 1993, for a summary of the fine distinctions between models of inference).

In the story about Bob's bike, the linear chain model predicts that the statement

He asked the salesperson about several models. (A6)

will be connected only to the immediately preceding statement

He went to the bike store. (A5)

In contrast, the global hypothesis has the reader connecting both of these statements not only to each other, but also to the original goal statement that sets up Bob's desire for a new 10-speed bike. So, the linear chain model predicts that when readers encounter statement A6 they will develop a link to A5, and this link can be tested experimentally by looking for effects on a variety of text-related tasks including word recognition, sentence reading and sentence verification. The global hypothesis also predicts an effect of A6 upon A5, but in addition it predicts an effect of A6 upon earlier statements.

These conflicting predictions were tested in van den Broek and Lorch's experiments using recognition priming in a sentence verification task. After subjects had read short stories, including the story about Bob's bike, they made yes/no decisions as to whether target sentences described events that occurred in one of the stories. A true instance was the target

Bob called several stores.

and while this sentence received a 'yes' response, the false sentence:

Bob called several car-rental stores.

received a 'no' response. These verification responses were timed, and formed the main measure in the experiments. Immediately prior to each target sentence the readers saw a priming sentence that was either neutral, or directed their attention to the previous sentence, or directed their attention to the goal statement. A neutral sentence reminded the readers of the story that was to be tested, but did not direct them to any particular statement, for example:

Remember the story about the bike.

An adjacent prime, for the test sentence that asked for verification of the A2 statement, was:

Remember that Bob looked through the yellow pages.

and a sentence that primed the goal statement was:

Remember that Bob wanted to buy a 10-speed bike.

The sentence verification times were facilitated by both types of priming sentence, relative to the neutral sentence. The neutral prime resulted in a 'yes' decision that took 2.272 sec., the adjacent prime had a decision time of 1.971 sec., and the non-adjacent prime had a decision time of 2.096 sec. A similar pattern was seen whether the target sentences were action statements, as in the example here, or were outcome statements. Both the linear chain hypothesis and the global hypothesis predicted the effect of a related adjacent prime upon verification of the targets, but the finding that goal statements predict the verification of action and outcome statements is only predicted by the global inference hypothesis. If readers only connect adjacent action/action statements it is difficult to describe a mechanism for the non-adjacent goal/action and goal/outcome priming in this experiment.

This sentence-priming experiment is consistent with the predictions of the global inference hypothesis in that sentence verification was facilitated by the prior presentation of a non-adjacent statement. The simple alternative to the global or causal network model – the linear chain model – failed to predict the results, but a modified version may be more successful. Non-adjacent statements are not linked directly, according to this linear model, but the facilitation effect may operate through mediating links. Distant statements are linked through intervening statements, and if the priming effect is not dissipated over distance then a goal statement can still prime an action statement. The so-called 'expanded mediational linear chain model' was tested in another of van den Broek and Lorch's (1993) experiments, by observing the priming effect on an action statement from a non-adjacent goal statement and from a non-adjacent action statement. Each priming sentence appeared in the original story eight statements prior to the probed target statement. The linear chain model, in its modified form, predicts similar priming effects. Primes should be connected to targets by identical chains of causally related events, and so equal priming effects should result. The global model makes a different prediction. The goal prime is directly related to the target and so priming is predicted, but the action prime is only indirectly related to the target, through eight intervening actions, and so little or no priming should be seen. The result was a straight-forward confirmation of the global hypothesis, with a 137 msec. priming effect from a goal statement and only 11 msec. priming from an action statement at similar distance. As in the first experiment, when adjacent statements were tested, similar priming effects were seen for action/action and goal/action statements. Non-adjacent statements are not linked except when they are causally related, but when they are related the link can be observed with a priming task.

This experiment, and those reported by Fincher-Kiefer (1993), Long and Golding (1993), Trabasso and Suh (1993), and others, suggest that as we read a passage we construct a mental model in which causal inferences link the story events. These inferences are formed over distances, not just between adjacent statements, and even when the passage is locally coherent. The passage about Bob's bike, for example, has local coherence, and van den Broek and Lorch found evidence of the formation of causal bridging inferences that was predicted by the global hypothesis. We understand a passage by constructing a model in which causal situations are represented. This conclusion conflicts with data from earlier studies of inference formation, using single-word recognition as a probe task, in which inferences appear to be constructed only in restricted contexts (McKoon and Ratcliff, 1986). Other inferences have been said to be only partially encoded in this minimal inference model, in that they would not be fully instantiated at the time of reading. The appearance of the on-line construction of inferences would then be a product of the method used in the experiment, with inferences being fully developed only at the time of testing. The method of testing inferences is currently being debated (see, for example, Fincher-Kiefer, 1993; Keenan *et al.*, 1990; Singer, 1993), and the use of inference probes in the form of complete sentences is now preferred to single-word probes. When Trabasso and Suh (1993) and van den Broek and Lorch (1993) used inference probes that contained propositions rather than single words, the construction of causal inferences was seen. If inferences are not stored as part of the textbase but are fully encoded in the reader's mental model then the most appropriate probe will be one that requires access to the mental model. Probing for the appearance of a single word might encourage a reading strategy in which inferences are unnecessary and in which a surface representation of the text is quite adequate for the purposes of the experiment.

Words, propositions, inferences, and the reader's mental model

This discussion of comprehension processes has been set in the context of a model of reading that entails three levels of representation. As the reader's eyes travel across a line of text the incoming visual information is first recognized as a series of words that together form a surface structure representation of the input, served by word identification processes. This is only the first level, and reading involves much more than word recognition, of course. This is said in spite of the impression given by the amount of attention from researchers to lexical decisions involving four-letter words (the authors include themselves as victims of this rebuke), and in spite of the disproportionate amount of space given to word recognition processes in this book versus the amount of space given to post-recognition processes.

This chapter has been concerned with the second and third levels of representation, in which words are first collected together into ideas or propositions; they then draw upon the reader's knowledge to go beyond the meanings provided by this propositional textbase to form a mental model or situational model in which the text is interpreted. The complexity of the propositional textbase allows us to predict the ease with which a passage will be read, and to predict the pattern of recall when readers attempt to describe it. The power of the propositional level of representation can also be seen in the success with which it can account for individual differences in reading. The identification of the constituent propositions of a text, and the formation of the textbase, correspond to the level at which the meaning of a passage is recognized. When a reader encounters the rather well-known sentence from Haviland and Clark (1974):

Herb took the picnic supplies from the car.

a propositional analysis is sufficient, unless some prior knowledge is available concerning, for example, Herb's preference for cars (possibly giving rise to predictions about the size of the picnic), or his tastes (predicting the composition of the picnic), or his chronic digestive problem (predicting a sad consequence to the picnic). Unless prior knowledge is integrated with the sentence, all of its meaning is available from a propositional analysis. When the next sentence in the passage is (inevitably):

The beer was warm.

the reader is invited to draw the elaborative inference that beer is one of the constituents of the picnic supplies. At this point a situation model is being formed, in that a link is made between two statements, and importantly, the link is not explicit but is in the mind of the reader. We can say that the passage is being interpreted. Perfetti (1989) has argued that the main difference between the level of representation at which propositions are identified, and the level at which the text is interpreted, is in the richness of the inferences that have been constructed. The situation model may even be a crude linguistic representation, and Johnson-Laird (1983) has also suggested that such models may be formed from perceptual constructs. The distinction suggested by Fincher-Kiefer (1993) suggests that while both representations can be constructed in parallel during reading, the situation model may not be formed completely at the time of reading. Both levels may be initiated as reading is started, with the propositional textbase retaining the explicit features of the text, and with formation of the situation model lagging behind in time and being developed from the propositions as they are identified. It is unclear whether these two levels of representation are separately identifiable or whether they more simply involve different points on a continuum in which the richness of inferential processing is the major component. For skilled readers, however, comprehension can be said to require the construction of a mental model in which the formation of inferences acts to link the individual propositions in a unified representation.

References

Abrams, S. G. and Zuber, B. L. (1972) Some temporal characteristics of information processing during reading. *Reading Research Quarterly*, 8, 40–51.

Andrews, S. (1986) Morphological influences on lexical access: lexical or nonlexical effects. *Journal of Memory and Language*, 25, 726–40.

Andrews, S. (1989) Frequency and neighbourhood effects on lexical access: activation or search? *Journal of Experimental Psychology: Learning, Memory and Cognition*, 15, 802–14.

Andrews, S. (1992) Frequency and neighbourhood effects on lexical access: Lexical similarity or orthographic redundancy? *Journal of Experimental Psychology: Learning, Memory and Cognition*, 18, 234–54.

Arthur, T. A. A., Hitch, G. J. and Halliday, M. S. (1994) Articulatory loop and children's reading. *British Journal of Psychology*, 85, 283–300.

Backman, J., Bruck, M., Herbert, M. and Seidenberg, M. S. (1984) Acquisition and use of spelling–sound correspondences in reading. *Journal of Experimental Child Psychology*, 38, 114–33.

Baddeley, A. D. (1986) *Working Memory*. Oxford: Oxford University Press.

Baddeley, A. D. (1990) *Human Memory: Theory and Practice*. Hove: Erlbaum.

Baddeley, A. D. (1992) Working memory. *Science*, 255, 556–9.

Baddeley, A. D. and Hitch, G. J. (1974) Working memory. In G. A. Bower (ed.) *The Psychology of Learning and Motivation 8*. New York: Academic Press.

Baddeley, A. D. and Lewis, V. (1981) Inner active processes in reading: the inner voice, the inner ear and the inner eye. In A. M. Lesgold and C. A. Perfetti (eds) *Interactive Processes in Reading*. Hillsdale, NJ: Erlbaum.

Baddeley, A. D., Ellis, N. C., Miles, T. R. and Lewis, V. J. (1982) Developmental and acquired dyslexia: a comparison. *Cognition*, 11, 185–99.

Bakker, D. J. (1972) *The Temporal Order and Disturbed Reading*. Rotterdam: Rotterdam University Press.

Balota, D. A. and Chumbley, J. I. (1984) Are lexical decisions a good measure of lexical access? The role of word frequency in the neglected decision stage. *Journal of Experimental Psychology: Human Perception and Performance*, 10, 340–57.

Balota, D. A. and Rayner, K. (1983) Parafoveal visual information and semantic contextual constraints. *Journal of Experimental Psychology: Human Perception and Performance*, 9, 726–38.

Baron, J. (1977) Mechanisms for pronouncing printed words: use and acquisition. In D. LaBerge and S. J. Samuels (eds) *Basic Processes in Reading: Perception and Comprehension*. Hillsdale, NJ: Erlbaum.

Baron, J. and Strawson, C. (1976) Use of orthographic and word specific knowledge in reading words aloud. *Journal of Experimental Psychology: Human Perception and Performance*, 2, 386–93.

Barron, R. W. and Baron, J. (1977) How children get meaning from printed words. *Child Development*, 48, 587–94.

Barry, C. and Richardson, J. T. E. (1990) Accounts of oral reading in deep dyslexia. In H. A. Whitaker (ed.), *Phonological Processing and Brain Mechanisms*, New York: Springer.

Bartlett, F. C. (1932) *Remembering: a Study in Experimental and Social Psychology*. London: Cambridge University Press.

Batt, V. (1993) Recognising polymorphemic words. Unpublished Ph.D. dissertation, University of Nottingham.

Batt, V., Underwood, G. and Bryden, M. P. (1995) Inspecting asymmetric presentations of words differing in informational and morphemic structure. *Brain and Cognition*, 49, 202–23.

Beauvois, M. F. and Derouesné, J. (1979) Phonological alexia: three dissociations. *Journal of Neurology, Neurosurgery and Psychiatry*, 42, 1115–24.

Bechtel, W. and Abrahamsen, A. (1993) *Connectionism and the Mind*. Oxford: Basil Blackwell.

Becker, C. A. (1976) Allocation of attention during visual word recognition. *Journal of Experimental Psychology: Human Perception and Performance*, 2, 556–66.

Becker, C. A. (1979) Semantic context and word frequency effects in visual word recognition. *Journal of Experimental Psychology: Human Perception and Performance*, 5, 252–9.

Becker, C. A. (1980) Semantic context effects in visual word recognition: an analysis of semantic strategies. *Memory and Cognition*, 8, 493–512.

Becker, C. A. (1982) The development of semantic context effects: two processes or two strategies? *Reading Research Quarterly*, 17, 482–502.

Becker, C. A. (1985) What do we know about context effects? In D. Besner, T. G. Waller and G. E. MacKinnon (eds), *Reading Research: Advances in Theory and Practice 5*. New York: Academic Press

Becker, C. A. and Killion, T. H. (1977) Interaction of visual and cognitive effects in word recognition. *Journal of Experimental Psychology: Human Perception and Performance*, 3, 389–401.

Besner, D. (1987) Phonology, lexical access in reading, and articulatory suppression: a critical review. *Quarterly Journal of Experimental Psychology*, 39A, 467–78.

Besner, D., Twilley, L., McCann, R. S. and Seergobin, K. (1990) On the connection between connectionism and data: are a few words necessary? *Psychological Review*, 97, 432–46.

Boder, B. (1973) Developmental dyslexia: a diagnostic approach based on three atypical reading–spelling patterns. *Developmental Medicine and Child Neurology*, 15, 663–87.

Bond, G. L. and Dykstra, R. (1967) The co-operative research program in first grade reading instruction. *Reading Research Quarterly*, 2, 5–142.

Bradley, L. and Bryant, P. E. (1978) Difficulties in auditory organisation as a possible cause of reading backwardness. *Nature*, 271, 746–7.

Bradley, L. and Bryant, P. E. (1983) Categorizing sounds and learning to read: a causal connection, *Nature*, 301, 419–21.

Bransford, J. D. and Franks, J. J. (1971) The abstraction of linguistic ideas. *Cognitive Psychology*, 2, 331–50.

Breitmeyer, B. G. (1980) Unmasking visual masking: a look at the 'why' behind the veil of 'how'. *Psychological Review*, 87, 52–69.

Breitmeyer, B. G. (1993) Sustained (P) and transient (M) channels in vision: a review and implications for reading. In: D. M. Willows, R. S. Kruk and E. Corcos (eds), *Visual Processes in Reading and Reading Disabilities*. Hillsdale, NJ: Erlbaum.

Briggs, P., Austin, S. and Underwood, G. (1984) The effects of sentence context in good and poor readers: a test of Stanovich's interactive-compensatory model. *Reading Research Quarterly*, 20, 54–61.

Brooks, L. R. (1977) Visual pattern in fluent word identification. In A. S. Reber and D. L. Scarborough (eds), *Towards a Psychology of Reading*. Hillsdale, NJ: Erlbaum.

Brown, B., Haegerstrom-Portnoy, G., Adams, A. J., Yingling, D. D., Galin, D., Herron, J. and Marcus, M. (1983) Predictive eye movements do not discriminate between dyslexic and control children. *Neuropsychologia*, 21, 121–8.

Bruce, D. J. (1964) The analysis of word sounds. *British Journal of Educational Psychology*, 34, 158–70.

Bryant, P. E., MacLean, M., Bradley, L. and Crossland, J. (1990) Rhyme and alliteration, phoneme detection, and learning to read. *Developmental Psychology*, 26, 429–38.

Bub, D., Cancelliere, A. and Kertesz, A. (1985) Whole-word and analytic translation of spelling-to-sound in a non-semantic reader. In K. E. Patterson, M. Coltheart and J. C. Marshall (eds), *Surface Dyslexia*. London: Erlbaum.

Buswell, G. T. (1922) *Fundamental Reading Habits: a Study of their Development*. Chicago: Chicago University Press.

Calfee, R. C. (1977) Assessment of individual reading skills: basic research and practical applications. In A. S. Reber and D. L. Scarborough (eds), *Towards a Psychology of Reading*. Hillsdale, NJ: Erlbaum.

Campbell, F. W. and Wurtz, R. H. (1978) Saccadic omission: why we do not see a grey-out during a saccadic eye movement. *Vision Research*, 18, 1297–303.

Carpenter, P. A. and Daneman, M. (1981) Lexical retrieval and error recovery in reading: a model based on eye fixations. *Journal of Verbal Learning and Verbal Behavior*, 20, 137–60.

Carpenter, P. A. and Just, M. A. (1983) What your eyes do while your mind is reading. In K. Rayner (ed.), *Eye Movements in Reading: Perceptual and Language Processes*. New York: Academic Press.

Clifton, C. (1992) Tracing the course of sentence comprehension: how lexical information is used. In K. Rayner (ed.), *Eye Movements and Visual Cognition: Scene Perception and Reading*. New York: Springer-Verlag.

Clifton, C., Speer, S. and Abney, S. (1991) Parsing arguments: phrase structure and argument structure as determinants of initial parsing decisions. *Journal of Memory and Language*, 30, 251–71.

Coeffe, C. and O'Regan, J. K. (1987) Reducing the influence of nontarget stimuli on saccade accuracy: predictability and latency effects. *Vision Research*, 27, 227–40.

Coltheart, M. (1978) Lexical access in simple reading tasks. In G. Underwood (ed.), *Strategies of Information Processing*. London: Academic Press.

Coltheart, M. (1980) Deep dyslexia: a right hemisphere hypothesis. In: M. Coltheart, K. E. Patterson and J. C. Marshall (eds), *Deep Dyslexia*, London: Routledge and Kegan Paul.

Coltheart, M. (1981) Disorders of reading and their implications for models of normal reading. *Visible Language*, 15, 245–86.

Coltheart, M. (1983) The right hemisphere and disorders of reading. In A. W. Young (ed.), *Functions of the Right Cerebral Hemisphere*. London: Academic Press.

Coltheart, M., Patterson, K. E. and Marshall, J. C. (eds) (1980) *Deep Dyslexia*. London: Routledge and Kegan Paul.

Coltheart, M., Patterson, K. E. and Marshall, J. C. (1987) Deep dyslexia since 1980. In M. Coltheart, K. E. Patterson and J. C. Marshall (eds), *Deep Dyslexia* (revd edn), London: Routledge and Kegan Paul.

Coltheart, M., Curtis, B., Atkins, P. and Haller, M. (1993) Models of reading aloud: dual-route and parallel-distributed-processing approaches, *Psychological Review*, 100, 589–608.

Coltheart, M., Davelaar, E., Jonasson, J. T. and Besner, D. (1977) Access to the internal lexicon. In S. Dornic (ed.), *Attention and Performance, VI*. Hillsdale, NJ: Erlbaum.

Coltheart, V., Laxton, V. J., Keating, G. C. and Pool, M. M. (1986) Direct access and phonological encoding processes in children's reading: effect of word characteristics. *British Journal of Educational Psychology*, 56, 255–70.

Coltheart, M., Masterton, J., Byng, S., Prior, M. and Riddoch, J. (1983) Surface dyslexia. *Quarterly Journal of Experimental Psychology*, 35A, 469–95.

Coslett, H. B. (1991) Read but not write 'idea': evidence for a third reading mechanism. *Brain and Language*, 40, 425–43.

Coslett, H. B. and Saffran, E. M. (1989) Evidence for preserved reading in 'pure alexia', *Brain*, 112, 327–59.

Coslett, H. B., Rothi, L. G. and Heilman, K. M. (1985) Reading: dissociation of lexical and phonological mechanisms. *Brain and Language*, 24, 20–35.

Critchley, M. (1970) *The Dyslexic Child*. Springfield, Ill.: Thomas.

Cunningham, A. E. (1990) Explicit versus implicit instruction in phonemic awareness. *Journal of Experimental Child Psychology*, 50, 429–44.

Daneman, M. and Carpenter, P. A. (1980) Individual differences in working memory and reading. *Journal of Verbal Learning and Verbal Behavior*, 19, 450–66.

Dennis, I., Besner, D. and Davelaar, E. (1985) Phonology in visual word recognition: Their is more two this than meats the I. In D. Besner, T. G. Waller and G. E. MacKinnon (eds), *Reading Research: Advances in Theory and Practice*, vol. 5. London: Academic Press.

Derouesné, J. and Beauvois, M. F. (1979) Phonological processing in reading: data from alexia. *Journal of Neurology, Neurosurgery and Psychiatry*, 42, 1125–32.

Doctor, E. A. and Coltheart, M. (1980) Children's use of phonology when reading for meaning. *Memory and Cognition*, 8, 195–209.

Downing, J. (1967) *Evaluating the Initial Teaching Alphabet*. London: Cassell.

Ehrlich, S. F. and Rayner, K. (1981) Contextual effects on word perception and eye movements during reading. *Journal of Verbal Learning and Verbal Behavior*, 20, 641–55.

Eisenberg, P. and Becker, C. A. (1982) Semantic context effects in visual word recognition, sentence processing, and reading: evidence for semantic strategies. *Journal of Experimental Psychology: Human Perception and Performance*, 8, 739–56.

Ellis, A. W. (1979) Developmental acquired dyslexia: some observations on Jorm (1979). *Cognition*, 7, 413–20.

Ellis, A. W. (1985) The cognitive neuropsychology of developmental (and acquired) dyslexia: a critical survey. *Cognitive Neuropsychology*, 2, 169–205.

Ellis, A. W. (1993) *Reading, Writing and Dyslexia* (2nd edn). Hove: Erlbaum.

Everatt, J. and Underwood, G. (1992) Parafoveal guidance and priming effects during reading: a special case of the mind being ahead of the eyes. *Consciousness and Cognition*, 1, 186–97.

Everatt, J. and Underwood, G. (1994) Individual differences in reading subprocesses: relationships between reading ability, lexical access, and eye movement control. *Language and Speech*, 37, 283–97.

Farnham-Diggory, S. and Gregg, L. W. (1975) Short-term memory function in young readers. *Journal of Experimental Child Psychology*, 19, 279–98.

Fincher-Kiefer, R. (1993) The role of predictive inferences in situation model construction. *Discourse Processes*, 16, 99–124.

Firth, I. (1972) Components of Reading Disability. Unpublished Ph.D. dissertation, University of New South Wales.

Fischler, I. and Bloom, P. A. (1979) Automatic and attentional processes in the effects of sentence contexts on word recognition. *Journal of Experimental Psychology: Human Perception and Performance*, 3, 18–26.

Fischler, I. and Bloom, P. A. (1980) Latency of associative activation in memory. *Journal of Experimental Psychology: Human Perception and Performance*, 4, 455–70.

Fishers D. F. and Shebilske, W. L. (1985) There is more than meets the eye than the eye–mind assumption. In R. Groner, G. McConkie and C. Menz (eds), *Eye Movements and Human Information Processing*. Amsterdam: Elsevier.

Fodor, J. A. (1983) *The Modularity of Mind*. London: MIT Press.

Forster, K. I. (1976) Accessing the mental lexicon. In R. J. Wales and E. Walker (eds), *New Approaches to Language Mechanisms*. Amsterdam: Elsevier.

Forster, K. I. and Davis, C. (1984) Repetition priming and frequency attenuation in lexical access. *Journal of Experimental Psychology: Learning, Memory and Cognition*, 10, 680–98

Frazier, L. and Rayner, K. (1982) Making and correcting errors during sentence comprehension: eye movements in the analysis of structurally ambiguous sentences. *Cognitive Psychology*, 14, 178–210.

Frith, U. (1985) Beneath the surface of developmental dyslexia. In K. E. Patterson, J. C. Marshall and M. Coltheart (eds), *Surface Dyslexia*. London: Erlbaum.

Funnell, E. (1983) Phonological processes in reading: new evidence from acquired dyslexia, *British Journal of Psychology*, 74, 159–80.

Gardner, H. and Zurif, E. (1975) BEE but not BE: oral reading of single words in aphasia and alexia. *Neuropsychologia*, 13, 181–90.

Garnham, A. and Oakhill, J. (1987) Interpreting elliptical verb phrases. *Quarterly Journal of Experimental Psychology*, 39A, 611–27.

Garrod, S. and Sanford, A. (1977) Interpreting anaphoric relations: the integration of semantic information while reading. *Journal of Verbal Learning and Verbal Behavior*, 16, 77–90.

Garrod, S., O'Brien, E. J., Morris R. K. and Rayner, K. (1990) Elaborative inferencing as an active or passive process. *Journal of Experimental Psychology: Learning, Memory and Cognition*, 16, 250–7.

Gathercole, S. E. and Baddeley, A. D. (1989) Evaluation of the role of phonological STM in the development of vocabulary in children: a longitudinal study. *Journal of Memory and Language*, 28, 200–13.

Gathercole, S. E. and Baddeley, A. D. (1990) Phonological memory deficits in language disordered children: is there a causal connection? *Journal of Memory and Language*, 29, 336–60.

Gathercole, S. E., Willis, C. and Baddeley, A. D. (1991a) Differentiating phonological memory and awareness of rhyme: reading and vocabulary development in children. *British Journal of Psychology*, 82, 387–406.

Gathercole, S. E., Willis, C., Emslie, H. and Baddeley, A. D. (1991b) The influences of number of syllables and word-likeness on the repetition of nonwords. *Applied Psycholinguistics*, 12, 349–67.

Gibson, E. J. and Levin, H. (1975) *The Psychology of Reading*. Cambridge, Mass.: MIT Press.

Gilbert, L. C. (1953) Functional motor efficiency of the eyes and its relation to reading. *University of California Publications in Education*, 11, 159–231.

Glanzer, M. and Ehrenreich, S. L. (1979) Structure and search of the internal lexicon. *Journal of Verbal Learning and Verbal Behavior*, 18, 381–98.

Glushko, R. J. (1979) The organisation and activation of lexical knowledge in reading aloud. *Journal of Experimental Psychology: Human Perception and Performance*, 5, 674–91.

Goldberg, H. K. and Arnott, W. (1970) Ocular motility in learning disabilities. *Journal of Learning Disabilities*, 3, 160–2.

Goldrich, S. G. and Sedgwick, H. (1982) An objective comparison of oculomotor functioning in reading-disabled and normal children. *American Journal of Optometry and Physiological Optics*, 59, 82.

Gonzalez, E. G. and Kolers, P. A. (1985) On the interpretation of eye fixations. In R. Groner, G. McConkie and C. Menz (eds), *Eye Movements and Human Information Processing*. Amsterdam: North-Holland.

Goodman, K. S. (1967) Reading: a psycholinguistic guessing game. *Journal of the Reading Specialist*, 4, 126–135.

Goodman, K. S. (1969) Analysis of oral reading miscues: applied psycholinguistics. *Reading Research Quarterly*, 5, 9–30.

Graesser, A. C., Hoffman, N. L. and Clark, L. F. (1980) Structural components of reading time. *Journal of Verbal Learning and Verbal Behavior*, 19, 135–51.

Grainger, J. (1990) Word frequency and neighbourhood effects in lexical decision and naming. *Journal of Memory and Language*, 29, 228–44.

Grainger, J., O'Regan, J. K., Jacobs, A. M. and Segui, J. (1992) On the role of competing word units in visual word recognition. *Perception and Psychophysics*, 45, 189–95.

Guttentag, R. E. and Haith, M. M. A. (1979) A developmental study of automatic word processing in a picture classification task. *Child Development*, 50, 894–6.

Guyer, B. L. and Friedman, M. P. (1975) Hemispheric processing and cognitive styles in learning-disabled and normal children. *Child Development*, 46, 658–68.

Haviland, S. E. and Clark, H. H. (1974) What's new? Acquiring new information as a process in comprehension. *Journal of Verbal Learning and Verbal Behavior*, 13, 512–21.

Henderson, J. M. and Ferreira, F. (1990) Effects of foveal processing difficulty on the perceptual span in reading: implications for attention and eye movement control. *Journal of Experimental Psychology: Learning, Memory and Cognition*, 16, 417–29.

Henderson, L. (1985) Toward a psychology of morphemes. In A. W. Ellis (ed.), *Progress in the Psychology of Language*, vol. 1. London: Erlbaum.

Hill, R. and Lovegrove, W. J. (1993) One word at a time: a solution to the visual deficit in SRDs? In S. F. Wright and R. Groner (eds), *Facets of Dyslexia and its Remediation*. Amsterdam: Elsevier.

Hinton, G. E., McClelland, J. L. and Rumelhart, D. E. (1986) Distributed representations. In D. E. Rumelhart and J. L. McClelland (eds), *Parallel Distributed Processing: Explorations in the Microstructure of Cognition*, vol 1. Cambridge, Mass.: MIT Press.

Hinton, G. E. and Shallice, T. (1991) Lesioning an attractor network: investigations of acquired dyslexia. *Psychological Review*, 98, 74–95.

Holmes, J. M. (1978) 'Regression' and reading breakdown. In A. Caramazza and E. B. Zurif (eds), *Language Acquisition and Language Breakdown*. Johns Hopkins University Press: Baltimore, Md. and London.

Huey, E. B. (1908) *The Psychology and Pedagogy of Reading*. New York: Macmillan.

Humphreys, G. W., Evett, L. J. and Taylor, D. E. (1982) Automatic phonological priming in visual word recognition. *Memory and Cognition*, 10, 576–90.

Humphreys, G. W., Riddoch, M. J. and Quinlan, P. T. (1988) Cascade processes in picture identification. *Cognitive Neuropsychology*, 5, 67–103.

Hyönä, J. (1995) Do irregular letter combinations attract readers' attention? Evidence from fixation locations in words. *Journal of Experimental Psychology: Human Perception and Performance*, 21, 68–81.

Hyönä, J., Niemi, P. and Underwood, G. (1989) Reading long words embedded in sentences: informativeness of word parts affects eye movements. *Journal of Experimental Psychology: Human Perception and Performance*, 15, 142–52.

Inhoff, A. W. (1987) Parafoveal word perception during eye fixations in reading: effects of visual salience and word structure. In: M. Coltheart (ed.), *Attention and Performance XII: The Psychology of Reading*. London: Erlbaum.

Inhoff, A. W. and Rayner, K. (1986) Parafoveal word processing during eye fixations in reading: effects of word frequency. *Perception and Psychophysics*, 40, 431–9.

Irwin, D. I. and Lupker, S. J. (1983) Semantic priming of pictures and words: a levels of processing approach. *Journal of Verbal Learning and Verbal Behavior*, 22, 45–60.

Jastrzembski, J. E. (1981) Multiple meanings, number of related meanings, frequency of occurrence, and the lexicon. *Cognitive Psychology*, 13, 278–305.

Javal, L. (1879) Essai sur la physiologie de la lecture. *Annales d'Occulistique*, 82, 242–53.

Johnson-Laird, P. N. (1983) *Mental Models*. Cambridge: Cambridge University Press.

Jorm, A. F. (1979a) The cognitive and neurological basis of developmental dyslexia: a theoretical framework and review, *Cognition*, 7, 19–33.

Jorm, A. F. (1979b) The nature of the reading deficit in developmental dyslexia: a reply to Ellis. *Cognition*, 7, 421–33.

Just, M. A. and Carpenter, P. A. (1980) A theory of reading: from eye fixations to comprehension. *Psychological Review*, 87, 329–54.

Just, M. A. and Carpenter, P. A. (1987) *The Psychology of Reading and Language Comprehension*. Newton, Mass.: Allyn and Bacon.

Just, M. A. and Carpenter, P. A. (1992) A capacity theory of comprehension: individual differences in working memory. *Psychological Review*, 99, 122–49.

Katz, J. L. and Lanzoni, S. M. (1992) Automatic activation of word phonology from print in deep dyslexia. *Quarterly Journal of Experimental Psychology*, 45A, 575–608.

Katz, S. and Gruenewald, P. (1974) The abstraction of linguistic ideas in 'meaningful' sentences. *Memory and Cognition*, 2, 737–41.

Keenan, J. M. and Kintsch, W. (1974) The identification of explicitly and implicitly presented information. In W. Kintsch, *The Representation of Meaning in Memory*. Hillsdale, NJ: Erlbaum.

Keenan, J. M., Potts, G. R., Golding, J. M. and Jennings, T. M. (1990) Which elaborative inferences are drawn during reading? A question of methodologies. In D. A. Balota, G. B. Flores d'Arcais and K. Rayner (eds), *Comprehension Processes in Reading*. Hillsdale, NJ: Erlbaum.

Kennedy, A. (1978) Reading sentences: some observations on the control of eye movements. In G. Underwood (ed.), *Strategies of Information Processing*. London: Academic Press.

Kennison, S. M. and Clifton, C. (1995) Determinants of parafoveal preview benefit in high and low memory capacity readers: implications for eye movement control. *Journal of Experimental Psychology: Learning, Memory and Cognition*, 21, 68–81.

Kimura, Y. and Bryant, P. (1983) Reading and writing in English and Japanese: a cross-cultural study of young children. *British Journal of Developmental Psychology*, 1, 143–54.

Kinsbourne, M. and Warrington, E. K. (1962) A variety of reading disability associated with right hemisphere lesions. *Journal of Neurology, Neurosurgery and Psychiatry*, 25, 339–44.

Kintsch, W. (1974) *The Representation of Meaning in Memory*. Hillsdale, NJ: Erlbaum.

Kintsch, W. (1975) Memory for prose. In C. N. Cofer (ed.), *The Structure of Human Memory*. San Francisco: Freeman.

Kintsch, W. and Keenan, J. M. (1973) Reading rate and retention as a function of the number of propositions in the base structure of sentences. *Cognitive Psychology*, 5, 257–74.

Kintsch, W., Kozminsky, E., Streby, W. J., McKoon, G. and Keenan J. M. (1975) Comprehension and recall of text as a function of content variables. *Journal of Verbal Learning and Verbal Behavior*, 14, 196–214.

Kirtley, C., Bryant, P. E., MacLean, M. and Bradley, L. (1989) Rhyme, rime, and the onset of reading. *Journal of Experimental Child Psychology*, 43, 129–44.

Kleiman, G. M. (1975) Speech recoding in reading. *Journal of Verbal Learning and Verbal Behavior*, 14, 323–39.

LaBerge, D. and Samuels, S. J. (1974) Toward a theory of automatic information processing in reading. *Cognitive Psychology*, 6, 293–323.

Lenel, J. C. and Cantor, J. H. (1981) Rhyme recognition and phonemic perception in young children. *Journal of Psycholinguistic Research*, 10, 57–68.

Levinson, H. N. (1980) *A Solution to the Riddle Dyslexia*. New York: Springer-Verlag.

Liberman, I. Y. (1983) Linguistic abilities and reading-spelling instruction. Paper presented at the 2nd World Congress on Dyslexia, Halkidiki, Greece, 27–30 June.

Liberman, I. Y. (1989) Phonology and the beginning reader revisited. In C. von Euler, I. Lundberg and G. Lennestrand (eds), *Brain and Reading*. London: Macmillan.

Liberman, I. Y., Shankweiler, D., Fischer, F. W. and Carter, B. (1974) Reading and awareness of linguistic segments. *Journal of Experimental Child Psychology*, 18, 201–12.

Lima, S. (1987) Morphological analysis in sentence reading. *Journal of Memory and Language*, 26, 84–99.

Long, D. L. and Golding, J. M. (1993) Superordinate goal inferences: are they automatically generated during reading? *Discourse Processes*, 16, 55–73.

Lovegrove, W. J. and Williams, M. C. (1993) Visual temporal processing deficits in specific reading disability. In D. M. Willows, R. S. Kruk and E. Corcos (eds), *Visual Processes in Reading and Reading Disabilities*. Hillsdale, NJ: Erlbaum.

Lovegrove, W. J., Martin, F. and Slaghuis, W. (1986) A theoretical and experimental case for a visual deficit in specific reading disability. *Cognitive Neuropsychology*, 3, 225–67.

Lovegrove, W. J., Bowling, A., Badcock, D. and Blackwood, M. (1980) Specific reading disability: differences in contrast sensitivity as a function of spatial frequency. *Science*, 210, 439–40.

Lundberg, I., Frost, J. and Petersen, O.-P. (1988) Effects of an extensive program for stimulating phonological awareness in preschool children. *Reading Research Quarterly*, 23, 264–84.

Lupker, S. J. (1985) Relatedness effects in word and picture naming: parallels, differences, and structural implications. In A. W. Ellis (ed.), *Progress in the Psychology of Language*, vol. 1. London: Erlbaum.

McCarthy, R. and Warrington, E. K. (1986) Phonological reading: phenomena and paradoxes. *Cortex*, 22, 359–80.

McClelland, J. L. and Rumelhart, D. E. (1981) An interactive activation model of context effects in letter perception: Part 1, An account of basic findings. *Psychological Review*, 88, 375–407.

McConkie, G. W. and Rayner, K. (1975) The span of the effective stimulus during a fixation in reading. *Perception and Psychophysics*, 17, 578–86.

McConkie, G. W. and Rayner, K. (1976) Asymmetry of the perceptual span in reading. *Bulletin of the Psychonomic Society*, 8, 365–8.

McKoon, G. and Ratcliff, R. (1986) Inferences about predictable events. *Journal of Experimental Psychology: Learning, Memory and Cognition*, 12, 82–91.

Mann, V. A. and Liberman, I. Y. (1984) Phonological awareness and verbal short-term memory. *Journal of Learning Disabilities*, 17, 592–9.

Marcel, A. J. (1980) Surface dyslexia and beginning reading: a revised hypothesis of the pronunciation of print and its impairments. In M. Coltheart, K. Patterson and J. C. Marshall (eds), *Deep Dyslexia*. London: Routledge and Kegan Paul.

Marcel, A. J. (1983) Conscious and unconscious perception: experiments on visual masking and word recognition. *Cognitive Psychology*, 15, 197–237.

Marshall, J. C. and Newcombe, F. (1973) Patterns of paralexia: a psycholinguistic approach. *Journal of Psycholinguistic Research*, 2, 175–99.

Marshall, J. C. and Newcombe, F. (1980) The conceptual status of deep dyslexia: an historical perspective. In M. Coltheart, K. E. Patterson, and J. C. Marshall (eds), *Deep Dyslexia*. London: Routledge and Kegan Paul.

Martin, R. C. (1982) The pseudohomophone effect: the role of visual similarity in nonword decisions. *Quarterly Journal of Experimental Psychology*, 34A, 395–409.

Masson, M. E. J. (1985) Rapid reading processes and skills. In G. E. MacKinnon and T. G. Waller (eds), *Reading Research: Advances in Theory and Practice 4*. New York: Academic Press.

Masterson, J., Laxon, V. and Stuart, M. (1992) Beginning reading with phonology. *British Journal of Psychology*, 83, 1–12.

Mattis, S., French, J. and Rapin, E. (1975) Dyslexia in children and young adults: three independent neuropsychological syndromes. *Developmental Medicine and Child Neurology*, 17, 150–63.

Meyer, D. E. and Schvaneveldt, R. W. (1971) Facilitation in recognizing pairs of words: evidence of a dependence between retrieval operations. *Journal of Experimental Psychology*, 90, 227–34.

Meyer, D. E., Schvaneveldt, R. W., and Ruddy, M. G. (1974) Functions of graphemic and phonemic codes in visual word-recognition. *Memory and Cognition*, 2, 309–21.

Morais, J., Cary, L., Alegria, J. and Bertelson, P. (1979) Does awareness of speech as a sequence of phones arise spontaneously? *Cognition*, 7, 323–31.

Morton, J. (1969) Interaction of information in word recognition. *Psychological Review*, 76, 165–78.

Morton, J. (1979) Facilitation in word recognition: experiments causing changes in the logogen system. In P. A. Kolers, M. Wrolstad and H. Bouma (eds), *Processing of Visible Language*, vol. 1. New York: Plenum Press.

Morton, J. and Patterson, K. E. (1980) A new attempt at an interpretation, or, an attempt at a new interpretation. In M. Coltheart, K. E. Patterson, and J. C. Marshall (eds), *Deep Dyslexia*. London: Routledge and Kegan Paul.

Murray, W. S. and Kennedy, A. (1988) Spatial coding in the processing of anaphor by good and poor readers: evidence from eye movement analysis. *Quarterly Journal of Experimental Psychology*, 40A, 693–718.

Murrell, G. A. and Morton, J. (1974) Word recognition and morphemic structure. *Journal of Experimental Psychology*, 102, 963–8.

Neale, M. D. (1966) *The Neale Analysis of Reading Ability*. London: Macmillan.

Neely, J. H. (1977) Semantic priming and retrieval from lexical memory: the roles of inhibitionless spreading activation and limited-capacity attention. *Journal of Verbal Learning and Verbal Behavior*, 20, 97–109.

Neely, J. H. (1991) Semantic priming effects in visual word recognition: a selective review of current findings and theories. In D. Besner and G. W.

Humphreys (eds), *Basic Processes in Reading: Visual Word Recognition*. Hillsdale, NJ: Erlbaum.

Neisser, U. (1964) Visual search. *Scientific American*, 210 (June), 94–102.

Neisser, U. (1967) *Cognitive Psychology*. New York: Appleton Century Crofts.

Nicolson, T. (1991) Do children read words better in context or in lists? A classic study revisited. *Journal of Educational Psychology*, 83, 444–50.

Noordman, L. G. M., Vonk, W. and Kempff, H. J. (1992) Causal inferences during the reading of expository texts. *Journal of Memory and Language*, 31, 573–90.

Norman, D. A. and Bobrow, D. G. (1975) On data-limited and resource-limited processes. *Cognitive Psychology*, 7, 44–64.

O'Brien, E. J., Shank, D. M., Myers, J. L. and Rayner, K. (1988) Elaborative inferences during reading: do they occur on-line? *Journal of Experimental Psychology: Learning, Memory and Cognition*, 14, 410–20.

O'Regan, J. K., Levy-Schoen, A., Pynte, J. and Brugaillere, B. (1984) Convenient viewing location within isolated words of different length and structure. *Journal of Experimental Psychology: Human Perception and Performance*, 10, 250–7.

Oakhill, J. and Garnham, A. (1992) Linguistic prescriptions and anaphoric reality. *Text*, 12, 161–82.

Oakhill, J., Yuill, N. and Parkin, A. (1986) On the nature of the difference between skilled and less-skilled comprehenders. *Journal of Research in Reading*, 9, 80–91.

Olson, R. K., Kliegl, R. and Davidson, B. J. (1983) Eye movements in reading disability. In K. Rayner (ed.), *Eye Movements in Reading: Perceptual and Language Processes*. New York: Academic Press.

Parkin, A. J. and Underwood, G. (1983) Orthographic vs. phonological irregularity in lexical decisions. *Memory and Cognition*, 10, 45–53.

Patterson, K. E. (1980) Derivational errors. In M. Coltheart, K. Patterson and J. C. Marshall (eds), *Deep Dyslexia*. London: Routledge and Kegan Paul.

Patterson, K. E. (1981) Neuropsychological approaches to the study of reading. *British Journal of Psychology*, 72, 151–74.

Patterson, K. E. (1982) The relation between reading and phonological coding: further neuropsychological observations. In A. W. Ellis (ed.), *Normality and Pathology in Cognitive Functions*. London: Academic Press.

Patterson, K. E. (1990) Alexia and neural nets. *Japanese Journal of Neuropsychology*, 6, 90–9.

Patterson, K. E. and Kay, J. (1980) How word-form dyslexics form words. Paper presented to a conference of the British Psychological Society, Exeter, March.

Patterson, K. E. and Kay, J. (1982) Letter-by-letter reading: psychological descriptions of a neurological syndrome. *Quarterly Journal of Experimental Psychology*, 34A, 411–41.

Patterson, K. E., Seidenberg, M. S. and McClelland, J. L. (1989) Connections and disconnections: acquired dyslexia in a computational model of reading processes. In R. G. M. Morris (ed.), *Parallel Distributed Processing: Implications for Psychology and Neuropsychology*. Oxford: Oxford University Press.

230   *References*

Pavlidis, G. T. (1978) The dyslexic's erratic eye movements: case studies. *Dyslexic Review*, 1, 22–8.

Pavlidis, G. T. (1981a) Do eye movements hold the key to dyslexia? *Neuropsychologia*, 19, 57–64.

Pavlidis, G. T. (1981b) Sequencing, eye movements, and the early objective diagnosis of dyslexia. In G. T. Pavlidis and T. R. Miles (eds), *Dyslexia Research and its Applications to Education*. Chichester: J. Wiley.

Pavlidis, G. T. (1985) Eye movements in dyslexia: their diagnostic significance. *Journal of Learning Disabilities*, 18, 42–50.

Pavlidis, G. T. (1986) Eye movements and the perceptual span: evidence for dyslexic typology. In G. T. Pavlidis and D. F. Fisher (eds), *Dyslexia: Its Neuropsychology and Treatment*. Chichester: J. Wiley.

Perfetti, C. A. and Goldman, S. R. (1976) Discourse memory and reading comprehension skill. *Journal of Verbal Learning and Verbal Behavior*, 14, 33–42.

Perfetti, C. A. (1989) There are generalised abilities and one of them is reading. In L. Resnick (ed.), *Knowing and Learning: Issues for a Cognitive Science of Instruction*. Hillsdale, NJ: Erlbaum.

Philpott, A. and Wilding, J. (1979) Semantic interference from subliminal stimuli in a dichoptic viewing situation. *British Journal of Psychology*, 70, 559–63.

Pirozzolo, F. J. (1979) *The Neuropsychology of Developmental Reading Disorders*. New York: Praeger.

Pollatsek, A., Bolozky, S., Wells, A. D. and Rayner, K. (1981) Asymmetries in the perceptual spans for Israeli readers. *Brain and Language*, 14, 174–80.

Pollatsek, A., Lesch, M., Morris, R. K. and Rayner, K. (1992) Phonological codes are used in integrating information across saccades in word identification and reading. *Journal of Experimental Psychology: Human Perception and Performance*, 18, 148–62.

Posner, M. I. and Snyder, C. R. R. (1975) Attention and cognitive control. In R. Solso (ed.), *Information Processing and Cognition: the Loyola Symposium*. Hillsdale, NJ: Erlbaum.

Rapp, B. C. and Caramazza, A. (1989) General to specific access to word meaning: a claim re-examined. *Cognitive Neuropsychology*, 6, 251–72.

Rayner, K. (1978) Eye movements in reading and information processing. *Psychological Bulletin*, 85, 618–60.

Rayner, K. (1979) Eye guidance in reading: Fixation locations within words. *Perception*, 8, 21–30.

Rayner, K. (1986) Eye movements and the perceptual span: evidence for dyslexic typology. In G. Th. Pavlidis and D. F. Fisher (eds), *Dyslexia: its Neuropsychology and Treatment*. Chichester: J. Wiley.

Rayner, K. and Duffy, S. A. (1986) Lexical complexity and fixation times in reading: effects of word frequency, verb complexity, and lexical ambiguity. *Memory and Cognition*, 14, 191–201.

Rayner, K. and Morris, R. K. (1992) Eye movement control in reading: evidence against semantic preprocessing. *Journal of Experimental Psychology: Human Perception and Performance*, 18, 163–72.

Rayner, K., Balota, D. A. and Pollatsek, A. (1986) Against parafoveal semantic preprocessing during eye fixations in reading. *Canadian Journal of Psychology*, 40, 473–83.

Rayner, K., Carlson, M. and Frazier, L. (1983) The interaction of syntax and semantics during sentence processing: eye movements in the analysis of semantically biased sentences. *Journal of Verbal Learning and Verbal Behavior*, 22, 358–74.

Reason, J. (1979) Actions not as planned: the price of automatization. In G. Underwood and R. Stevens (eds), *Aspects of Consciousness 1*. London: Academic Press.

Reicher, G. M. (1969) Perceptual recognition as a function of meaningfulness of stimulus material. *Journal of Experimental Psychology*, 81, 274–80

Rubenstein, H., Garfield, L. and Millikan, J. A. (1970) Homographic entries in the internal lexicon. *Journal of Verbal Learning and Verbal Behavior*, 9, 487–94.

Rubenstein, H., Lewis, S. S. and Rubenstein, M. A. (1971) Homographic entries in the internal lexicon: effects of systematicity and relative frequency of meanings. *Journal of Verbal Learning and Verbal Behavior*, 10, 57–62.

Rubin, G. S., Becker, C.A. and Freeman, R. H. (1979) Morphological structure and its effect on visual word recognition. *Journal of Verbal Learning and Verbal Behavior*, 18, 757–67

Rumelhart, D. E. and McClelland, J. L. (1982) An interactive activation model of context effects in letter perception: Part 2. *Psychological Review*, 89, 60–94.

Rumelhart, D. E. and McClelland, J. L. (1986) On learning the past tenses of English verbs. In D. E. Rumelhart and J. L. McClelland (eds), *Parallel Distributed Processing: Explorations in the Microstructure of Cognition*, vol 1. Cambridge, Mass.: MIT Press.

Rutter, M. (1978) Prevalence and types of dyslexia. In A. L. Benton and D. Pearl (eds), *Dyslexia: An Appraisal of Current Knowledge*. New York: Oxford University Press.

Sartori, G., Barry, C. and Job, R. (1984) Phonological dyslexia: a review. In R. M. Malatesha and H. Whitaker (eds), *Dyslexia: A Global Issue*. The Hague: Nijhoff.

Sartori, G., Bruno, S., Serena, M. and Bandin, P. (1984) Deep dyslexia in a patient with crossed aphasia. *European Neurology*, 23, 95–9.

Sasanuma, S. (1980) Acquired dyslexia in Japanese: clinical features and underlying mechanisms. In M. Coltheart, K. E. Patterson, and J. C. Marshall (eds), *Deep Dyslexia*. London: Routledge and Kegan Paul.

Scarborough, D. L., Cortese, C. and Scarborough, H. S. (1977) Frequency and repetition effects in lexical memory. *Journal of Experimental Psychology: Human Perception and Performance*, 3, 1–17.

Schank, R. C. and Abelson, R. (1977) *Scripts, Plans, Goals and Understanding*. Hillsdale, NJ: Erlbaum.

Schlapp, U. and Underwood, G. (1988) Reading, spelling and two types of irregularity in word recognition. *Journal of Research in Reading*, 11, 120–32.

Schneider, W. and Shiffrin, R. M. (1977) Controlled and automatic information processing: I, Detection, search and attention. *Psychological Review*, 84, 1–66.

Schuberth, R. E. and Eimas, P. D. (1977) Effects of context on the classification of words and nonwords. *Journal of Experimental Psychology: Human Perception and Performance*, 3, 27–36.

Schvaneveldt, R. W., Meyer, D. E. and Becker, C. A. (1976) Lexical ambiguity, semantic context and visual word recognition. *Journal of Experimental Psychology: Human Perception and Performance*, 2, 243–56.

Schwartz, M . F., Saffran, E. M. and Marin, O. S. M. (1980) Fractionating the reading process in dementia: evidence for word-specific print-to-sound associations. In M. Coltheart, K. E. Patterson, and J. C. Marshall (eds), *Deep Dyslexia*. London: Routledge and Kegan Paul.

Seidenberg, M. S. and McClelland, J. L. (1989) A distributed, developmental model of word recognition and naming. *Psychological Review*, 96, 523–68.

Seidenberg, M. S. and McClelland, J. L. (1990) More words but still no lexicon: reply to Besner *et al.* (1990). *Psychological Review*, 97, 447–52.

Seymour, P. H. K. and Elder, L. (1986) Beginning reading without phonology. *Cognitive Neuropsychology*, 3, 1–36.

Seymour, P. H. K. and Porpodas, C. D. (1980) Lexical and non-lexical processing of spelling in developmental dyslexia. In U. Frith (ed.), *Cognitive Processes in Spelling*. London: Academic Press.

Shallice, T. (1981) Neurological impairment of cognitive processes. *British Medical Bulletin*, 37, 187–92.

Shallice, T. and Coughlan, A. K. (1980) Modality specific word comprehension deficits in deep dyslexia. *Journal of Neurology, Neurosurgery and Psychiatry*, 43, 866–72.

Shallice, T. and Saffran, E. M. (1986) Lexical processing in the absence of explicit word identification: evidence from a letter-by-letter reader. *Cognitive Neuropsychology*, 3, 429–58.

Shallice, T. and Warrington, E. K. (1975) Word recognition in a phonemic dyslexic patient. *Quarterly Journal of Experimental Psychology*, 27, 187–99.

Shallice, T. and Warrington, E. K. (1980) Single and multiple component central dyslexic syndromes. In M. Coltheart, K. E. Patterson and J. C. Marshall (eds), *Deep Dyslexia*. London: Routledge and Kegan Paul.

Shallice, T. and Warrington, E. K. and McCarthy, R. (1983) Reading without semantics. *Quarterly Journal of Experimental Psychology*, 35A, 111–38.

Singer, M. (1979) Processes of inference in sentence encoding. *Memory and Cognition*, 7, 192–200.

Singer, M. (1980) The role of case-filling sentences in the coherence of brief passages. *Discourse Processes*, 3, 185–201.

Singer, M. (1993) Global inferences of text situations. *Discourse Processes*, 16, 161–8.

Singer, M. and Ferreira, F. (1983) Inferring consequences in story comprehension. *Journal of Verbal Learning and Verbal Behavior*, 22, 437–48.

Smith, E. E., Shoben, E. J. and Rips, L. J. (1974) Comparison processes in semantic memory. *Psychological Review*, 81, 214–41.

Smith, F. (1971) *Understanding reading: a Psycholinguistic Analysis of Reading and Learning to Read*. New York: Holt, Rinehart and Wilson.

Smith, F. (1973) *Psycholinguistics and Reading*. New York: Holt, Rinehart and Wilson.

Smith, P. T. and Sterling, C. M. (1982) Factors affecting the perceived morphemic structure of written words. *Journal of Verbal Learning and Verbal Behavior*, 21, 704–21.

Snowling, M. (1987) *Dyslexia: a Cognitive Developmental Perspective*. Oxford: Basil Blackwell.

Stanley, G., Smith, G. A. and Howell, E. A. (1983) Eye movements and sequential tracking in dyslexic and control children. *British Journal of Psychology*, 74, 181–7.

Stanners, R. F. and Forbach, G. B. (1973) Analysis of letter strings in word recognition. *Journal of Experimental Psychology*, 98, 31–5.

Stanovich, K. E. (1980) Toward an interactive-compensatory model of individual differences in the development of reading fluency. *Reading Research Quarterly*, 16, 32–71.

Stanovich, K. E. and Bauer, D. W. (1978) Experiments on the spelling-to-sound regularity effect in word recognition. *Memory and Cognition*, 6, 410–15.

Stanovich, K. E. and West, R. F. (1979) Mechanisms of sentence context effects in reading: automatic activation and conscious attention. *Memory and Cognition*, 7, 77–85.

Stanovich, K. E. and West, R. F. (1981) The effect of sentence context on ongoing word recognition: tests of a two-process theory. *Journal of Experimental Psychology: Human Perception and Performance*, 7, 638–78.

Sullivan, K. P. H. (1991) Unpublished Ph.D. dissertation, University of Southampton.

Sullivan, K. P. H. and Damper, R. I. (1992) Novel-word pronunciation within a text-to-speech system. In: G. Bailly, C. Benoit and T. R. Sawallis (eds), *Talking Machines: Theories, Models and Designs*. Amsterdam: Elsevier.

Swinney, D. A. (1979) Lexical access during sentence comprehension: (re)consideration of context effects. *Journal of Verbal Learning and Verbal Behavior*, 18, 645–59.

Taft, M. (1979a) Recognition of affixed words and the word frequency effect. *Memory and Cognition*, 7, 263–72.

Taft, M. (1979b) Lexical access via an orthographic code: the Basic Orthographic Syllabic Structure (BOSS). *Journal of Verbal Learning and Verbal Behavior*, 18, 21–39.

Taft, M. (1981) Prefix stripping revisited. *Journal of Verbal Learning and Verbal Behavior*, 20, 289–97.

Taft, M. (1985) The decoding of words in lexical access: a review of the morphographic approach. In D. Besner, T. G. Waller and G. E. MacKinnon (eds), *Reading Research: Advances in Theory and Practice 5*. New York: Academic Press.

Taft, M. (1991) *Reading and the Mental Lexicon*. Hove: Erlbaum.

Taft, M. and Forster, K. I. (1975) Lexical storage and retrieval of prefixed words. *Journal of Verbal Learning and Verbal Behavior*, 14, 638–47.

Taft, M. and Forster, K. I. (1976) Lexical storage and retrieval of polymorphemic and polysyllabic words. *Journal of Verbal Learning and Verbal Behavior*, 15, 607–20.

Tanenhaus, M. K., Carlson, G. and Trueswell, J. C. (1989) The role of thematic structures in interpretation and parsing. *Language and Cognitive Processes*, 4, 211–34.

Taraban, R. and McClelland, J. L. (1988) Constituent attachment and thematic role assignment in sentence processing: influences of content-based expectations. *Journal of Memory and Language*, 27, 597–632.

Taylor, E. A. (1957) The spans: perception, apprehension and recognition as related to reading and speed reading. *American Journal of Ophthalmology*, 44, 501.

Taylor, H. G., Lean, D. and Schwartz, S. (1989) Pseudoword repetition ability in learning-disabled children. *Applied Psycholinguistics*, 10, 203–19.

Tinker, M. A. (1958) Recent studies of eye movements in reading. *Psychological Bulletin*, 55, 215–31.

Trabasso, T. and Suh, S. (1993) Understanding text: achieving explanatory coherence through on-line inferences and mental operations in working memory. *Discourse Processes*, 16, 3–34.

Trabasso, T. and van den Broek, P. (1985) Causal thinking and the representation of narrative events. *Journal of Memory and Language*, 24, 612–30.

Treiman, R. (1985) Onset and rimes as units of spoken syllables: evidence from children. *Journal of Experimental Child Psychology*, 39, 182–201.

Treiman, R. and Baron, J. (1981) Segmental analysis: development and relation to reading ability. In G. E. MacKinnon and T. G. Waller (eds), *Reading Research: Advances in Theory and Practice 3*. New York: Academic Press.

Treisman, A. M. (1960) Contextual cues in selective listening. *Quarterly Journal of Experimental Psychology*, 12, 242–48.

Underwood, G. (1976) Semantic interference from unattended printed words. *British Journal of Psychology*, 67, 327–38.

Underwood, G. (1977) Contextual facilitation from attended and unattended messages. *Journal of Verbal Learning and Verbal Behavior*, 16, 99–106.

Underwood, G. (1982) Attention and awareness in cognitive and motor skills. In G. Underwood (ed.), *Aspects of Consciousness 3*. London: Academic Press.

Underwood, G. and Briggs, P. (1984) The development of word recognition processes. *British Journal of Psychology*, 75, 243–55.

Underwood G. and Everatt J. (1992) The role of eye movements in reading: some limitations of the eye–mind assumption. In: E. Chekaluk and K. R. Llewellyn (eds), *The Role of Eye Movements in Perceptual Processes*. Amsterdam: Elsevier.

Underwood, G. and Thwaites, S. (1982) Automatic phonological coding of unattended printed words. *Memory and Cognition*, 10, 434–42.

Underwood G., Bloomfield, R. and Clews, S. (1988) Information influences the pattern of eye fixations during sentence comprehension. *Perception*, 17, 267–78.

Underwood, G., Briscoe, T. and MacCleary, L. (1992) How obligatory are parsing strategies? Unpublished experiment in G. Underwood and J. Everatt, The role of eye movement in reading. In E. Chekaluk and K. R. Llewellyn (eds), *The Role of Eye Movement in Perceptual Processes*. Amsterdam: Elsevier.

Underwood, G., Clews, S. and Everatt, J. (1990) How do readers know where to look next? Local information distributions influence eye fixations. *Quarterly Journal of Experimental Psychology*, 42A, 39–65.

Underwood, G., Clews, S. and Wilkinson, H. (1989) Eye fixations are influenced by the distribution of information within words. *Acta Psychologica*, 72, 263–80.

Underwood, G., Hubbard, A. and Wilkinson, H. (1990) Eye fixations predict reading comprehension: the relationship between reading skill, reading speed and visual inspection. *Language and Speech*, 33, 69–81.

Underwood, G., Petley, K. and Clews, S. (1990) Searching for information during sentence comprehension. In R. Groner, G. d'Ydewalle and R. Parham (eds), *From Eye to Mind: Information Acquisition in Perception, Search and Reading*. Elsevier: North-Holland.

Underwood G., Roberts, M. and Thomasson, H. (1988) Strategical invariance in lexical access: the reappearance of the pseudohomophone effect. *Canadian Journal of Psychology*, 42, 24–34.

Underwood, N. R. and Zola, D. (1986) The span of letter recognition of good and poor readers. *Reading Research Quarterly*, 21, 6–19.

Upward, C. (1992) Teaching literacy first, traditional English orthography second. In C. M. Sterling and C. Robson (eds), *Psychology, Spelling and Education*. Clevedon: Multilingual Matters.

van den Broek, P. and Lorch, R. F. (1993) Network representations of causal relations in memory for narrative texts: evidence from primed recognition. *Discourse Processes*, 16, 75–98.

van Dijk, T. A. and Kintsch, W. (1983) *Strategies of Discourse Comprehension*. New York: Academic Press.

Vellutino, F. R. (1979) *Dyslexia: Theory and Research*. Cambridge, Mass.: MIT Press.

Vonk, W., Hustinx, L. G. M. M. and Simons, W. H. G. (1992) The use of referential expressions in structuring discourse. *Language and Cognitive Processes*, 7, 301–33.

Warrington, E. K. (1971) Neurological disorders of memory, *British Medical Bulletin*, 27, 243–7.

Warrington, E. K., Logue, V. and Pratt, R. T. C. (1971) The anatomical localisation of selective impairment of auditory verbal short-term memory. *Neuropsychologia*, 9, 377–87.

Warrington, E. K. and Shallice, T. (1980) Word form dyslexia, *Brain*, 102, 43–63.

Warrington, E. K. and Weiskrantz, L. (1973) An analysis of short-term and long-term memory defects in man. In J. A. Deutsch (ed.), *The Physiological Basis of Memory*. New York: Academic Press.

Waters, G. S. and Seidenberg, M. S. (1985) Spelling-sound effects in reading: time course and decision criteria. *Memory and Cognition*, 13, 557–72.

Wells, F. L. (1906) Linguistic lapses. In J. McK. Cattell and F. J. E. Woodbridge (eds), *Archives of Philosophy, Psychology and Scientific Methods* 6. New York: Science Press.

West, R. F. and Stanovich, K. E. (1978) Automatic and contextual facilitation in readers of three ages. *Child Development*, 49, 717–27.

West, R. F., Stanovich, K. E., Feeman, D. J. and Cunningham, A. E. (1983) The effect of sentence context on word recognition in second- and sixth-grade children. *Reading Research Quarterly*, 19, 6–15.

Wheeler, D. D. (1970) Processes in word recognition. *Cognitive Psychology*, 1, 59–85.

Wickelgren, W. A. (1969) Context-sensitive coding, associative memory, and serial order in (speech) behavior. *Psychological Review*, B76, 1–15.

Winnick, W. A. and Daniel, S. A. (1970) Two kinds of response priming in tachistoscopic recognition. *Journal of Experimental Psychology*, 84, 74–81.

Wright, S. F. and Groner, R. (1993) *Facets of Dyslexia and its Remediation*. Amsterdam: Elsevier.

Yuill, N. and Oakhill, J. (1988) Effects of inference awareness training on poor reading comprehension. *Applied Cognitive Psychology*, 2, 33–45.

Subject Index

Name Index